Sidney Harry Fox

NOTABLE BRITISH TRIALS SERIES

General Editor—HARRY HODGE

Trial	Date of Trial	Editor
Mary Queen of Scots	(1586)	A. Francis Steuart
Guy Fawkes	(1605-6)	Donald Carswell
King Charles I.	(1649)	J. G. Muddiman
The Bloody Assizes	(1678)	J. G. Muddiman
Captain Kidd	(1701)	Graham Brooks
Jack Sheppard	(1724)	{ Horace Bleackley { S. M. Ellis
Captain Porteous	(1736)	William Roughead
The Annesley Case	(1743)	Andrew Lang
Lord Lovat	(1747)	David N. Mackay
Mary Blandy	(1752)	William Roughead
James Stewart	(1752)	David N. Mackay
Eugene Aram	(1759)	Eric R. Watson
Katharine Nairn	(1765)	William Roughead
The Douglas Cause	(1761-1769)	A. Francis Steuart
Duchess of Kingston	(1776)	Lewis Melville
Deacon Brodie	(1788)	William Roughead
"Bounty" Mutineers	(1792)	Owen Rutter
Abraham Thornton	(1817)	Sir John Hall, Bt.
Henry Fauntleroy	(1824)	Horace Bleackley
Thurtell and Hunt	(1824)	Eric R. Watson
Burke and Hare	(1828)	William Roughead
J. B. Rush	(1849)	W. Teignmouth Shore
William Palmer	(1856)	Eric R. Watson
Madeleine Smith	(1858)	F. Tennyson Jesse
Dr. Smethurst	(1859)	L. A. Parry
Mrs. M'Lachlan	(1862)	William Roughead
Franz Muller	(1864)	H. B. Irving
Dr. Pritchard	(1865)	William Roughead
The Wainwrights	(1875)	H. B. Irving
The Stauntons	(1877)	J. B. Atlay
E. M. Chantrelle	(1878)	A. Duncan Smith
Kate Webster	(1879)	Elliott O'Donnell
City of Glasgow Bank	(1879)	William Wallace
Charles Peace	(1879)	W. Teignmouth Shore
Dr. Lamson	(1882)	H. L. Adam
Adelaide Bartlett	(1886)	Sir John Hall, Bt.
Mrs. Maybrick	(1889)	H. B. Irving
J. W. Laurie	(1889)	William Roughead
The Baccarat Case	(1891)	W. Teignmouth Shore
T. N. Cream	(1892)	W. Teignmouth Shore
A. J. Monson	(1893)	J. W. More
G. Chapman	(1903)	H. L. Adam
S. H. Dougal	(1903)	F. Tennyson Jesse
Adolf Beck	(1904)	Eric R. Watson
Oscar Slater	(1909-1928)	William Roughead
H. H. Crippen	(1910)	Filson Young
J. A. Dickman	(1910)	S. O. Rowan-Hamilton
Steinie Morrison	(1911)	H. Fletcher Moulton
The Seddons	(1912)	Filson Young
George Joseph Smith	(1915)	Eric R. Watson
Sir Roger Casement	(1916)	George H. Knott
Harold Greenwood	(1920)	Winifred Duke
Bywaters and Thompson	(1922)	Filson Young
Ronald True	(1922)	Donald Carswell
H. R. Armstrong	(1922)	Filson Young
J. P. Vaquier	(1924)	R. H. Blundell
J. D. Merrett	(1927)	William Roughead
Browne and Kennedy	(1928)	W. Teignmouth Shore
Dr. Knowles	(1928)	Albert Lieck
Sidney H. Fox	(1929)	F. Tennyson Jesse
A. A. Rouse	(1931)	Helena Normanton
The Royal Mail Case	(1931)	Collin Brooks

IN PREPARATION.

Gardiner (Peasenhall)   Field and Gray
Robert Wood

Fox.

Trial of Sidney Harry Fox.

Sidney Harry Fox

Trial of
SIDNEY HARRY FOX

EDITED BY

F. Tennyson Jesse

Author of "Murder and its Motives," &c.

EDINBURGH AND LONDON
WILLIAM HODGE & COMPANY, LIMITED

MADE AND PRINTED IN GREAT BRITAIN
BY
WILLIAM HODGE AND COMPANY, LTD.
GLASGOW AND EDINBURGH

September, 1934.

THIS BOOK IS DEDICATED TO

SIR VINCENT BADDELEY, K.C.B.,

UNOFFICIAL PROOF READER AND KINDEST OF FRIENDS

PREFACE.

THE EDITOR wishes to acknowledge her grateful thanks to Mr. St. John Hutchinson, Mr. J. D. Cassels, K.C., Mr. C. Pensotti, Captain Glynes Bruty, Mr. E. H. W. Meyerstein, Mr. Wilfred Auckorn, and to Mr. and Mrs. Harding of the Hotel Metropole, Margate, for their invaluable help and courtesy, without which this trial could not have been compiled. My thanks are also due to Professor Smith for the care he has taken in revising the report of his evidence.

CONTENTS.

CONTENTS.

FOURTH DAY—SATURDAY, 15TH MARCH, 1930.

Evidence for the Prosecution (continued).

FIFTH DAY—MONDAY, 17TH MARCH, 1930.

Evidence for the Prosecution (continued).

SIXTH DAY—TUESDAY, 18TH MARCH, 1930.

Evidence for the Prosecution (concluded).

SEVENTH DAY—WEDNESDAY, 19TH MARCH, 1930.

Evidence for the Defence.

EIGHTH DAY, THURSDAY, 20TH MARCH, 1930.

Evidence for the Defence (concluded).

APPENDICES.

CONTENTS.

FRIDAY, 7TH FEBRUARY, 1930.

FRIDAY, 14TH FEBRUARY, 1930.

FRIDAY, 21ST FEBRUARY, 1930.

LIST OF ILLUSTRATIONS.

SIDNEY HARRY FOX.

INTRODUCTION.

I.

The trial of Sidney Harry Fox on the charge of murdering his mother, Rosaline Fox, aroused great interest, not only in those people who always take an interest in such things, but in the public mind. Vulgar as the crime was—it was committed purely for gain—there was a flavour of the monstrous and horrible about it which appealed to the imagination. Matricide is uncommon, but even apart from this obvious truth, there was something so peculiar, not only about the character of the son, but about that of the mother, that the case remains to a certain extent mysterious to this day.

Two ideas have persisted, as ideas have a way of doing even in the face of plain fact. One is that Mrs. Fox, in her devotion to her worthless son, and in her desire to procure money for him by what seemed the only possible means, consented to her own murder. The other rumour —even more persistent—is that Rosaline Fox was not the young man's mother, but an old mistress.

The first rumour may have had its foundation in the undoubted fact that Mrs. Fox was a consenting party to her son's frauds, and it may even be possible that he told her he was insuring her against illness or accident, and that she consented to be half-suffocated and made ill, not realising that it was her life which had been insured, and that illness alone would have been useless. That she consented to her own death, and a painful death at that, is an absurd supposition. Maternal affection has been known to go to great lengths, but hardly to such lengths as that.

The story that she was not his mother, but his mistress,

Sidney Harry Fox.

is a complete fabrication. The sexton of Great
Fransham, where Rosaline Fox had lived in girlhood
and during her life, had, when a boy, attended the little
village school with her, had known her all her life, and
knew her sons. He unhesitatingly identified the body.
This cannot have been difficult, for Rosaline Fox was an
extraordinary personality, and it is in the deeps of that
personality rather than in the shallows of her son's, that
the mystery of the case will always lie.

She both married into the railway and took a lover
from it, her husband being a railway signalman, and the
man she lived with, after parting from her husband,
being employed as a porter. Sidney Fox, her fourth and
last son, was probably the child of this man, but he
unfortunately came to suspect—or to pretend that he
suspected—that he was of noble origin, although born on
the wrong side of the blanket, and this encouraged him
in those tastes which would be extravagant in the son
of a porter, and peculiar in a man of any rank of life.

His talents, such as they were—they mainly consisted
of a real genius for forgery and a faculty for mimicry
which enabled him to pass himself off as a public-school
boy—were wasted in the sphere of life in which he had
been born. Stage-doors and dressing-rooms, supper
parties, and pleasant meals with men friends at clubs
were the things that Fox enjoyed, and the sort of atmosphere in which he felt at home. There may perhaps
have been good blood in his veins which made it
distasteful to him to earn an honest living. Certainly
he was quite different from his three brothers.

William Edgar Fox, the eldest, had settled down to
a useful career as a monitor at a mental home, the Queen
Alexandra Hospital, Cosham. The second son was killed
in France in the war, and the third was killed at
Woolwich Arsenal in 1915.

Of her sons the scapegrace Sidney, who forged and
stole, and spent his life going in and out of prison, was

2

Introduction.

the dearest in his mother's eyes. It was with him that she went on a dreary and somewhat perilous round of hotels, without luggage, always cheating the management by getting away without paying. There can be no doubt that her financial morality was little, if at all, better than that of her son. And the old white-haired woman with the big genial face, and the loose, smiling lips, the shuffling gait, and the trembling hands, was a confederate in the young man's criminal escapades.

Besides being a thief and a forger, Fox was an invert, and it is a curious thing, worthy of note, that he was vain of his inversion. He could not bear even his own counsel to think that he had ever gone with a woman save for the money he might get from her. He took a pride in the fact that his pleasure lay entirely with his own sex.

Whether he were of noble origin or not it was certain that Fox had to earn his living. He started to make money in rather an ingenious fashion at the age of eleven or twelve, when he undertook to collect on behalf of some charity. He went from house to house in the district, obtaining contributions and writing the amounts down in his collecting book. He then appropriated about fifteen shillings of the money and gummed two pages of the book together, so that the donations amounting to that sum should not be traced. It was an ingenious idea, but one cannot think of everything at such a tender age, and it was noticed that one of the pages of the book was thicker than it should have been, and the fraud was discovered. The matter was put in the hands of the police, and Sidney was birched.

Later he and his mother moved to London, and Sidney obtained the position of house-boy to the late Sir John and Lady Constance Leslie, and every day Fox could be seen leading the old gentleman round Manchester Square. He was a great success as a page-boy, was apparently devoted to his employers, and took the greatest care of

3

Sidney Harry Fox.

them. He became, indeed, quite a pet in the family, and was known as " Cupid " because of his charming looks and frank expression.

With his fellow-servants he was not as popular as with his employers. He always threw the blame, if anything went wrong, upon the other servants, and did so with such a cherubic smile that he was at first believed, though not by them. His tastes, even at the age of sixteen, were too expensive for his wages, so he stole some silver, and, beginning seriously to get to work, made overtures to an elderly housemaid, and got her entire savings out of her. Fox had been three years in his situation, but though his employers thought a great deal of him for his care and devotion to them, they had to send him away, though they did not prosecute.

The next position that Fox obtained seems to have been in a bank—an admirable step from his point of view, as he developed a talent for forgery. This talent was to prove of great service to him later, when he made frequent and unauthorised use of his mother's name. Again a mistaken clemency was exercised on Fox's behalf, and he was given the chance of being prosecuted or joining the army. He chose the army, and eventually became a cadet in the Royal Flying Corps.

His next exploit, however, was to lead him to prison. He went down to Brighton and called on an elderly lady there who knew Lady Constance Leslie and her family well. Fox, who knew all the ramifications of the Leslie family, passed himself off as a grandson whom the old lady happened never to have known. He had by this time picked up all the patter of the class which he was attempting to imitate. He always dressed well, and it is not surprising that he was able to pass at his own valuation. Naturally the lady at Brighton was charmed to see the grandson of her old friend. She plied him with questions about the family, all of which he was able to answer. At last the young man said casually:

4

Introduction.

" I wonder if you could cash me a cheque? I've run
short, and don't know any one in Brighton whom I can
ask."

The good lady was only too anxious to be helpful, and
replied that she had not enough money in the house, but
that her greengrocer would cash a cheque if she asked
him. So the lady sent her maid round to the greengrocer's with Fox, and the obliging tradesman gave him
five pounds for a cheque on the Arundel branch of the
London, County, and Westminster Bank. The cheque in
due course came back marked " No account." The
grandson of Lady Constance Leslie, whom Fox had
impersonated, was found, and the fraud was made plain.

As luck would have it, an assistant provost marshal of
the Eastern Command (Captain Glynes Bruty) was
taking a few days' holiday—it was Christmas of 1917
—at Brighton, and like the proverbial busman on
holiday, he spent much time with the local authorities
discussing cases and comparing notes, and in this way
he came to hear of the nameless young man who had
cheated the greengrocer. He was told of a youth called
Fox who had at one time been house-boy to Lady
Constance Leslie, and that he might perhaps be the
culprit, since it was obvious that whoever it was he
had intimate and detailed knowledge of the Leslie
family.

On his return to London the A.P.M. took up the case.
Having ascertained the facts of Fox's life both in
Manchester Square and at the bank, he sent a military
policeman in plain clothes to call on Mrs. Fox, who
readily gave the information that her son, " Lieutenant
Fox " as she called him, was a member of the Royal
Automobile Club. Inquiries at the club proved that he
was not a member, but that he was using the club
unknown to the authorities, and that letters came to him
there addressed to " The Honourable S. H. Fox." A
watch was accordingly set for him. There was, indeed,

5

Sidney Harry Fox.

a letter awaiting him on the very day that the inquiries were made; it had been left by an elderly officer, and was marked " Await arrival." The letter was opened by the authorities and proved to be of a most compromising nature. Indeed, it led to the dismissal and disgrace of the unfortunate officer who had written it.

At half-past seven that evening " The Honourable Sidney Fox " arrived and opened the letter, which had by then been put back in the rack. He tore it up and threw the pieces into a wastepaper basket, from which they were retrieved by a plain clothes military policeman. At the same moment the A.P.M. approached Fox, who was sitting on the long seat at the top of the steps that lead to the waiting-room at the R.A.C.

The A.P.M. asked him whether he were entitled to the courtesy title of " Honourable," to which Fox replied that he was, but when pressed to say how and why could only reply: " My mother's father was a gentleman."

" Doubtless," said his interlocutor, " but that does not entitle you to this prefix."

" I thought it did," said Fox.

" Are you a member of this club? " was the next question.

" Certainly I am."

" When did you join? "

" Well, I filled up the papers for joining."

" That does not make you a member, and you are not a member. Are you an officer? "

" Certainly I am."

" When did you get your commission? "

" I got a chit to say I was going to be gazetted when I was in hospital."

" That does not make you an officer, and you are not an officer. You must come with me."

At headquarters Fox came very badly out of his ordeal. He was first made to empty his pockets, and one of the things that came to light was the cheque book which he

Introduction.

had used in Brighton. He had to admit that he had no account at the Arundel branch of the London, County, and Westminster Bank or, indeed, at any branch. He had also to admit that he had stolen the cheque book while he was in hospital. Nothing serious had been the matter with him, and he was employed to hand round the letters to the patients in bed. Guessing from the shape of the envelope that it contained a cheque book, he had pocketed it, and proceeded to forge cheques. Blank cheques on at least five other banks, packets of correspondence, rouge, and a scented booklet of *papier poudré* also came out of Fox's pocket. While this examination was going on the military policeman was piecing together the torn letter and pasting it on tissue paper. This letter had been written on the notepaper of a famous club, and was signed only with initials, but when he saw it, Fox gave away the name of the writer. His unfortunate correspondent was cashiered.

Fox was handed over to the civil arm, and received three months hard labour; part of his routine was to consist of training for the army.

Sidney Fox was one of those young men whom war conditions brought to their finest and most impudent blossoming. His war service, in respect of which he drew ever afterwards a pension of eight shillings a week, was performed in England, and he continued to be the particular friend of officers placed more highly than he in the military hierarchy, and when the war was over became the friend of certain young men who mixed in theatrical circles, where Fox enjoyed himself thoroughly.

But even Fox's luck could not hold for ever; in 1919 he served eight months' hard labour for forgery, and in 1920 he was given six months for victimising London stores by using the names of regular customers.

Mindful of his devoted service to the old baronet, a kindly interest was still taken in Fox by the Leslie family, and while he was in jail they consulted with the

7

Sidney Harry Fox.

Governor, and had him taught the trade of a carpenter. His health improved while he led this regular life, but when he came out of prison it was only to pass from one crime to another, obtaining credit by fraud, larceny, theft, and forgery. He occasionally used to pose as an old Etonian, and as an officer of the R.A.F. His private life was as infamous as were what might be termed his public activities. Mr. J. D. Cassels, for the defence, was certainly being kind when he said that accused " from his youth up has known no companion but his mother."

In spite of various prison terms, Fox always found his mother ready to receive him on his release. She, meanwhile, supplemented the pension of ten shillings a week which she had been awarded in respect of her son killed in the war, by going out as a cook and charwoman. When her son came out of prison, they renewed their more luxurious life, staying in the best hotels, and leaving without paying. Thus the years after the war passed with fluctuating fortunes.

II.

In 1927 Mrs. Fox struck up a friendship with a Mrs. Morse, a middle-aged Australian lady, and the two women took a flat in Southsea. Mrs. Morse was the wife of a captain in the Merchant Service, who was at the time in the Far East. Fox obtained a job in the offices of an insurance company in the neighbourhood, and it is worthy of note that in such an office he may well have found and studied a copy of Taylor's " Medical Jurisprudence," though this, of course, is mere surmise. What is certain is that he was living with his mother and Mrs. Morse, and that he aroused an autumnal passion in the breast of the last-named lady, and was even able to make her believe that he was in love with her. Their association led to a successful action for divorce brought

8

Introduction.

about by Captain Morse. This action is remarkable, if not unique, for the fact that it was brought while Fox was lying under sentence of death. Another curious thing of note from the legal point of view is that Fox was, as far as the present writer is aware, the first murderer convicted not to appeal.

While Fox was outraging his own personal and peculiar morality in making love to the lady, it apparently occurred to him that there were other means of obtaining her money than by having to continue to cohabit with her, and he took out a policy for £3000 upon her life, and also induced her to make a will in his favour. One night Mrs. Morse awoke to find her room full of gas. She managed to crawl out of bed, fling open the window, and give the alarm. Fox was the first to arrive on the scene. The lighting in the flat was electric, but there was a gas tap hidden behind the chest of drawers in Mrs. Morse's room, and it was discovered afterwards that the tap of the gas jet could not be turned on save purposely. Fox knew of the presence of this tap; indeed, he declared himself that he had been warned by the owner, Mrs. Fleming, to be careful of it. Fox insisted that the tap must have got turned on accidentally by some careless movement of the chest of drawers. Whether Mrs. Morse suspected anything or not is unknown, but it is probable that she did, for soon after the establishment was broken up. Fox took his mother to other lodgings, but not before he had forced open a locked drawer in the flat and, discovering some jewellery therein, had stolen it. This theft was traced to him, and he was eventually run to earth and committed for trial at the assizes. He was sentenced to fifteen months' imprisonment. Mrs. Morse left for Australia, alarmed by the incident of the gas, taken in conjunction with the theft of the jewellery.

It is said that she revoked her will at once—some accounts say she destroyed it—but apparently Fox was

Sidney Harry Fox.

unaware of this, for he took either the will or a copy of it, and also the insurance policy on the life of Mrs. Morse, about with him during his various peregrinations. Indeed, these were the documents he placed in a sealed envelope and handed to the hotel manager with the intimation that they were valuable securities which he wished to be kept in safe custody. When the reports of Mrs. Fox's death at Margate were published in the newspapers, Portsmouth detectives remembered the gas incident at Southsea, and this, combined with the suspicions of Mr. Harding, manager of the Hotel Metropole at Margate, showed Sidney's activities to be, at the least, curious. It is not without interest to record that Fox's mother met her death in a room with a gas fire, but that the death was planned to look like death from asphyxiation by smoke, and—although it must always remain a subject of speculation—it may well have been that Fox did not dare to attempt the murder of his mother through the simple turning on of the unlit gas jet because of that curious little incident in his past which had nearly resulted in the death of Mrs. Morse.

After he had served his time for the theft of the jewels, Sidney Harry Fox once more emerged from prison and started to take up life again more or less where he had left it, always with the exception of Mrs. Morse, who was now a missing quantity, though, as will be seen, Fox still had hopes of her. He found that his mother had been cared for during his enforced absence by the Guardians; she had been taken out of the workhouse and passed into the infirmary because of the state of her health.

In March of 1929 Fox took his mother away from St. Mary's Hospital, Portsmouth, and the curious life of luxury and anxiety was resumed. On 21st April she made her will, in which she left everything to her youngest son, Sidney. It was nine days after this will was made that Sidney took out the first of the accident

Introduction.

policies on his mother's life, and started asking the officials of the insurance company such questions as: " Would this policy cover the case of drowning in a bath? Would it apply supposing a person was poisoned, let us say, by food at a restaurant? " Therefore, it may well be that from 1st May, 1929, to 23rd October, when Mrs. Fox died, her course was already set for her. How long before that 1st May Fox had dallied with the notion of his mother's end no one can tell, but it is certain that he had always wanted to live in luxury. He must always have felt that with any luck he would one day establish himself comfortably for life; but with all his cunning he had that admixture of stupidity and an ostrich-like quality which, fortunately for the run of common men, is apt to lead the lone adventurer to the prison and the gallows.

It seems fairly well established that Fox had taken his mother abroad to see the grave of his brother who had been killed in the war. Until this expedition abroad (when, if Sidney had only known it, he could have murdered his mother and been sympathised with by every one, from the mayor downwards, for in a French town he would hardly have been suspected of matricide) he and she continued on their strange career of cheating hotels and living from the pawnshop to the mouth. In fact this mode of livelihood went on long enough to try Sidney's patience too highly. There is no doubt that he came to the conclusion that something must be done, and done quickly. He was still cherishing the notion of going to Australia, although Mrs. Morse, having come to her senses, had finished with him. Fox may well have trusted to his own powers of charming even an unwilling victim, and hoped that once he met Mrs. Morse again all would be well. The divorce suit instituted by Captain Morse had by then been started, and had Fox succeeded in overcoming Mrs. Morse's extremely natural suspicions, he might have hoped to marry her.

11

Sidney Harry Fox.

Some plan certainly was being turned over in Fox's mind when he arrived at Margate with his mother; the details of that plan no one will ever know. Whether or not they included an optimistic attempt on the affections of Mrs. Morse must remain a matter for conjecture.

III.

Mrs. Fox and her son arrived at the Hotel Metropole, Margate, having left the County Hotel, Canterbury, where they had stayed from the 12th October to the 15th. They had left that hotel with a brown paper parcel, which comprised all the luggage that they possessed in the world, and before that they had been staying at the Royal Pavilion Hotel, Folkestone, which they not only left without paying their bill, but where they had succeeded in obtaining £15 5s. credit, without disclosing that Sidney Fox was at the moment an undischarged bankrupt.

Nothing could have been less sensational than this entry of Fox and his mother into the Hotel Metropole, and nothing could have been more sensational than the manner of Mrs. Fox's exit. From an apparently adored mother she was to become known to the world as a helpless victim, and from being a trivial and apparently modest young swindler, her son was to spring into sudden prominence as her murderer.

On that October evening this apparently harmless couple walked into the hotel—she with her shuffling gait, for she suffered from *paralysis agitans*, he guiding and supporting her with that care which made every one think him such a good son. Although they had no luggage—Fox remarked vaguely that it had been " sent on "—they looked so respectable, she with her silver hair, he with his frank gaze and charming smile, that it hardly needed his usual trick of confiding to Miss Hopper, the receptionist, the care of a packet of

12

Introduction.

" valuable papers," for her to allot him rooms without a qualm of suspicion.

But Mr. Harding, the manager, was not as unsuspicious as Miss Hopper, and he sent Fox's account in to him every day. Mrs. Fox and her son had no luggage. They had not even any night-wear, or anything serious in the way of washing-things, and yet they were allowed to stay on day after day in one of the best commercial hotels in England. When Mrs. Fox left her bedroom each morning, she wore her only two dresses, both of stockinette, one over the other for added warmth. Every stitch she possessed was on her body, unless perchance she had left her coat in the wardrobe. She used a handkerchief as a wash-rag, and had no nightgown. Fox had neither nightshirt nor pyjamas. He shaved himself, so it is presumed he had a razor, and he took care to keep his only suit cleaned with petrol (a fact which was to prove of rather illusory interest later on).

But apart from this very limited outfit those strange migrants seemed not to have been troubled with the problem of cleanliness. There must be many people like them, or chambermaids would express more surprise and suspicion. Nevertheless, the Fox family seemed so typical of hotel swindlers that Mr. Harding watched them with caution. The placing of " papers " in a hotel safe is an old trick; and although to lose luggage is a thing that may happen to any of us, the usual procedure is to go out and buy a toothbrush and some night attire, and then, after the lapse of twenty-four hours or so, a change of underclothing. But the only things that Fox bought were a half-bottle of port, some grapes, and three bottles of tonic for his mother.

It was on Wednesday that Fox took rooms for himself and his mother at the Metropole, saying it was only for one night, and the following morning he again went to the receptionist and told her they would want to keep

13

Sidney Harry Fox.

the rooms on for another night, as there were friends he wished to see. On Friday, the 18th, Fox, who apparently had formed the habit of chatting pleasantly with Miss Hopper, told her that his mother was unwell, and had a headache, and asked if they could stay on. Every day he mentioned his bill, thereby giving the impression that he was anxious not to go beyond his means.

He incited a womanly sympathy for himself and his poor old mother in Miss Hopper's mind. He told her his usual tale of having had three brothers killed in France, and how he had just taken the old lady to see the graves. She became quite anxious lest his mother had not a warm enough coat for the journey—for Fox explained that they were going on to a new house, whither their luggage and furniture had already gone before them—and Miss Hopper offered the loan of her own fur coat for his mother's use.

On the 18th October, two days after their arrival, Fox also talked with Mr. Harding, the manager, and asked him to recommend him a solicitor. This, like depositing the " valuable " papers, seemed to argue at least some slight affluence, as solicitors are apt to be costly. Certainly Fox had business dealings of some kind, because that same day he went to Ramsgate, and insured Rosaline Fox with Messrs. Pickfords, agents for the Ocean Accident and Guarantee Corporation, Ltd., for the sum of £1000 in the event of her death from external, accidental means. The premium was only 2s., though that was a large sum for Fox at the moment.

On Sunday, 20th October, Fox went again to Mr. Harding and told him that his mother was lying in a faint. The manager went along to her room, and found the old woman lying fully dressed on the bed. He gave her some drops of sal volatile, and suggested that a doctor should be sent for. He also suggested that they should give up their rooms, which had no fires, and move into Nos. 66 and 67. Room 66 not only had a gas fire,

14

Introduction.

but it also had a communicating door into room 67. It was the first time that Fox and his mother had had communicating rooms at any of the hotels at which they had stayed, and it is only fair to Fox to remember that it was at Mr. Harding's suggestion that the change to a room with a gas fire was made. A Dr. Austin was sent for, and he found very little the matter with Mrs. Fox, and ordered a simple tonic.

It may be remembered that George Joseph Smith, better known to infamy as the Brides in the Bath murderer, always called in a doctor before murdering his brides, and on each occasion the doctor found very little wrong with the woman who was so soon to die, and only prescribed simple remedies.

At about 2.30 that afternoon, a page-boy was sent from the hotel to the Tivoli Road branch of Messrs. V. J. Woolls, Ltd., and returned with an 8-ounce bottle containing the medicine. In spite of already having this bottle of the tonic, Fox went himself later on in the day, at about 6.30, to another branch of Messrs. Woolls—that in Cecil Square. Here he offered in payment a cheque written out on a piece of hotel notepaper, and signed "Rosaline Fox." The cheque was made out for £2, and was drawn on Lloyds Bank at Norwich. Fox asked the chemist, Mr. Farmer, to take the money for the medicine out of this and give him the change, but there was only a penny stamp on the cheque, and Mr. Farmer declined it, whereupon Fox left the shop.

That Sunday Rosaline Fox dined upstairs in her room, and Sidney received his bill, which amounted to £5 6s. 11d. Fox said a curious thing about the bottle of medicine to Miss Hopper and to the barmaid at the Hotel Metropole. He said that the chemist had had to break down the prescription, for it was dangerous as written by the doctor. There was not a word of truth in this statement. The prescription was a very simple one—

15

Sidney Harry Fox.

one dram and a half of nux vomica, half an ounce of sal volatile, and chloroform water.

In spite of this rebuff, Fox was evidently convinced that the chemist's shop was the best hope of obtaining some money, and he went into it again at 10.30 on Monday morning and ordered another bottle of the same tonic, and also a bottle of cascara tablets. He again offered a cheque in payment, and Mr. Farmer once more refused it. However, the arrangement was made that the prescription was to be made up and Fox was to return for the medicine at mid-day. Now, at mid-day Mr. Farmer went for his lunch, and Miss Allen, the assistant, was in charge of the shop when Fox again made his appearance. He produced his cheque, asked her to cash it, to take the cost of the two bottles of medicine and the cascara tablets from the money, and give him the rest.

" It's quite all right," added Fox airily. " I saw Mr. Farmer about it, and he told me to go to the bank. I've been to the bank, and they said it would be quite all right if I affixed another penny stamp and endorsed it, which I have done."

Miss Allen deducted four shillings for the medicine and tablets, and handed Fox the balance, consisting of £1 16s.

So close to the edge of daily circumstance was Fox living that this was quite a useful sum to him. He and his mother between them had pensions amounting to eighteen shillings a week, and they were living at the rate of more than that for the half-day. It is true that they never made any attempt to pay their bills, but they needed money for railway tickets so that they could get away and start the game all over again elsewhere. This particular sum, in addition to paying for those luxuries for his mother which made him appear such a good son, was to pay for his fare to London when he went to extend certain policies on her life.

It was before leaving for this trip that he bought his

16

Mrs Rosaline Fox

Introduction.

mother the bunch of grapes, and he also tipped the chambermaid 7s. 6d.—he certainly had the grand manner, and knew when it was wise to tip with a lavishness disproportionate to his means—and off he went to London.

So worried was he about his mother that he telephoned from London that Monday night to inquire after her, and again on Tuesday morning. He was building up the impression of an excellent and devoted son in the Hotel Metropole. It was to stand him for a brief while in good stead. Could a devoted son have done more? When his mother felt faint, he called in the manager of the hotel. He had already chatted to Miss Hopper about his mother, and shown much solicitude concerning her. He had bought her no fewer than three bottles of tonic in three days, to say nothing of the bunch of grapes, and he had telephoned twice from London. All these things made their impression.

The good folk at the Hotel Metropole would have been rather surprised if they could have known how Fox had spent his time in London. He had secured from the Cornhill Insurance Company an extension of a £2000 policy, so that it would become payable to him if his mother died of an accident before midnight on Wednesday, 23rd October. He also called at the head office of Pickfords, and obtained an extension of their £1000 policy to cover the same date. He returned to the Hotel Metropole on Tuesday with these policies in his pocket.

Now, the previous year Fox and his mother had stayed at an apartment house kept by a Mrs. Platt at Liverpool Street, King's Cross, and on the morning of Tuesday, 22nd October, Mrs. Platt received a telephone message from somebody unknown asking her to tell Fox, should she see him, that his mother had been taken very ill, and that he was to return at once. Shortly afterwards Fox did telephone Mrs. Platt. He told her a lie. He told her that he was going to spend the night in London, and asked if she could put him up. He was already in London, and had no intention of stopping the night. Mrs. Platt duly delivered the message which she imagined some one else had sent him, but there can be no doubt that it was Fox himself who was responsible for both telephone calls. In the first case he gave the bogus message to the office boy from the business next door, to be taken to Mrs. Platt; the second time he asked for Mrs. Platt herself. When Mrs. Platt told him that his mother was ill, and he was asked to return at once, Fox replied: "That's funny, she was quite well when I left this morning. What am I to do? I haven't enough money to get home. Do you think you could lend it to me?"

Mrs. Platt, who obviously knew her Fox rather better than he guessed, declined this, and suggested he might get the money by pawning something. He replied that he had nothing valuable left. She said that probably the railway company would let him pay at the other end. There was nothing left for poor Fox to do but to say: "That's a good idea. I hadn't thought of that," and to ring off.

Somehow or other Fox succeeded in getting the money for the fare, and arrived back at the Hotel Metropole late on Tuesday evening.

IV.

Wednesday dawned, and several curious things happened during the course of the day. Louise Bickmore, the chambermaid, after calling Fox, went to the communicating door and tried to open it, to take the old lady her morning tea, as she had done every morning. This morning the door was bolted on the inside, and Louise Bickmore had to go out into the corridor again and open the door of room 66. To her surprise, she saw Mrs. Fox's false teeth—two complete dentures—lying on

Introduction.

the carpet beside the bed, instead of being in the tumbler of water as usual.

At about 6.30 on the evening of that day, Fox went into the bar of the Metropole and spoke to Mrs. Wager, the barmaid (to whom he had previously made the incorrect statement about Dr. Austin's prescription) and informed her that they would be leaving for Lyndhurst next day—in fact, they were going to that mythical house to which his mythical luggage had already '' gone on.'' He said that his mother was very much better, and added, '' Mother and I have had a sham fight, which shows she is well.''

This statement of Fox's about the '' sham fight '' is one of the most macabre things in the whole case. At a later date he amplified the statement, and explained that he and his mother were apt to indulge in playful boxing matches. What a picture—the old and half-paralysed woman and the young devoted son wrestling together, and giving and receiving blows out of pure merriment of heart! It is indeed a little difficult of credence. Did the fight perhaps take place on the Tuesday evening? And was that why Mrs. Fox had bolted her door, and why her dentures were lying on the carpet? Or was it that Fox feared bruises might be discovered on her body, and so he had invented an explanation that would account for them? He would even be able to say: '' Oh yes, I told Mrs. Wager that we had been having a sham fight; we often did.''

He came up again from this odd conversation in the Metropole bar to fetch his mother down to dinner. Louise Bickmore again came into the room, and found Mrs. Fox sitting by the gas fire, reading a newspaper. It was the last time she was to see her alive. There was hot and cold water laid on in the room, and Sidney had just finished washing his hands and was wiping them. Like Pilate, he cleansed his hands before the commission of a crime.

19

Sidney Harry Fox.

Then the devoted son and the invalid mother went down to the dining-room. The old lady ate quite a good dinner, and drank half a pint of beer. Not content with the beer, Fox, when he had assisted his mother back to her room, went out and bought a half-bottle of port for her. This he purchased at the Hoy Hotel for the sum of 3s. He took this bottle of port upstairs, and nothing more was heard of the Fox family until twenty minutes before midnight, except for two curious happenings. Early in the evening Fox had been overheard by Mr. Harding telephoning from the box in the hall—which is fairly public at the Hotel Metropole—he heard him mention the word " insurance." The thought may have crossed his mind that Fox had little to insure, but the notion of murder was as yet far from Mr. Harding's mind.

Later on that night, after, according to his story, Fox had put his mother to bed, he came down and drank in the lower bar of the Hotel Metropole. As he left the bar he ran into Mr. Harding in the hall. Always before Fox had stopped for a few pleasant words, but now he stood and stared at the manager as though he had seen a ghost; and then without a word he ran quickly up the stairs, leaving Mr. Harding to stare after him and wonder what could be the matter. And even now just how much was the matter at that moment we shall never know. Whether Mrs. Fox lay already strangled behind her bolted door, and Fox was drinking to reassure himself and to nerve his hand at the further task of building the fire; or whether he had just come down to take these few extra drinks which were going to make it possible for him to lift that hand against his mother's life. Only one thing is certain : that her death was already part of his mind whether the deed lay just ahead of him or was already achieved.

The present writer has often wondered how, once he had left the bar, Fox gauged the time—a most essential part

20

Introduction.

of his plan—for were he to break the news five minutes after midnight the insurance on his mother's death would cease to be effective. No one at the Metropole remembers seeing Fox with a watch, old or new, and, indeed, everything he could turn into cash was already pawned. The answer is very plainly to be seen in front of the Hotel Metropole. A large clock tower, bearing a big clock illuminated at night, stands there for all to see. Fox could not see it from his own room, but he could from his mother's room, and he must have waited until it seemed to him that the time was ripe, watching that bland and luminous dial, until he struck a match and lit the pile of newspapers he had arranged beneath the armchair.

His next appearance was a public one. Mr. Hopkins, a commercial traveller who was staying at the Hotel Metropole, had been out to a place of entertainment, and had returned to the hotel at about 11.20 p.m. He sat for some time in the lounge. Suddenly he was startled by the sight of a man, naked except for his shirt, running down the stairs towards him. It was Fox, very agitated, and calling out: " Where is the ' boots '? Where is the ' boots '? I believe there's a fire! Where is the ' boots '? There's a fire! "

Mr. Hopkins, who seems to have kept his head admirably, ran up six steps—not those of the main staircase—that led to the room of the " boots," and also towards the billiard saloon.

The " boots " was not immediately forthcoming, and Mr. Hopkins shouted to the people in the billiard room that there was a fire. He then turned and went upstairs after Fox, the other people from the billiard room following. Fox went straight to the door of room 67, his own door. The room was full of smoke, and the communicating door into his mother's room—the door that he had opened when he smelled smoke—was shut. Fox and Mr. Hopkins came out again into the corridor.

21

Sidney Harry Fox.

Fox pointed to the door of room 66, and said: "My mother is in there."

There seems to be some confusion as to who opened the door of No. 66, but the important fact is that it was closed. Somebody opened it, and the room was found to be dense and black with smoke. Mr. Hopkins could only see a faint glimmer on the left, which he thought must be from the gas fire or from flames. He attempted to get into the room with a handkerchief tied over his mouth, but was driven back by the smoke. He then went down as low as he could on his hands and knees, and crawled into the room, for he had noticed that there were 5 or 6 inches of clear air close to the floor. He groped to the bed, and his hands came in contact with the bare legs of Mrs. Fox hanging over the bed's edge. He still could not see her, but he at once stood up, put his hands under her arms, and dragged her off the bed on to the floor. He succeeded in getting the heavy old woman outside into the corridor before he himself collapsed. He remembered hearing Sidney say, "My mummy, my mummy . . .," but it was Mr. Hopkins, exhausted as he was, who took off his raincoat and wrapped it round the sprawling body that was naked except for a small vest. He dragged her along the corridor to the top of the stairs, and then collapsed.

Two other commercial travellers, Mr. Henry Dickens Miller and Mr. Reginald Reed, managed to get into room 66 through Fox's room and to switch on the electric light which gave only a very faint glow owing to the density of the smoke.

Mr. Miller was beaten back by the smoke. Mr. Reed dropped on his knees, crawled through, and saw immediately in front of him a burning armchair. He tried to extinguish the flames, but unsuccessfully, so he dragged the chair into the corridor—according to his own recollection through the communicating door into room 67—according to that of Mr. Harding directly

22

Introduction.

into the corridor through room 66—in either case various people succeeded in putting out the flames.

All this time Fox seems to have confined his own efforts to wringing his hands and calling out: " My mummy! " Mr. Reed shouted for water, and when it was brought, threw it over the chair in the corridor. He then went back into the room where the smoke was now less dense, and dragged out a small area of carpet that was alight. This area of burning carpet, about 18 inches square, had been exactly under the blazing chair.

Mr. Frederick George French, a sales engineer, managed to get into room 66, and opened the window, and then he and a Mr. William Arthur Underwood helped Mr. Reed to extinguish the burning chair. Even out in the corridor a certain amount of smoke still came from it, so Mr. French and Mr. Underwood carried it downstairs and put it on the pavement outside the hotel. They then noticed a pair of stockings still hanging over the arm, and a pair of corsets and a handbag on the seat. Mr. Underwood handed all three articles to a police officer. Mr. Underwood took hold of the bag and shook it; there seemed to be nothing in it. It was closed at the top, and burned at the bottom.

While all this was going on Rosaline Fox had been carried down to the entrance hall and efforts were being made to revive her by artificial respiration. Dr. Austin was sent for, and examined her. He diagnosed that the old lady was dead, and stopped the artificial respiration. He noticed that her face was very flushed, and he certified her death as being due to shock and suffocation. Dr. Nichol, who was also called in, did not examine Mrs. Fox, but said that her face was very pale and composed—as did most of the other witnesses—the notable exception being Inspector Palmer of the Margate Borough Police, who described the dead woman's face as being reddish-blue. Thus at once in this case we have the conflict of opinion in medical matters that marks

23

Sidney Harry Fox.

all murder trials, and which was on this occasion to be particularly noticeable.

Dr. Nichol and Dr. Austin, with Mr. Hammond, the chief officer of the fire brigade, and various police officers, went upstairs. The window had been opened and the gas fire turned out, but the room was still smoky; the armchair had been removed, and it could be seen that the area of burned carpet was disconnected from the most obvious source of ignition, namely the gas fire, for there was an unburned strip of carpet between the fender and the site that had been occupied by the armchair. Dr. Nichol's impression was that there seemed to be no obvious connection between the gas fire and the charred portion of the floor. (Later it was one of the chief points for the prosecution that there was this wide strip of unburned carpet between the fender and the site occupied by the armchair.) It was noticed that there was a mass of charred newspapers, amongst them the remnants of a French paper. This was one of the most telling pieces of evidence against Fox. It was proved that his mother could not read a word of French. The French newspaper must have been bought when Fox and his mother were abroad, and yet was amongst the burned papers upon the carpet. Fox's argument was that his mother must have been reading the English evening paper, which he had taken particular pains to obtain for her on that evening (and on that evening alone . . .). But what would an old lady who knew no French have been doing with an old French newspaper?

Every one who examined the room had the impression that whoever had lain upon the bed that evening had lain upon it crosswise. The pillow which, according to the evidence of the chambermaid, was always beneath Mrs. Fox's head when she called her in the morning, was discovered to be upon the pedestal table beside the bed, and there was a patch of urine in the centre of the bed. A shock such as strangulation might have caused

24

Introduction.

this flow of urine, but so might the shock to an old woman in a poor condition of health, of awakening and finding the room filled with smoke.

Dr. Nichol received the impression, to which he could not swear, that the dead woman's teeth were lying in a basin. Police Constable Bray, who had carried out the artificial respiration, and Police Sergeant Fleet, who had put his fingers in the dead woman's mouth to make sure that there was no obstruction of the air passages, were quite certain that the dentures were not in her mouth when they were attempting to restore life.

Room 66 was examined that night and the following day, by the hotel manager, the doctors, Mr. Hammond, and the police. The false teeth were discovered to be in the wash-hand basin.

The only other things found in the room on that first investigation were Mrs. Fox's coat and fur necklet, and her two stockinette dresses, which were hanging behind the door, her shoes and her stockings, the two bottles of tonic (the third one was never traced), a bottle of cascara, and a bottle of petrol which Fox used for cleaning his clothes (this petrol was apparently not used for starting the fire and was dropped out of the case), a telegram relating to the position of the grave at Arras, a railway excursion handbill, and a beret. A piece of burned woollen undergarment, probably the top of her combinations, was found on the floor near the fender.

There was also in the room a small cane chair which had one leg burned. It was found nowhere near the site of the fire, but by the window. The commercial travellers who first made incursion into the smoky room swore it had not been in their path or they would have knocked against it, so apparently it must have been moved before Fox gave the alarm. This can only mean that some one must have been in the room at the time the fire was started, and that person must have moved the chair before leaving the room and shutting the door on the conflagration. The bottle of petrol, and the third, and totally unnecessary, bottle of tonic are little mysteries of no great importance, but this cane chair with the burned leg is a very different sort of problem.

Though the little group of men had observed the pillow on the pedestal table, the patch of urine on the bed, the impression of the body that had lain crosswise, the isolated patch of burning on the carpet, still no suspicion was aroused. Mr. Hammond came to the conclusion that a garment, probably the burned combination, had been left hanging over the armchair, had caught fire, and originated the tragedy. All that most people in the hotel thought was that a devoted son had lost his mother. It must be remembered that no one knew that any insurances had been taken out on Mrs. Fox's life.

V.

Fox was not present while Dr. Austin was examining his mother. Mrs. Harding was comforting the young man, stroking his head and telling him that he must not be sure that his mother was dead, that she might be alive after all—had she known it, a very poor form of comfort for Fox. Fox had thick bushy hair, and when Mrs. Harding came to go to bed that night she suddenly smelt smoke upon her hands. She stood and stared at her husband: " That boy's hair is full of smoke," she said, " and he says he never went near the room! " The Hardings gazed at each other, a worse suspicion than that of swindling breaking upon their minds.

Meanwhile Dr. Nichol went to see Fox and break the news to him that his mother was dead. The doctor asked Fox several questions, and told him that he was doing so for the benefit of the coroner. Fox asked what coroner, and Dr. Nichol explained to him that an

26

Introduction.

inquiry always had to be made in cases of violent death. Fox became very agitated at this, seeming, in Dr. Nichol's own words, to " double up."

Dr. Nichol, a scrupulously fair witness, laid stress in his evidence before the magistrates that in his opinion the accused did not collapse because the coroner was mentioned, indeed, at the time, the doctor received the impression that Fox " doubled-up " when he realised that his mother was dead. Nevertheless, in the light of later knowledge, it is interesting to reflect that the last Fox had seen of his mother was when the police were trying to revive her by artificial respiration—that he knew very little about death, and that he might very well have been alarmed lest his mother should not have been beyond all hope of recovery. Waiting in that little downstairs sitting-room, what must his fears have been if this thought came into his mind? Suppose those bluish lips had once again drawn in the breath of life and had murmured his name in condemnation? Dr. Nichol's assurance of his mother's death would agitate Fox perhaps even more if he were guilty than if he were innocent.

Fox then asked to see his mother again, and Dr. Nichol took him upstairs to the room where the body had been placed. Fox walked into the room—again to use Dr. Nichol's graphic phrasing—" in the most natural way imaginable."

In olden days it was considered to prove innocence if the accused could touch the body of the dead person, the notion of the medieval mind being that the dead person would bleed at a guilty touch. Later, for all practical purposes, this resolved itself into the idea that no guilty man could bear to be confronted with the body of his victim, an idea which surely must have been shattered by the complete calm of Troppmann when he saw the bodies of the Kinck family lying before him. Fox walked up to his mother, looked at her and touched her.

27

Sidney Harry Fox.

He stayed by her for a few minutes, and then came out, his eyes full of tears. *Homo sapiens* is a strange animal, and his grief may not have been entirely assumed.

In fact, considering that Sidney Fox had burdened himself with his old mother for several years, and had even taken her out of the charitable institution in Portsmouth where she had been living, it may well be assumed that, after his fashion, he did care for her. He probably, in his reluctance to make use of her, saved her up for his last effort; he had run the gamut of forgery, fraud, blackmail, and—in the case of Mrs. Morse—attempted murder; and at last there was nothing left for him to turn to account but his mother. It is even possible that as he saw that dread necessity coming nearer and nearer he flinched at its application. For many weeks or months there may have been at the back of his mind the knowledge that his mother would have to be his last asset. But if at any moment some confiding elderly woman or perverted rich man had come his way, Rosaline Fox would probably have been the human being with whom he would have shared his spoils.

At the trial the defence made as much play as they could with the undoubted fact that Fox's mother could have been murdered at a previous period for a larger sum than that for which she was insured when death overtook her, but, as Mr. Justice Rowlatt so pertinently said in his summing-up:

"The defence on the question of the insurance have pointed out that there were times when Mrs. Fox had been insured for £4000 as against £3000 at the time of her actual death. It has been said that if she had died then Fox would have come into more money. It is one thing to plot this kind of thing, and another thing to find the opportunity for it. The nerve might fail, you know."

The management gave Fox another room in which to sleep, and Dr. Nichol went with him there and tried to calm him. Fox said that his mother had always been

Introduction.

a wonderful woman to him, and that he only wished he had gone into her room again to see her, as he often did before going to bed himself. He had not done so for fear of disturbing her. He had last seen her sitting by the gas fire reading an evening paper. Sidney Fox remarked to the doctor that his mother was a friend of Walburga, Lady Paget, who had met her death in a very similar way shortly before. It is extremely unlikely that Lady Paget knew Mrs. Fox, but it is within the bounds of probability that Lady Paget's death by fire suggested to Fox the manner of his mother's death. Fox also said that there must have been notes to the value of £24 in his mother's bag, which seems a curious remark for a son distraught with grief.

The doctor gave him an injection of morphine, and he grew calmer. When Inspector Palmer of the Margate Borough Police entered the room to question him, Fox gave his version of the night's events lucidly. He told also of the visit to the graves of the " brothers killed in the war," described how he had lit the gas fire for his mother, and asked if he should wait to turn out the lights. She apparently replied in the negative, and said that it would be all right. According to his own account Fox then left her, went downstairs to the bar for a drink, and came back at about 9.45, and went to sleep. He was aroused about 11.30 p.m. by what he thought was a window rattling, and noticed a smell of fire. He closed the window and went to his mother's room to see if the smell emanated from there. He found her room full of smoke, tried to enter it, but was beaten back. He then ran downstairs for help. Fox also told Inspector Palmer that he was of independent means, and that his mother was of independent means, and that his permanent address would be Lyndhurst, Hants, which seems to have been unjustifiable optimism on his part.

During the inspector's questionings, Fox broke down and cried and asked for a glass of water. Nevertheless,

he was collected enough to tell the inspector that there
had been £24 in his mother's handbag, as he had cashed
a cheque for his mother at her bank in London the
previous day. These notes had as much objective
existence as the luggage and the house at Lyndhurst.

Dr. Nichol came back into the room and asked the
inspector to leave Fox to go to sleep as soon as possible,
and the inspector left the room and asked Police
Constable Bray to show him the handbag. He found
that one side of it was burned, but the inner compartment was intact, save for one tiny scorch mark : of the
notes which Fox declared he had obtained in London,
there was no trace anywhere.

Fox was himself again the next morning, and repeated
his story of the notes to every one with whom he came
in contact. He insisted that he was sure about them,
for he had cashed a cheque for £25 at Lloyds in Threadneedle Street, kept £1 and given the rest to his mother.
Inspector Palmer asked him if his mother had any
jewellery or odd change, and Fox replied that the
jewellery was in the luggage that had " gone on " to
Lyndhurst. Inspector Palmer said to him : " Your
mother had no night attire," and Fox replied calmly :
" My mother has worn none for some time." Inspector
Palmer remarked : " Lyndhurst is rather a large village.
Is there no further address? Is there a name to the
house? " To which Fox replied : " Yes, ' End View.'
My mother recently bought it, and we have been abroad
whilst it was being redecorated and the furniture removed
from our house at Norwich." He went on to add that
his father had died at East Dereham in 1913, and that he
had been proprietor of Fox's Flour Mills. He also said
that he had been educated at Framlingham College and
that his mother had a good income, and that he had
never had to work. The only truth in the whole of this
rigmarole is the undoubted fact that he certainly never
worked if he could possibly avoid it.

Introduction.

Meanwhile, the day following the death, Mr. Harding received a telephone message from the Royal Pavilion Hotel, Folkestone, stating that Fox had been there and that, following the same tactics, although not carrying them to the extremes of a fire and a death, he had left without paying his bill. Mr. Harding then went to the Chief of Police, Mr. Hancock, and expressed his suspicions which had grown on his mind with deadly certainty since Mrs. Harding's deadly discovery of the smoke in Fox's hair. The police told Mr. Harding to charge Fox with obtaining food and accommodation by false pretences, and this was done on the 3rd November.

Fox was held on the charge of fraud while the body of his mother was exhumed. Meanwhile, until this arrest, all seemed to be going well with Fox. The inquest was held on the 24th October. It was very short. A verdict of " Accidental death " was returned, and the incident seemed closed. Mrs. Bugg, a waitress at the Hotel Metropole, condoled with Fox on his mother's death, and added: " You'll have to get married," to which Fox replied: " I shouldn't have done that before she died, I promised her that. I shall be going abroad."

He then told her the story of the notes having been burned in the handbag. Fox also told Miss Hopper how much upset he was at his mother's death, and how he had hoped to have her with him for another twenty years.

Meanwhile, besides receiving the sympathy of the hotel staff he obtained more practical consolation from Mr. Wilson, a Margate solicitor. He placed his affairs in the hands of Mr. Wilson, and on the strength of the insurance and Mrs. Fox's will, the solicitor advanced him on the 25th October the sum of £25, and, three or four days later, he advanced him a further £15.

Fox left the Metropole on Friday, 25th October, still keeping up his tradition of not paying the bill, which

31

Sidney Harry Fox.

then amounted to £12 14s. Probably nobody liked to insist on such a mundane thing as payment from a bereaved son. His mother's funeral took place at Great Fransham, and her childhood friend dug the grave truly. On the day before the burial Fox wrote to Miss Hopper, giving his address as a hotel in Norwich, as follows:—

> " My dear Miss Hopper,
> "I am sending a small book, which I hope you will like. I am not feeling very well. I do wish to-morrow had passed. It doesn't seem possible that this time last week the poor dear soul was well. How I shall miss her."

Fox had been playing what may vulgarly be called " the highbrow racket " with Miss Hopper, who was interested in books, and he had talked of books to her. On leaving the Hotel Metropole, he had taken from her custody the packet that he had confided to her care. Fox, although his tastes did not seem to have drawn him towards women, yet undoubtedly had a way with them. Everybody sympathised with him at the hotel, as can be seen by his little conversations with the chambermaid, the waitress, and Miss Hopper. It must always be remembered that nothing was known at the hotel about any insurances, and it must have seemed incredible to decent and kindly women that this charming young man, with his ready smile and his pleasant manners, could have murdered his mother.

It must have seemed to Fox at this moment that he had not done so badly after all. He had already a considerable sum of money—his mother was buried, her clothes had been thrown away on the municipal dump-heap, which shows how dirty and shabby they must have been, and the false teeth had been given by the chambermaid, Louise Bickmore, to another maid at the Metropole. Not one of the hotels to which he owed money was suing him; the inquest had passed off without

32

Room 66 after the fire, with the burned chair replaced in position

Introduction.

a hitch. If only his lies did not find him out, if only his " stumer " cheques did not return to roost too soon, he could draw the insurance money and go to Australia. Yet, had he known it, he was already in the most serious position, for the insurance companies were suspicious.

There is probably no one so versed in the trickeries of human nature, from the meanest little fraud to the worst crime of all, as an official of an insurance company, and it was to such an official who examined the papers relating to the insurance of Mrs. Fox, that Sidney owed his downfall. The plain, stark fact of murder was writ large upon those papers to the official eye. An ex-policeman employed by one of the insurance companies came down to Margate, and started to make inquiries. It is recorded that this investigator wired to his head office : " Extremely muddy water in this business," and the insurance companies placed Scotland Yard in possession of the facts relating to the policies. Indeed, once suspicion was aroused, facts piled upon each other with deadly effect. The insurance companies, which had not had before their eyes the spectacle of the devoted son, but who merely knew Fox in a business capacity, saw little to recommend him. What was apparent to the insurance companies was that Fox had gone up to London on Monday, 21st October, to extend the policies on his mother's death by accident, until midnight on Wednesday, 23rd October. She was discovered dead—by an accident, as the policies required, twenty minutes before the policies expired. On that Wednesday night Fox was committed to leaving the hotel the following day. He had no money to pay his bill; he had no money to pay a railway fare; he had forged " stumer " cheques. Unless his mother died by external violence before midnight, he had no means of dealing with these difficulties. If, on the other hand, she did die by external violence in that short space of time left to him, he could not only settle his bills and call in his forgeries, but would also be in possession of a large sum of money—£3000—which would enable him to start life afresh.

Looked at from this angle it is difficult to see how Fox ever imagined he could, in the slang phrase, get away with it. Nevertheless, he had a very good defence in which he had trusted. From the 1st May down to the 23rd October he had taken out policies which covered 167 days out of the 176. Mrs. Fox, who was doubtless agreeable to the frauds, which she was unaware threatened her life, had agreed with him to take out these policies, and he was able to say that his mother never liked to travel without an insurance. He had been able also to say that, out of the money he had spent, practically half of their joint income had been upon premiums, and that he personally had received nothing.

All might have been well for Fox if at the first breath of investigation a complicated web of lies had not been revealed. He declared that there had been £24 in his mother's handbag, because he had that day cashed a cheque for that amount in Lloyds in Threadneedle Street. This statement was, of course, easily proved to be a lie. A fantastic amount of pawntickets, given for objects ranging from a gold wrist watch to a pair of trousers, was discovered in Fox's possession. His account of himself as having been a student at Framlingham College was easily proved to be untrue. His statement that his father had been the owner of Fox's Flour Mills at East Dereham was exploded by the simple discovery that there were no such mills. His statement that his mother had bought a house named " End View " at Lyndhurst, and had sent her luggage there also ceased to have any weight when it was discovered that there was no house called " End View " at Lyndhurst, and that no luggage had arrived at that station for any one of the name of Fox.

In fact, once questions began to be asked, the whole elaborate façade that Sidney Fox had built up between himself and a trusting world crumbled and fell away.

34

Introduction.

The defrauded hotels and the insurance companies were too much for Fox, and Sergeant Fleet of the Margate Police Force, one of the officers who attempted artificial respiration on the body of Mrs. Fox, went to Norwich on the 3rd November, and brought back Sidney Fox to Margate. There the young man appeared before the Recorder, Mr. G. Malcolm Hilbery, K.C., on six charges relating to frauds.

The insurance companies communicated with Scotland Yard, and Mr. Hambrook, Chief Inspector of Police, now Superintendent Hambrook, and the late Detective Sergeant Ayto, were sent down to Margate on the 7th November to make inquiries. Both officers were present at exhaustive tests made by Mr. Hammond, who besides being chief officer of the Margate Fire Brigade, was a member of the Institute of Fire Engineers, and had twenty-nine years' experience of fires. Mr. Hammond tried to burn, both with and without the aid of petrol, pieces of carpet, newspapers, a merino vest, horsehair stuffing, such as was in the armchair, and cotton wool, and he found that every time he used no petrol only the pile of the carpet was burned; when he used petrol, the carpet was burned through. He set fire to a piece of underclothing hanging over a cane chair, and found that the top rail was almost burned away, but not the leg, as had been the case with the cane chair found by the window in the bedroom. He also found it was extremely difficult to set fire to a solid stuffed armchair, and more difficult still to set fire to a carpet laid flat upon the floor. He came to the conclusion that such a conflagration as there had been in room 66 could not possibly have been accidental. In fact, not only must it have been deliberate, but it must have been carefully nursed.

To this day it seems that no one knows exactly what it was that Fox used to cause such a dense black and greasy smoke that even by the time Chief Inspector

Sidney Harry Fox.

Hambrook arrived upon the scene the nostrils and finger nails of those who went into room 66 became filled with soot. No wonder it caused Fox's hair to smell even while he had been lighting and tending the fire.

It is an interesting little point of psychology, that while Fox was still held on charges of fraud, Inspector Hambrook, who had had cause to arrest him in the days when he had been nothing but a thief and a forger, and who knew him well, passed by him on several occasions in the anteroom to the Court at Margate, and always Fox stared past him as though he had never seen him.

" Good morning, Fox," said Mr. Hambrook at last.

" I don't know you," muttered Fox.

Had Fox been a little cleverer he would have sent for Mr. Hambrook and said to him. " You know, and I know, that I am a bad lot, and that I have done this and that, but you know I could not be a murderer."

Fox, however, said no such thing. He persisted in his ostrich-like policy.

The grand jury returned a true bill against Fox upon the charges of fraud, but the accusation against him was then altered to that of murder. On 9th January, 1930, he was brought before the Magistrates, and the clerk, Mr. Maugham, read aloud the accusation :

> " That on 23rd October, 1929, you, Sidney Harry Fox, did feloniously, wilfully, and with malice aforethought, kill and murder Rosaline Fox at the Hotel Metropole, Paradise Street, in the Parish of St. John the Baptist, Margate, in the County of Kent."

Fox pleaded " Not guilty." He was defended by Mr. George Hindle, and Mr. Sefton Cohen appeared for the Director of Public Prosecutions.

The proceedings in front of the magistrates ran the normal course, and Fox was committed for trial at Lewes Assizes.

36

Introduction.

VI.

The trial of Fox for the murder of his mother opened at Lewes on Wednesday, 12th March, 1930, before Mr. Justice Rowlatt.

The counsel for the Crown were: The Attorney-General, Sir William A. Jowitt, K.C., M.P.; Sir Henry Curtis Bennett, K.C.; Mr. St. John Hutchinson, and Mr. Gerald Thesiger.

The counsel for the accused were: Mr. J. D. Cassels, K.C.; Mr. S. T. T. James, and Mr. C. Pensotti. Mr. E. H. Bain held a watching brief for two insurance companies.

The trial was chiefly noticeable for the extraordinary conflict of expert medical evidence. It may indeed be said that several things besides the guilt of Fox were proved beyond a doubt—such as the amazing innocence of solicitors, the trustfulness of women (if that needed proof), the courage of commercial travellers, and the discord always ready to flare up among doctors, more particularly amongst those known as experts. There is another point for which this trial should attract particular notice, and, let us hope, an alteration in the law. Mr. Robert Eric Hawkins, assessor in the service of the Ocean Accident and Guarantee Corporation, Ltd., of London, in the evidence which he gave at the Quarter Sessions, testified to the fact that a proposal form against accident for twenty-four hours does not need to be signed, though the policy does have to be signed by the person insured. However, as we know, Rosaline Fox would have signed anything that her " clever " son gave her to sign, and it should surely not be possible to take out a twenty-four hours' insurance against death by accident on the life of another human being. Mr. Hindle, who cross-examined him for the defence, asked—

" Does your company issue thousands of those day policies particularly in conjunction with travel tickets? "

Sidney Harry Fox.

Mr. Hawkins replied in the affirmative.

" They are usually sold by being canvassed for when persons buy travel tickets? " continued Mr. Hindle.

" Yes."

" Messrs. Pickfords are your agents and they canvass for you? "

" Yes, they get commission and are out to get all they can."

" So there is nothing very unusual about it? "

" No."

It is therefore to the defence that we owe our knowledge of this shocking state of affairs. There is nothing to prevent a son, a wife, or a husband (the relationship is of no matter) getting some one's life insured against accident for twenty-four hours, and this is almost asking for the commission of the crime of murder. There are many people in this world in a state of mental failure, or entirely under the domination of some other human being, who would sign whatever was asked of them. It must be remembered that at one time there was nothing to prevent a person insuring the life of some one else without even mentioning the fact. Those were the great days for the poisoners, and the law was amended, yet it seems that there is still further protection needed for an insured person. Indeed, so deadly was the coincidence of Fox's insurance of his mother's death against accident, and that same death, that it was an official of an insurance company who first declared openly that murder must have been committed.

The Attorney-General was deadly both in his speeches and in his cross-examinations, although strictly correct in everything he said. Yet, deadly as he was, he probably did not do Fox as much harm as Fox did himself. Again it was shown how inexorable is the ordeal of the witness-box for a guilty man. The isolation of the dock, that focus of a Court-room, is relentless enough in bringing out every unpleasing physical attribute of the accused

Introduction.

—there are very few of us who would not seem to be of the alleged " criminal type " in the fierce light which beats upon the dock—but the witness-box, where speech brings a man to life, so that the twists of his thought and of his personality are laid bare, is an even more deadly exposure, save to the man wrongly accused.

Very often the mere perusal of a trial will leave the reader surprised at the verdict—he has not allowed for the effect the accused has made upon the jury in the witness-box. Innocent men have been saved by going into the box, but it is the most unsafe spot in the world for those who are guilty. Such an one would be well advised to leave his defence to his counsel, and the onus of proving the case upon the Crown, instead of hindering the former, and doing the work of the latter.

Fox's conceit would have made such a course impossible to him. He had gone through life trusting, with a very fair measure of success, to his charm and personality, which had always served him well, and he could see no reason why these assets should fail him now.

Patrick Mahon, the murderer of Emily Bealby Kaye at the Crumbles, was of the same vain type as Fox. Mahon was extremely good looking, and the present writer has had it on the authority of an eminent counsel present at the trials of both men that before he stood his trial (in the same Court-house as Fox) he sent out for the bottle of a patent preparation guaranteed to produce a manly sunburn.

Fox did not do this, his face showed the prison pallor, but he looked smart and dapper enough. He wore a black tie and black overcoat, and he remained perfectly confident throughout the whole of his ordeal. Mr. E. H. W. Meyerstein, who was present through the trial, says that his voice was of the " acquired-genteel type," but that when after sentence had been passed he uttered the words: " My lord, I never murdered my mother," his

Sidney Harry Fox.

voice took on a crooning inflection, as though he were saddened by the heartlessness of the world. He did not, according to the same eyewitness, look like a man likely to be guilty of a murder by violence, but then neither did Patrick Mahon, nor James Canham Read, nor Devereux, nor many others of unholy memory. His personality has been summed up to the writer by Mr. Meyerstein as expressed by the word "plausible."

He was perfectly calm all through the gruelling cross-examination of the Attorney-General, and only brushed the corners of his eyes with a handkerchief as his own counsel rose to re-examine.

Patrick Mahon, when in the witness-box, also used a handkerchief—he was wearing a plum-coloured suit and had bought a mauve silk handkerchief which he had arranged with care in his breast pocket. When he affected to break down on telling of Miss Kaye's death, he took out a handkerchief and put it to his eyes, but it was an ordinary linen one from his trousers pocket, the carefully arranged folds of mauve silk remained undisturbed. . . . Yet Mahon really broke down during a curious incident which Fox survived unmoved. At each trial when the accused was in the box, there came a terrific clap of thunder, and the Court darkened. Mahon lost his nerve when this happened, and never recovered it, but Fox remained calm and unmoved. It was indeed that calm of Fox's which did him so much harm in the box, just as Seddon's calm had told against him years earlier in the box at the Central Criminal Court.

Fox, in fact, did himself almost more harm—save for one exception—in examination in chief than he did in cross-examination. He smiled in a pleasant, social manner at his solicitor and counsel, and he also did so when illustrating the " sham fight " which he had already described as being an occurrence that took place frequently between him and his mother when the old lady was feeling in good form.

Introduction.

The questions of the Attorney-General were so deadly that a certain sympathy—the same sort of sympathy the English are apt to feel for any animal, human or otherwise, that has been driven into a corner—might have been evoked, but when Fox's own counsel asked him: "What was the feeling between you and your mother," and Fox replied: "Excellent—the ordinary feeling between mother and son," he spoke in such a cold matter-of-fact tone that he might just as well have been saying that she was, in insurance terms, "a first-class life." He used the cliché "the day of the tragedy" in speaking of his mother's death, in the same manner. But, after all, what really finished Fox was his answer to the Attorney-General when questioned as to the closing of the door of room 66.

It will be remembered that according to Fox's own account he smelt smoke, opened the door into his mother's room, saw a fire blazing, and the room dense and black with fumes, and yet shut the door again before running downstairs for help.

"Did you," asked the Attorney-General, "realise when you opened the communicating door that the atmosphere of the room was such as would probably suffocate anybody inside?"

"If I had stayed in three or four minutes I should have been suffocated," replied Fox.

"So that you must have been greatly apprehensive for your mother?"

"I was."

"Fox, you closed the door?"

"It is quite possible I did."

"Can you explain to me," demanded the Attorney-General, "why it was that you closed the door instead of flinging it wide open?"

Then Fox made the fatal reply: "*My explanation of that now is that the smoke should not spread into the hotel.*"

41

Sidney Harry Fox.

Such a gasp went up from the crowded Court-room
while every one present drew in a breath of horror, as to
be definitely audible.

The Attorney-General returned to the attack.

" So that you left your mother, as you say, with the
communicating door closed, and with the door of room
67 [Fox's own room] closed. You passed the door of
No. 66 [the door of Mrs. Fox's room, which gave upon
the corridor], but you did not open that, and you knew
your mother was inside that room? "

The truth of the matter was that Fox did not dare
take any risks, just in case his mother had not been dead
after his hands had closed about her throat, and after
he had set the room on fire. He felt forced to leave her
in that choking atmosphere till the last moment. The
facts, so unanswerable by the defence, of the strip of
unburned carpet between the gas fire and the armchair,
of the cane chair damaged by fire, yet found by the
window, of the French newspaper, and the motive
supplied by the insurance policies, all these things were
not more deadly than Fox's reply in the witness-box as
to why he had not thrown open the doors of his mother's
room.

Sir Bernard Spilsbury, who had conducted the post-
mortem examination, was, of course, a very heavy gun
brought by the prosecution. No other medical expert
in the case entirely agreed with him.

Professor Sidney Smith, Regius Professor of Forensic
Medicine in Edinburgh University, and Dr. Brontë,
formerly Crown Pathologist for All Ireland, were in
direct opposition to Sir Bernard Spilsbury. Dr. H. D.
Weir, pathologist to the National Hospital for Diseases
of the Heart, was, in the main, in agreement with Sir
Bernard, and where he was in disagreement, that disagreement was, from the layman's point of view, so
slight that it hardly affected the issue—in other words,
Sir Bernard Spilsbury stated definitely that the deceased

Introduction.

had not died as the result of the fire—that she was already dead before the fire had been set alight, from asphyxia, due to manual strangulation, whereas Dr. Weir was of opinion that there was sufficient disease of the heart for Mrs. Fox to have died of heart failure, following on strangulation. To quote his own words: " the strangulation itself did not cause death, but brought on heart failure." It is unnecessary to point out to the reader that even if this latter hypothesis be the true one, Mrs. Fox was, none the less, murdered.

Professor Smith's contention was that Mrs. Fox's heart was sufficiently feeble for her to have died from heart failure because of the additional strain imposed by sudden fright on awakening and finding the room full of smoke and attempting to get up. Dr. Brontë was of the same opinion and gave it as his view that Mrs. Fox died of heart failure as the result of disease of vessels and muscles of the heart exaggerated by shock. Again it is unnecessary to point out that if—as was undoubtedly the case—the fire was lit feloniously—even only to commit arson—Mrs. Fox none the less died of its effects, according to Professor Smith and Dr. Brontë, so that at the very least a charge of manslaughter would lie against the lighter of the fire.

In the evidence of these experts and of those of the other doctors in the case, there is a mass of highly technical material which presents a difficulty for the lay mind, but the broad issue between the opposing camps is as stated above. The only other medical things which it is necessary for the lay mind to grapple with are the causes for this division of opinion.

Sir Bernard Spilsbury had attended the exhumation of Mrs. Fox's body, and conducted a post-mortem examination. Dr. Roche Lynch, Senior Official Analyst to the Home Office, examined the stomach and its contents and other organs, which Sir Bernard Spilsbury took from the dead woman's body. It must be remembered that

Sidney Harry Fox.

when Sir Bernard Spilsbury went down to Great
Fransham there was no idea that Mrs. Fox had been
strangled; the possibility of the presence of poison and
the effects of suffocation by smoke and the state of the
heart were the first things to be considered. Dr. Roche
Lynch found no trace of poison, and merely a little
quantity of alcohol in the stomach, such as would remain
if Mrs. Fox had taken a glass of port before her death.
Sir Bernard Spilsbury found no external marks or signs
of violence upon the body, but he found the heart to be
moderately enlarged, though the cavities were healthy.
There was a patch of fibrosis on the wall of the heart
and slight disease of the aorta, and of the left coronary
artery of the heart, but he thought this amount of heart
disease not enough to account for sudden death from
heart failure. There was no deposit of soot on the linings
of the air passages even under a microscopic examination,
neither was there any carbon monoxide in the blood such
as one might have expected to find if Mrs. Fox had died
from the fumes given off by the fire. Sir Bernard stated
definitely that he would eliminate as a cause of death the
effects of the fire in room 66. At the back of the larynx
Sir Bernard maintained that he had found a recent bruise
about the size of half-a-crown, which would have been
caused by violence, and it was then that he had the first
indication pointing to the conclusion which he eventually
drew, and to which he firmly adhered, that death was
due to strangulation.

He continued his dissection, but found no injury to
the cartilages or bones of the larynx. An examination
of the tongue disclosed a minute bruise about midway
down the tongue, only visible with the help of the
microscope. He formed the opinion that this bruise on
the tongue, which was about a quarter of an inch in
diameter, had been inflicted during life or within a
minute or so after the heart had stopped beating, and
had probably been caused by the pressure of artificial

44

Introduction.

teeth in the mouth. On the whole he thought it more likely to have been caused before the heart ceased to beat than after. The " half-crown bruise," as it came to be known, must, he said, have been caused before death, either by the larynx being pressed back against the spine, or by some upward movement, pushing the larynx up towards the mouth. This latter he considered the more likely, and the same action might have caused the biting of the tongue by forcing the jaws back. The epiglottis was congested and had some small marks indicating bleeding, conditions characteristic of death from strangulation. Sir Bernard also found a small dark area on the surface of the thyroid gland which, in his view, confirmed his opinion that death had occurred by strangulation, when the dentures were in the mouth.

Professor Smith and Dr. Brontë, however, did not take the same view, and Dr. Weir dissented slightly, and for that reason Sir Bernard Spilsbury preferred not to lay too much stress upon the possible injury to the thyroid gland. Nothing, however, shook him as to the other three symptoms, the half-crown bruise, the bruise on the tongue, and the marks on the epiglottis.

It was about this half-crown bruise that the medical warfare was waged most fiercely. Unfortunately the larynx was not at once preserved, and by the time Sir Bernard got it to his laboratory it had putrified, so it was Sir Bernard alone who saw the bruise. Professor Smith and Dr. Brontë were of the opinion that the mark at the back of the larynx was not a bruise at all, but a post-mortem change—they maintained that if it had been a bruise it could not possibly have been made without some external marks being left upon the neck. A point in favour of the accused was that the hyoid bone—a tiny bone in the larynx, was found by Sir Bernard to be unbroken, and the hyoid bone is very brittle. Sir Bernard admitted that death by strangulation would have been more evident if the hyoid bone had been found broken. However, there have been several cases of strangulation in which the hyoid bone has not been fractured.

" In your experience of strangulation cases, have you ever known a case with fewer signs than this? " asked Mr. Cassels of Sir Bernard Spilsbury, who replied : "No, I have not."

Professor Smith gave it as his definite opinion that Mrs. Fox had died of heart failure. In his view Mrs. Fox wakened up to find the room full of smoke, had tried to get up out of bed, and the exertion and fear brought about death from heart failure. To the suggestion that the pillow (which it will be remembered was found on the pedestal table) might have been pressed over Mrs. Fox's face, which would account for the lack of external signs of manual strangulation, he said he would have expected a stain of saliva, or even a blood stain to have been found on the pillow. Dr. Brontë agreed on all these points. He gave it as his opinion that Mrs. Fox died of heart failure as the result of her heart disease, accelerated by shock. He had not seen the half-crown bruise himself, so, with great correctitude, refused to swear to its existence. He maintained that had a pillow been used to suffocate Mrs. Fox there must have been froth round her mouth and nose which would have been bound to have stained the pillow.

Sir Bernard maintained that the half-crown mark at the back of the larynx could not possibly have been a mark of putrefaction. " It was a bruise and nothing else. There are no two opinions about that. If it had been putrefaction, the mark would not have been red in colour, but green." At the time that Dr. Brontë and Professor Smith saw the mark it was green—" overlaid," said Sir Bernard, " by the uniform green colour of putre-faction." Dr. Brontë declared that putrefaction changes would have magnified the bruise and made it easier to detect.

In short, there was the usual complete disagreement

46

Introduction.

among the medical experts which is to be found in every murder trial. Professor Smith and Dr. Brontë both refused to accept the famous " half-crown bruise." Sir Bernard Spilsbury stood by his statement undaunted.

Professor Smith and Dr. Brontë gave it as their convinced opinion that the deceased had not died from asphyxia—a process of some length—and both these experts were of opinion that Mrs. Fox had died of heart failure through shock, though Professor Smith admitted that death might occur suddenly in asphyxia when it was due to heart failure. All this may seem to the layman to be a distinction without a difference—especially since every one eventually dies of heart-failure—but the exactitude of scientific evidence in England is deservedly rated high, and each witness was giving an opinion from which it would have been impossible for him to deviate.

Mr. Justice Rowlatt put the following question to Professor Smith: " Supposing the woman had been found lying dead in the position she was with the body externally and internally in the condition it was, and there had been no question of a fire, could you have given an opinion as to the cause of death? "

Professor Smith answered: " In such a case I would have been of opinion that she died from heart failure."

" Heart failure just by pure accident? " asked the judge.

" Yes, my lord," replied Professor Smith.

Dr. Weir, who was unable, by the time he saw the larynx, to discern the " half-crown bruise," yet was of opinion that there were sufficient bruises to rule out the question of a purely accidental death. In his opinion, except for the bruises, there was sufficient disease in the heart to account for death from natural causes, but he said definitely: " In my opinion death was due to heart failure due to partial strangulation—to commencing strangulation—in other words that the strangulation itself did not cause death, but brought on heart failure."

Sidney Harry Fox.

Therefore we see that there were three experts for death from heart failure. Professor Smith and Dr. Brontë did not deny that the sight of the fire—always provided she was alive when the fire started—might have brought on the heart attack from which they maintained she died.

Dr. Weir's opinion has already been given.

Sir Bernard Spilsbury definitely diagnosed that death was due to strangulation, and that the fire was not the cause of her death, since under a microscopical examination he found no traces of soot in the throat and ear passages nor any carbon monoxide in the blood. The pillow as a smothering agent was not considered seriously. Sir Bernard Spilsbury said that suffocation by a pillow could not have produced the changes he found in the corpse, and Professor Smith and Dr. Brontë agreed there would have been a stain on the pillow caused by froth from the mouth and nose had it been used for the purposes of suffocation.

In fact the only thing on which the experts seemed to agree was the elimination of the pillow, and, indeed, it is not very difficult for the ordinary layman with common sense to account for its position on the side table. It may easily have fallen off the bed and been hastily placed there by the murderer.

It will be seen at once that the three theories, both of the medical gentlemen for the prosecution and those for the defence, led to one thing—murder.

Sir Bernard Spilsbury and Dr. Weir were definite that death was caused, or precipitated, by strangulation, and indeed the probabilities are that Fox did not light the fire before his mother was dead. Whichever of the medical experts was in the right, the fact still remains that the fire was without doubt feloniously lit; and hence if a jury had come to the conclusion that Fox contemplated the fire might so frighten a woman with a weak heart as to cause death (on the supposition that he was

48

a reasonable enough man to have contemplated this eventuality), then the jury might still have brought in a verdict of murder. Even if the jury decided he could not so have contemplated, they would still have had to bring in, at the least, a verdict of manslaughter.

It is needless to say that counsel both for the prosecution and the defence made the utmost of these disagreements among experts, and that Mr. Justice Rowlatt held the scales with the most admirable fairness in his summing-up.

VII.

When Fox was found guilty, after the jury had been absent for an hour and ten minutes, and was duly sentenced to death, a woman spectator, who was possibly hysterical—and certainly foolish—cried out: " If his own mother were here, she would forgive him."

Whether the lady expected the disembodied spirit of Mrs. Fox to manifest itself, or whether she meant that Mrs. Fox would forgive her son had she been present in the flesh, in which case there would have been no trial at all, is not known. In any case the feelings of Mrs. Fox, even if ascertainable, could hardly be used as a measure by which to mete that justice which is designed for the protection of the citizen.

Rosaline Fox herself had never been law-abiding—I am not referring to the personal and hence less important matter of sex, which the English-speaking world so arbitrarily means when it refers to " morality," but to those more serious sins against honesty which can so cruelly affect the community. She had liked " living soft," and she had done so as regardless of unpaid landladies with arduous livings to earn as of big hotels, about which latter she may have said to herself that if people would be so trusting and foolish they had only themselves to blame. She had committed the meanness of trading on the generosity and kindly feelings of

Sidney Harry Fox.

every one with whom she came in contact at the Margate hotel, trusting to her " clever " son to get them both away unharmed as he had so often done before.

She must sometimes have envisaged the risk of prison, familiar as she had been with it in relation to Sidney; she may even have realised that in case of exposure there would be unpleasantness for herself, though it was most unlikely that a Bench of magistrates would send an old woman suffering from *paralysis agitans* to prison. But whatever thoughts passed through that queer, distorted mind of hers, we can be fairly sure that there was one which did not—and that was the thought that her son Sidney would take her life.

Imagine that last scene in room 66 as it must, more or less, have taken place. There is no doubt that Sidney Fox was guilty of the premeditated murder of his mother. Which, then, is the more likely proposition, that he had laid and " coaxed " the fire beneath the armchair while his mother was still living, and able to press the bell and call for help, or that he had killed her first and lit the fire afterwards in safety, gathering together the newspapers, even that old French paper which was to prove so fatal to him, setting fire to the slow-burning underclothing, waiting anxiously to make sure that his mother was really dead and that the fire would really burn, whilst the time factor must have been ever present in his mind? For it had to be before twelve o'clock that the dread discovery was made or all his planning would have been for nothing.

Fox had the advantage of counsel for the defence making the last speech, and Mr. Cassels made the most of the fact that (as usual) experts had disagreed, and drew attention to the fact that if Fox had it in his heart to murder his mother it would have been easier, instead of staging a fire, for him simply to have turned on the gas after the old woman was asleep. " What easier," asked Mr. Cassels, " than to fill the slot of the gas meter, and while his mother lay asleep to go and turn on that

50

Introduction.

gas and leave her to suffocate in that atmosphere? What easier than to explain that this suffering old woman in turning out the fire had turned it on again? "

Nothing easier—had it not been for Mrs. Morse, for although according to English law that strange incident of the gas turned on in Mrs. Morse's bedroom had not been brought to light in Court, the guilty consciousness of it was present in Fox's mind, and he knew, too, that the Portsmouth police knew of it.

Also, he only had until midnight. Supposing he had killed his mother, placed her, face down, with her fingers on the gas tap with the gas turned on unlit, and had then waited in the next room and had smelt no gas, he would still have had to rush downstairs with the news of the death well before midnight. People might have made experiments afterwards and found out that for many hours the gas escaped up the chimney and that in Fox's room it could not be smelt. Had he had the whole night, and could his mother have been discovered lying by the stove in the morning matters might have been different, but by then the policy would have expired—and in any case it is unlikely, with the figure of Mrs. Morse always in the background of his mind, that he would have dared to make the attempt.

Taking everything in conjunction—the unburned strip of carpet between the gas fire and the armchair, the fact that the armchair had caught fire from beneath, the position of the scorched cane chair which, burned by the fire, was yet found by the window, and so showed that some one must have been present at the conflagration, the unprecedented half-bottle of port, the strange position of the body, and the patch of urine which showed sudden shock, and above all that fatal shutting of the door upon the intense smoke, the taking out of the accident policy until midnight, and the impossible financial condition Fox would have found himself in on the following day had his mother not died from an

51

accident—all these things outweighed the fact that Sir Bernard Spilsbury agreed that he had never known a case of strangulation with fewer signs than that of Mrs. Fox, and that other medical experts disagreed with him as to the cause of death being strangulation.

There is about an English jury a saving common sense which, crude as all human adjustments must be when it comes to the understanding by any one mind of the processes of another, yet on the whole works out extremely fairly and, if anything, to the benefit of the accused. The difference of medical experts, the suggestion of an easier method of murder, the devotion of Fox to his mother, testified to by many witnesses— none of these things counted compared with Fox's own demeanour in the box, his conduct on the night that his mother died, and, above all, the fatal matter of the insurances.

Chance can be kind—every year, as we know, there are lucky people who win the Calcutta Sweep and the Irish Sweepstake. But there is a limit to the lucky chances of life, and that a man who had no resources should have insured his mother up till midnight from death by accident and have found her dead by accident at twenty minutes to twelve was really too much for the jury. It will be remembered that in the case of George Joseph Smith, his reply to the fact that three of his wives had died in their baths was that it was just his bad luck, but the series of coincidences was too much for the common sense of Mr. Justice Scrutton and of the jury.

Fox, like Smith, had been lucky for so long that he had trusted his luck beyond the margin of safety.

What is beyond the possibility of doubt (in so far as one can say that of any human happening) is that Fox was guilty of matricide, and hence it follows that he must have suffered a great deal of his punishment on that fatal Wednesday night in the hotel. Was she really dead? How could he be sure? The room was too full

Introduction.

of smoke by then for him, with his murderer's nerves stretched to breaking point, to go in and make sure. Just as George Joseph Smith may have wondered, when artificial respiration was being applied to each of his brides, whether those lips he had thought stilled for ever might not open and breathe one condemnatory sentence, so must Fox have wondered when he saw the same methods being applied to his old mother, whom fat, dirty, and naked save for a small vest, he had allowed to be dragged out by strangers, so that a brave man, who was also a compassionate Samaritan, covered the body with his coat.

It will be noticed that it was on that night that Fox showed sign of nerves. Afterwards, reassured by the sympathy of the staff of the hotel, he plucked up heart and went on with the dreadful business of hypocritical grief.

When Fox died there was removed from this world an unscrupulous egoist, and the same may well be said of his mother, but she at least had real affection for her son, and trusted him, although she knew his life, like her own, was a gigantic sham.

There is a mediæval legend, put into verse by one Miss Adelaide Ann Proctor, of a woman who was allowed to revisit this earth for a glimpse of her husband, and saw him making love to her successor, and when she returned to purgatory she was told that she was free to go on into paradise, that her purgatory had all taken place in that one moment. It is difficult to measure time or space, but it takes merely an ordinary human being to realise that if Rosaline Fox had that moment of knowledge and terror to which the evidence points, it must have in great measure paid for all her sins.

Fox died without confession. It is unfair to credit him with all the sanctimonious outpourings which the papers published as from his pen.

He was executed at Maidstone Gaol on Tuesday, 8th April, 1930.

53

Leading Dates in the Sidney Harry Fox Case.

1916   Fox defrauded a greengrocer at Brighton.

1918   Fox arrested in London and sentenced to three months hard labour. Mrs. Fox was at this time in receipt of 10s. a week pension in respect of one of her sons killed in the war.

1919   Fox given eight months hard labour for forgery.

1920   Six months for victimising London stores.

1922   Twelve months for obtaining credit from a London hotel by fraud.

1924   Twelve months hard labour for larceny and fraud.

1927   Mrs. Fox and Mrs. Morse took a flat in Southsea, and were joined by Fox.

1928   20th February. Mrs. Fox admitted to St. Mary's Hospital, Portsmouth, as an indigent person.

      March. Fox sent to prison for fifteen months for stealing jewellery from a furnished flat.

1929   March. Mrs. Fox taken away from St. Mary's Hospital, Portsmouth, by Sidney Harry Fox.

      21st April. Mrs. Fox's will was made.

      1st May? Fox insured his mother for the first time.

      NOTE.—*The brief of the prosecuting counsel says Fox insured his mother nine days after the will—this would be 30th April, not 1st May.*

      Wednesday, 16th October. Fox took rooms for himself and his mother at Hotel Metropole, Margate, saying it was only for one night.

      Sunday, 20th October. Fox called in Dr. Austin. Their rooms were changed for Nos. 66-67. Room 66 had a gas fire. Fox tried and failed to cash cheque through Mr. Farmer, chemist, who made up medicine for him.

      Monday, 21st October. Fox succeeded in cashing cheque through Messrs. Woolls, Ltd., chemists.

Sidney Harry Fox.

1929   Monday, 21st October.   Fox went to London and arranged the insurance policies, to expire at midnight of Wednesday, 23rd October.

Wednesday, 23rd October, 9.30 p.m.   Fox bought half a bottle of port at the Hoy Hotel, Margate.   Fire in room 66 and death of Mrs. Fox.

Thursday, 24th October.   Inquest.

Friday, 25th October.   Fox left Metropole Hotel.

Tuesday, 29th October.   Funeral of Mrs. Fox at Great Fransham.

Sunday, 3rd November.   Police Sergeant Fleet, of the Margate Police Force, went to Norwich and returned to Margate with the accused who was later charged with fraud.

Thursday, 7th November.   Scotland Yard called in.

Saturday, 9th November.   Exhumation of the body of Mrs. Fox.

1930   Thursday, 9th January.   Fox charged with the murder before the Margate magistrates.

Friday, 10th January.   Fox appeared before the Recorder on six charges relating to frauds.   Grand jury returned a true bill. Indictment transmitted to the next Kent Assizes.

Friday, 17th January.   Proceedings before the magistrates resumed.

Friday, 21st February.   Fox committed for trial.

Wednesday, 12th March.   Trial opens at the County Hall, Lewes.

Friday, 21st March.   The Verdict.

Tuesday, 8th April.   Fox executed.

THE TRIAL

AT THE

SUSSEX ASSIZES,

COUNTY HALL, LEWES,

ON

WEDNESDAY, 12TH MARCH, 1930.

Judge—

MR. JUSTICE ROWLATT.

Counsel for the Crown—

THE ATTORNEY-GENERAL (Sir William A. Jowitt, K.C., M.P.),
Sir HENRY CURTIS BENNETT, K.C.,
Mr. ST. JOHN HUTCHINSON, and
Mr. GERALD THESIGER.

Counsel for the Accused—

Mr. J. D. CASSELS, K.C.,
Mr. S. T. T. JAMES, and
Mr. C. PENSOTTI.

Mr. E. H. Bain held a watching brief for two
Insurance Companies.

First Day—Wednesday, 12th March, 1930.

The CLERK OF COURT—Sidney Harry Fox, you are charged on indictment that on the 23rd of October in last year you murdered your mother, Mrs. Rosaline Fox, in room 66, at the Hotel Metropole, Margate. Well, Sidney Harry Fox, are you guilty or not guilty?

The ACCUSED—Not guilty.

Opening Speech for the Crown.

The ATTORNEY-GENERAL—My lord and gentlemen of the jury, the accused in your hands and over whose destiny you have control is charged with the most serious crime known to our law. He is charged with the crime of murder, and you have the highest and most important duty which citizens of this country can be called upon to perform. In a case of this sort, as indeed in any criminal case, it is for the prosecution to establish the guilt of the accused beyond reasonable doubt, and not for the accused to establish his innocence. For myself as Attorney-General, and for any counsel engaged in the prosecution in criminal cases, it is our duty without rhetoric simply to call to your attention the facts of the case so far as we know them, whether they tell against the accused or whether they tell in his favour, so that on hearing these facts you may do justice according to the evidence.

What makes this case happily almost unparalleled in this country is that Rosaline Fox, with whose murder Fox is accused, was his mother. The case for the prosecution is this, that on the 23rd October of last year he strangled his mother, and strangled her in order that he might reap financial benefit by her death. I think I shall start my story by taking you back to Wednesday, 16th October, of last year. Had you on that day chanced to have been at the Hotel Metropole, Margate, about six o'clock in the evening you would have seen a couple come into the hotel

59

Sidney Harry Fox.

who might perhaps have attracted your attention. They were the accused and his mother. Mrs. Rosaline Fox had been the wife—I think her husband is dead—of a man employed on the railway, and she had lived most of her married life at a village called Great Fransham. She had four sons. The eldest son, who is still alive, is a hospital attendant at Cosham, and he will be called before you as a witness. The second son served in France, and was killed in the war in 1917. The third son was killed at Woolwich Arsenal, I presume by some explosion, in 1915; and the fourth and youngest son is Sidney Harry Fox, the accused. As regards the old lady—she was not really an old lady, but old for her years, she being sixty-three years old—I will content myself for the moment by telling you this : she had been in the infirmary at Portsmouth, near where her eldest son was a hospital attendant, as a sick and destitute person for rather more than a year—from 20th February, 1928, until 27th March, 1929. She left in the charge of her youngest son, the accused. She was in receipt of a pension of 10s. a week. She was rather old for her years, and to see her walk she was obviously suffering from some type of paralysis, which seemed to prevent her from having complete control over her muscles. As she walked she was observed rather to shuffle along.

The accused, the youngest son, had during the war performed some military service in this country, and was in receipt of a pension of 8s. a week by reason of some aggravation of some condition or other said to have been caused by that service. He was educated at the village school at Great Fransham. You will see that the joint pension coming to these two people who walked into the Hotel Metropole amounted to 18s. a week. They came from the County Hotel, Canterbury, where they had been from 12th October to 15th October. On 15th October they left that hotel with a brown paper parcel, which comprised the only luggage they had in the world.

The accused is charged with murder. Whether you take a favourable view or an unfavourable view as to his conduct in certain matters which are incidental to this case is

Opening Speech for the Crown.

The Attorney-General

neither here nor there. You are not concerned with any matters of that sort at all. You are here to say only whether he is guilty of murder or not. But I cannot leave out those matters for this reason : it is essential in judging this case that you should bear this fact clearly in mind, that it is manifest from what I am going to say that the accused and his mother were in desperate financial straits. They were spending every day a good deal more than the joint weekly pension of 18s., and while they were staying at the County Hotel, Canterbury, where they had arrived on 12th October, they incurred a bill of £4 16s. Leaving that hotel on 15th October, they were unable to pay more than £2, and there was a balance of £2 16s. unpaid. They took with them the only luggage they had in the world, a brown paper parcel. After leaving Canterbury they went to the Savoy Restaurant, Dover, for one night, incurring a debt of 14s. 6d., of which only 4s. 6d. was paid. On 16th October they arrived at the Hotel Metropole, Margate. Upon arrival at the Hotel Metropole, the accused told the receptionist, Miss Hopper, that he wanted two single rooms with communicating doors for one night, and explained the absence of any luggage by saying it had been sent on. As regards the clothing they had, the deceased had some kind of overcoat, a little piece of fur, one undergarment, two pairs of stockings, a pair of shoes, and two stockinette dresses, which she wore one on the top of the other. She had no night attire or washing materials, and had two plates of artificial teeth, as she had no teeth of her own, or even stumps. The accused was in the same state in regard to clothes, he having nothing except what he stood up in. On the evening he arrived, the accused handed an envelope to Miss Hopper asking her to put it in the safe. You will probably hear that there was nothing much in that envelope, but you can readily understand that when a person asks for an envelope to be put in the safe, it makes the hotel people think that he has valuables about him, and that it is quite all right to trust him. He explained to Miss Hopper that he and his mother had been visiting the graves of his three brothers who had been killed in the war. You will realise that, in fact, only one brother was killed in the

Sidney Harry Fox.

war. They had originally arranged to stay only one night. The accused asked Miss Hopper if he might stay another day, as he had friends to see in the neighbourhood. He is a well-spoken young man, and, obviously from his handwriting, he is well educated and intelligent. Plausible as he was in his manner, no objection was taken to his staying on.

On 17th or 18th October the accused went to Ramsgate, and there obtained from Messrs. Pickfords an insurance policy for £1000 in the event of the holder's death from external accidental means. The premium was 2s., and the document purported to be signed by Rosaline Fox, but whether or not it was so signed is not a matter on which I express any view. I do not think it very much matters, but I should think it is not improbable that this old lady would have signed any document her son asked without clearly understanding what it was. You may have to consider whether it was her signature or not on that and two similar documents.

On the evening of 18th October the accused told Mr. Harding, the manager of the hotel, that he would like to be introduced to a firm of local solicitors about some insurance business, and the name of a firm was given to him. Whether he really wanted to I should think was very doubtful. It may have been like the envelope in the safe—to give Mr. Harding the impression that he was a man of substance and a man of affairs.

They were still at the hotel on Sunday, 20th October, and on that day the accused went to the hotel manager, Mr. Harding, and told him that his mother appeared to be in a faint. Mr. Harding went to the room and found the deceased lying fully dressed on the bed. He administered some drops of sal volatile and suggested sending for a doctor. He also suggested that they should give up their rooms 68 and 70, which had no fires, and remove into rooms 66 and 67. Room 66 had a gas fire, and it had a communicating door which enabled one to pass into the adjoining room, which was occupied by the accused, without going into the passage outside. Dr. Austin, who had been sent

Opening Speech for the Crown.

The Attorney-General

for, arrived about luncheon time, and found very little the matter with the deceased, and prescribed a simple tonic—

> 1½ drs. nux vomica.
> ½ oz. sal volatile.
> Make up to 8 oz. bottle with chloroform water.
> To be taken every four hours.

A bottle would last approximately three days. Dr. Austin prescribed that tonic and arranged that he would call back the following day. The medicine was obtained by a page-boy from Messrs. Woolls, chemists. On that day a bottle containing petrol was observed to be in the possession of the accused, and he and a chambermaid were seen using it to clean his and his mother's coats. It may be wrong to attach very much importance to that petrol bottle, but if the accused was to keep up a certain appearance with only one suit of clothes it would not be unnatural that he should get some petrol to keep himself as smart as he could. You will hear that this bottle of petrol was found in room 66 after the tragedy had taken place. There was a fire in the room, and the suggestion of the prosecution is that, after the murder had taken place, the fire was lit, not accidentally, but purposely, to make it appear that the woman, who had been previously strangled, lost her life through the fire. I do not attach too much importance to that bottle. You will see the significance of the petrol, although very little appears to have been taken out of that bottle.

Mr. Justice Rowlatt—Is there very much in it? I think I should drop it out.

The Attorney-General—I do not think I could take the responsibility of doing that, my lord, but at any rate there is not much in the point of the bottle.

The accused told Miss Hopper and a barmaid that the chemist had to break down the doctor's prescription for his mother for fear of an overdose. You will have to ask yourselves what possible point there was in telling that sort of story unless you think it showed that he was at that time casting about in his mind to try to think of a method of achieving what he wanted to achieve.

On 21st October the accused obtained a second bottle of

Sidney Harry Fox.

tonic from the chemist, and, after the chemist had declined
to cash a cheque for him, he returned and induced the
assistant to do so, saying that the chemist had said it would
be all right. That shows the desperate straits in which this
man was put to raise money. That same day the accused
took his mother a bunch of grapes, and, giving the chambermaid 7s. 6d., asked her to look after his mother, as he was
going to London. He telephoned from London that night
and the next morning, inquiring after his mother. No
doubt my learned friend will press this point and say,
" Look how careful and solicitous this son was." On the
other hand, it is quite possible you may come to the conclusion that these telephone calls and a tip to the chambermaid were all of a piece to impress people that he was a
solicitous and thoughtful son.

I will now deal with the accused's visit to London on
22nd October. We do not know where he stayed, but we do
know something that he did. At about twelve mid-day on
Tuesday, 22nd October, he went to the Cornhill Insurance
Company and saw the clerk in the renewal department and
asked that two insurance policies should be extended until
midnight on 23rd October, one for £2000 and one for £1000.
The previous extensions of the £2000 policy had expired at
noon on various dates, but on applying for the extension
of the 23rd the accused said, " I want it not until noon, but
until midnight." The accused then rang up a boarding-
house keeper, who told him of a message that he was to
return to Margate as his mother was ill. He tried to
borrow the fare from her, but failed. Now, you have a man
coming back to Margate in desperate financial straits with
two policies in his pocket, one for £2000 and one for £1000,
which would become payable to him if by any chance his
mother died by violent, visible external means during the
following day.

On the morning of 23rd October, when the chambermaid
Bickmore took tea into room 66 she found for the first time
that the communicating door was locked on room 66 side,
and that Mrs. Fox's dentures were on the floor instead of
being in their usual place in the usual basin. In the even-

64

The Attorney=General (Sir William A. Jowitt, K.C.)

Opening Speech for the Crown.

The Attorney-General

ing the pageboy went to the chemist and brought back a third bottle of the tonic, and that evening the accused said, " I am going to Lyndhurst with Mrs. Fox to-morrow. She is ever so much better. We have had a sham fight, which shows she is well." You may think to yourselves that that was a most extraordinary statement to make. The idea of a young man in the prime of early life having a sham fight with a partially paralysed woman of sixty-three who happens to be his mother is a most extraordinary thing. You will ask yourselves what is the significance attached to it. There is, perhaps, some significance in the fact that they had this sham fight, and the fact that that morning the communicating door was bolted on her side and her teeth were found on the floor by the side of the bed. Was it, perhaps, this, that on the 23rd October the accused was minded to do something to his mother? And supposing there was going to be as a result some tell-tale bruise, might it not have occurred to a man of great cunning and great resource how useful it would be if he could explain that bruise by saying, " Oh, we had a sham fight. It is not a thing I made up on the spur of the moment. I told Mrs. Wager." At 9.30 that night the accused went out and purchased a half-bottle of port. You may wonder why he went to another hotel to buy a bottle of port. He had to pay for it there—3s.—and he brought it back. You will have very little doubt that he took it upstairs. He asked Mrs. Wager for the *Evening Standard*, and was seen going in the direction of the room, but he does not stay there. He goes back again to Mrs. Wager's bar and has some drinks. There is no suggestion that he was drunk. At about 10.40 Roberts, the porter, sees the accused going up the stairs on his way to his room 67. Just ask yourselves as men and women of the world what his thoughts were as he walked up the stairs to room 67 at twenty minutes to eleven on the 23rd of October. Observe this, he was committed to going next day. This pleasant stay at the Hotel Metropole at Margate had come to an end. He had told several people that he was going to Lyndhurst. He had in one pocket the hotel bill for £10 11s. 8d., and you will know that he

Sidney Harry Fox.

had not the means with which to pay that bill. He had another pocket, and in that he had two policies. If by any chance Mrs. Rosaline Fox died by violent external means in the course of the next hour and twenty minutes he was entitled to receive £3000.

What happened in room 66 during the next hour happened in silence. There was no sound; there was no cry; and there was no bell. Roberts, the porter on duty in the hall, would have heard a bell. It was not until 11.40 p.m. within twenty minutes of the end of 23rd October, and within twenty minutes of the time when those two policies came to an end, that a Mr. Hopkins, a commercial traveller, who was sitting downstairs in the hall of the Metropole, saw the accused running downstairs, clad scantily in his undergarments, shouting, " Where is the boots? I believe there is a fire. There is a fire." Hopkins calls for the boots, and summons to his aid some of the commercial travellers who are in the billiard room. They go up the stairs— Hopkins, Miller and Reed, three commercial travellers, and the accused. They get up to the corridor. In the passage outside there is very little indication that there is anything the matter. There is little smoke. When they go up they find the door leading into room 66 and the door leading into room 67 are both closed. The accused opens the door of room 67. In room 67 there is a good deal of smoke. Then the accused opens the door leading into room 66 and says, " My mother is in there." Room 66 is in a terrible condition of smoke. Hopkins tries to enter; he puts his handkerchief over his mouth and he tries to go in, but he cannot; he has to come out. The accused does not go in. Hopkins then thinks he might be able to go in on his hands and knees, and with considerable courage Hopkins proceeds to crawl on his hands and knees into room 66. He sees a faint glimmer, the atmosphere is very thick. Probably the faint glimmer was the gas stove, which was alight. He can see nothing at all. As he crawls in he has to grope with his hands. He finds the deceased woman on the bed. Then he relieves his crawling position and stands up in that atmosphere. He puts his hands under her armpits and

66

Opening Speech for the Crown.

gets her on to his back, and so in that position he gets back out of the room. He lays her in the corridor some three or four yards away from the door of room 66. Miller and Reed, the other two commercial travellers, had also gone up. As Hopkins was crawling into room 66 he saw dimly a figure coming in through the communicating door. That figure was the figure of Reed. He finds a portion of the carpet which is burning with short flames and in a well-defined area. He also finds an armchair which is resting immediately above where the carpet is burning. He endeavours to stamp out the flames, but cannot do so, but he does succeed in getting hold of the chair, and he succeeds in dragging the chair out to the corridor. After that they enter room 66, turn out the gas fire, and then stamp out the flames on the carpet. On the chair were a pair of stockings, a pair of corsets, and a lady's handbag. When the chair was brought out of the room these articles were not on it. In the confusion which arose it may be that somebody had put them on. They carried the deceased to the top of the stairs, and it is the fact that there were no teeth in her mouth; she had not got her dentures in. She was pallid, pale, when she lay there awaiting medical attention. It is not for you to say whether life was extinct or whether it was not.

Then, as you can readily understand, large numbers of people begin to arrive. The police arrive first. Police Constable Bragg opened another window in room 66 and carried Mrs. Fox to the foot of the stairs. In case a spark of life should still be there they tried artificial respiration. More police arrived on the scene. The doctors then arrived, Dr. Austin first and then Dr. Nichol. Dr. Austin found life to have been extinct for some little time. The body was taken and laid out in room 126. By this time room 66 has become free of smoke; the windows are open. You will have a considerable number of witnesses who will tell you about the precise condition of room 66. On the floor was found a quantity of burned and scorched newspapers, some were down at the fender. One of the newspapers was the *Evening Standard.* You will perhaps think it worthy of

Sidney Harry Fox.

your special attention that one of the newspapers which was partially burned—not entirely burned—was a French newspaper. Next, the bed was quite undamaged and had been slept on; it had the impression of somebody having lain on the left-hand side of the bed. The clothes were roughly pulled back, and, most important of all, the pillow was found, not on the bed, but on a little pedestal cupboard by the side of it. There was a patch of urine on the bed which had gone right through to the ground below. I do not know whether you attach importance to it or not; it is a common result of shock. It is precisely what you would expect to happen when a woman was throttled; but, on the other hand, it is also something which might quite possibly happen through nervous shock if a woman woke up and found the room full of smoke. You will hear what the doctors say. You will probably come to the conclusion that it is a feature of the case which does not point conclusively either to one side or the other. The deceased's teeth were intact in the basin. Two tonic bottles and one cascara bottle were found on the mantelpiece; one was full and the other half-full. The third tonic bottle was missing. There was a petrol bottle there in the room. Mrs. Fox was dead. She had died about an hour before the policies expired.

Dr. Nichol then saw the accused, who appeared to be in a state of great mental distress. Ladies and gentlemen, you will have to ask yourselves whether that distress which he manifested, the nervous strain which he must have undergone whichever story is true—you will have to ask yourselves whether you do not consider it a significant fact that while he is in that condition—" out of the fullness of the heart the mouth speaketh "—he says this to Dr. Nichol, " Has the money been found? The £24 in her bag—have they got that? " It is a fact that there never was £24 in her bag. It is at the moment when this man seems to be tortured with anguish that he tells that story—I presume in the hope of getting an additional £24. He asks to see the body. If the prosecution's story is right, he must have been most anxious to see if there was any outward and visible sign

Opening Speech for the Crown.

which might lead to trouble. As regards the lies he told about the £24, about there being a house at Lyndhurst, about his being educated at Framleigh College, and so on, these may be merely the stories of a boastful braggart. In any case, you will take no notice of them. You may think that it was done for the purpose of stopping inquiries about bills. They have that effect. The accused has been throughout a most plausible man. He professes to be a devoted son. After his mother's death he obtained a loan and was seen to be flush with cash. As regards the hotel bill, he had told them to send it in to his solicitor. Having made the necessary funeral arrangements with a Mr. Gore, he left the hotel.

No one has heard about the policies up to this point, but after the burial, which took place on the 29th of October, an order was made for the exhumation of the body. The death was on the 23rd, the burial six days later, on the 29th, and the exhumation was some thirteen days later. Sir Bernard Spilsbury made the examination. By a stroke of good chance the handbag, stockings, corsets, and the piece of the *Evening Standard* which had been discarded and put in the dustbin after the inquest were recovered from the Corporation dustbin. I think we have got everything back with the exception of that piece of undergarment. Dr. Lynch made an examination of the stomach contents. I am not going to trouble you very much about that except to say that he found no poison of any sort, but he found what he would expect to find consistent with a quantity of port being consumed shortly before death. Sir Bernard Spilsbury will tell you it was a case where putrefaction had not gone on at its usual rate, and there was rather less smell than usual; consequently the body was in such a condition that Sir Bernard was able without difficulty to make such investigation as he desired. The facts of the fire which I have described to you were recounted to him, and he would go down and make his explorations with the immense experience which he has had to see how far the symptoms which he found would coincide with the story which he went to investigate. You will be told this, first of

69

Sidney Harry Fox.

all, there were certain negative things which he found—(1) He looked most carefully to see if there was any deposit of soot, slight particles such as you might get up your nose or down the windpipe or tubes. If a woman or anybody had been for a short time in a room such as is described *alive,* they must have drawn down this smoky atmosphere into their lungs, down their windpipe. Of course, if the body was dead there would be no question of anything being drawn down. The first thing, therefore, to see is whether the linings of the windpipe contain any traces at all of that which must have been there had there been a living body in a room full of smoke. There was none. Microscopical examination of the linings of the windpipe revealed that the windpipe was completely free of these minute particles. (2) If a person is in a room and there is a fire in the room, very probably if the room is closed, if you get a fire and not very much oxygen, you must get generated the gas carbon monoxide. Carbon monoxide is for an expert in this matter a comparatively simple matter to test. The gas finds its way into the blood, and having got into the blood would remain there until the process of putrefaction had gone so far. He tested to see if there was any carbon monoxide. There was none. Therefore this woman had not been poisoned by any fumes such as would be given off by a fire of this sort. What you will have to consider is whether or not death had taken place before the fire was lit.

Coming to the positive things which Sir Bernard Spilsbury found, if your lordship will permit it, Sir Bernard will, when giving his evidence, produce a model of the larynx. He found at the back of the larynx a clear recent bruise of about the size of half a crown. He will tell you that that bruise could only have been caused by what he calls manual strangulation—strangulation by the hand. He found at the top of the epiglottis various small spots of bleeding because there has been some rupture, probably by violence, of the little, tiny blood vessels, and an escape of blood from those little blood vessels. He found in the course of his investigation a bruise on the tongue about the size of a pea, on the side of the tongue about opposite to one's

70

Opening Speech for the Crown.

The Attorney-General

farthest back teeth. It is a clear bruise. It has not gone through the surface as it would have done in time. It must have been quite recently caused, just before death. That bruise could have been caused by, and must have been caused by, the pressure of two hard surfaces. It is manifest therefore that it was caused by the upper denture pressing against the lower denture, or the lower against the upper, and it was caused at a moment of time when the woman must have had her tongue or the edge of her tongue in some way or other just lapping over her teeth. Perhaps she had her mouth open, her teeth in her mouth, and the edge of the tongue just overlapping the teeth. Suppose you had a woman asleep with dentures in; suppose she had not, as people very often do not, entirely closed her mouth; suppose she had that side of her tongue just between her teeth so that if she had closed her teeth the tongue would have been caught; suppose that whilst she slept a hand came and caught her there and went up like that (indicating), you will see that you will at once get a pressure, and if the tongue happens to be between the two dentures you will get exactly the sort of bruise which you do find in this case. This much is plain. That bruise could not possibly have been caused if the teeth were out. Therefore it becomes a matter of great importance to remember that when these people enter the room on the evening of the 23rd the teeth are found in the basin. Who put the teeth in the basin? If in truth the teeth had been in the mouth, how did the teeth get to the basin? If, on the other hand, you did have a manual strangulation you might get displacing of the teeth, first of all pressure of the tongue down against the denture, and then you might get the jaw dropping and the teeth displaced or partially displaced, and then if any murderer had been there he would have had to take the teeth and put them in the basin. You will have to consider very anxiously the position of that bruise on the tongue—whether you do not think that that bruise points almost conclusively to the fact that it was done whilst this poor woman slept.

It is right to add that externally on the neck or to the outward edge there was no mark. The mark, the size of

71

Sidney Harry Fox.

a half-crown, which Sir Bernard Spilsbury saw, was upon these delicate internal structures, some highly coloured with blood vessels. It will be said, how could the inside bruise be done without an outside bruise? This much at least is plain : the inside bruise is there. It is there, and what Sir Bernard Spilsbury will tell you is this, that if you are trying manually to strangle a person the degree of force which would be required to do it would naturally tend to leave marks on the outside; yet if you are dealing with a poor old woman partially paralysed, lying asleep in her bed, it does not require so very much force from a young man in the prime of life. It merely requires sufficient pressure kept on to prevent the air going down the windpipe just long enough, and everybody agrees with this, if the man who does that is sufficiently determined to apply and keep on pressure, the bruising then would not show, because bruising is caused by the escape behind of blood from the minute blood vessels, and very shortly after death the blood ceases to flow and does not escape from ruptured blood vessels; there was no external mark, therefore because this poor old woman did not give very much resistance, or because, resist though she did, the pressure was kept on for about a couple of minutes. In that connection you will recollect one fact—the position of the pillow.

There are some people who do not use a pillow, they like to lie with their head flat. No so with Mrs. Fox. Mrs. Fox had always used her pillow. When they went into the room after this the pillow was not on the bed, the pillow was on the pedestal cupboard at the side of the bed. Is it not obvious that if any murderer had been prepared to attack the old lady as she slept he would have had to guard against the possibility of a cry, and the soft pillow, whilst her throat is caught with one hand, could be snatched from under her with the other hand, in her sleep, and pressed down over her nostrils—that would cause suffocation—the right hand holding the victim in position, the left hand pressing down the pillow on her face? It is not for the prosecution to construct a theory as to the precise way in which this was done. We shall never see what happened behind the walls

Opening Speech for the Crown.

of room 66 between 10.40 p.m. and 11.40 p.m., but I shall ask
you from Sir Bernard Spilsbury's evidence to say that he
is right when he says that the symptoms, negative and
positive, which he found were symptoms which were incon-
sistent with death from asphyxia from the fumes of a fire,
but were consistent and consistent only with manual strangulation before the fire had taken place. To strangle an old
woman does not require much force, but the possibility of
a cry may have to be guarded against; a soft pillow is all
that is required for this purpose.

Now I must tell you about the fire. I have got here the
carpet of this room. I have got here the armchair. You will
see the carpet and you will see the chair. You may have an
opportunity of seeing the room and seeing exactly the
position of the burned patch of carpet. The fire was more
or less under the armchair and seems to have spread towards
the gas stove without reaching it. There is a gap. You
will find that there is an unburned piece of the carpet
between the seat of the fire where the chair was and the
gas fire. This fire cannot have spread as is suggested.
Is it possible that when this old lady went to bed, by
perhaps throwing down carelessly her combinations, and
throwing down carelessly the *Evening Standard*, and throwing down for some reason or other the French newspaper, is
it possible that you may have had a bridge leading from
the gas fire and the other end? Elaborate experiments have
been made with this very carpet, reproducing the conditions
as nearly as we can with this very fender, and the Chief
of the Margate Fire Brigade made these experiments. These
experiments revealed that without using petrol he failed to
burn the carpet. I am not going to say any more about
this matter except that either this fire was the work of an
incendiary or it was an accident. If it was the work of
an incendiary the only person who had both the opportunity
and the motive was the accused. You will have to make
up your minds whether or not it was an accident. You
will have to bear in mind the position of the fire, the difficulty in setting the carpet alight, and the presence of the
French newspaper. If somebody had made a bonfire of

Sidney Harry Fox.

whatever paper or material he had in his possession, if he had made a bonfire under the chair, I could well understand he would use a French newspaper as well as an English newspaper. It is an odd feature of the case. How on earth could a fire manage to spread from the gas stove, hopping over certain bits of carpet and then starting to burn fiercely round the armchair? There was a small cane chair which had one leg burnt. An odd feature of the case is that that cane chair was not near the fire. That cane chair had been moved. That is a matter which you will have to consider.

Now, if any murderer has done this act of manual strangulation, what has he to do next? He has got to create some method to account for the death. Consequently, he would, if he had committed this manual strangulation by hand, try to create some other explanation, and so you might have a fire; and so in this case you find these features about a fire which indicate that it was not a genuine fire which spread from the gas stove, but it was a bogus fire or a bonfire which was purposely made underneath that chair. You will examine the chair and you will find that the chair is scorched and burnt on all sides, so that it seems plain that the fire must have concentrated under that chair. When this room was examined these two stockinette dresses were hung up on the door. You will be told by the maid that on all previous occasions the dresses were just flung carelessly down on the chair. It is an odd thing that this particular night of all others Mrs. Fox should have been so much more careful and should have selected this night to do what she had not done before—and you remember this was the night when she had her half-bottle of port, and when she went to bed with the gas fire on—and this was the night when it must be said that she left her combinations in such a way that they actually touched or were lit by that fire, and yet this is the night when you find these dresses for the first time put carefully upon the door.

Then we come to the next thing. I pointed out about the matter of this closed door. When I pointed it out to you you had not heard the explanation which the accused gave. He

74

Opening Speech for the Crown.

The Attorney-General
said he found the room full of smoke. Supposing that is
true, supposing he had gone into his mother's room and
found the room full of smoke, is it conceivable that a man
in these circumstances would have shut the door afterwards?
The communicating door is shut when these people come up.
The door of No. 67 is shut and the door of No. 66 is shut.
Ask yourselves whether a man would not have flung open
the door of No. 66 where his mother was and then gone
downstairs. You have already heard me deal with the pillow
on the cupboard by the side of the bed. This lady always
slept on her pillow in the ordinary way. Why was it that
the pillow was discovered on that pedestal cupboard? Then
this bruise along the side and the back of the tongue, which
must have been done by the pressure of the two dentures
against each other and must have been done when the dentures were in the mouth. When these people come into the
room the dentures are found in the basin. You have to
ask yourselves for the explanation, if explanation there be,
of some of the statements the accused made. Why did this
man tell this story about the chemist, about the danger of an
overdose? Why do you think there were these three bottles of
medicine? One of them is gone. Then there is the explanation of this extraordinary story of the sham fight. In the
presence of Sergeant Fleet the accused, the day after the
fire, when discussing the matter with the coroner, said, " She
was quite cheerful. In fact, just before she went to bed
we were having a sham fight—you know, a boxing match.''

Ladies and gentlemen, the case for the prosecution is this,
that the accused went up the stairs in the Hotel Metropole
at 10.40 p.m. on the night of 23rd October, committed as
he was to going away the next day, with a bill which he
could not pay, with no money, with two policies which would
expire in an hour and twenty minutes, and which would
entitle him to receive £3000 if the woman died by violent
death of this sort—that he went up then with murder in
his heart. He did not, of course, when he went into his
room neglect the more obvious precautions. If murderer
he was, you can have no doubt of the cunning and skill.
His bed, for instance, had been slept on. This story would

75

Sidney Harry Fox.

have broken down at once if it had been seen that his bed had not been laid on. He came down these stairs partially undressed in his undergarments when he called for the boots and said, " I believe there is a fire." In all these cases some mistakes are made. Fortunate it is that they are, and you may think that these matters which I have touched upon—the closed door and the pillow, and various other things, altogether apart from the evidence of the fire, and apart altogether from the evidence of Sir Bernard Spilsbury—show what the true facts of this case are.

I have endeavoured to select from the vast mass of material what I believe to be the most relevant points. I must now tell you something more about the position as regards these policies. On 10th November, 1913, a small policy had been taken out on Mrs. Fox's life by another brother called Reginald. It was quite unlike these policies. It was an ordinary life policy for £10. When she died Reginald was entitled to receive £10 or 10 guineas. That policy was the only policy which existed prior to the making of her will. That policy lapsed and came to an end in August, 1928. The next date to remember is March, 1929, when she left the infirmary, and the first step taken was to reinstate this little policy, which was done on the 9th of April, 1929. On the 21st of April, 1929, Mrs. Fox made her will. It is probable that the handwriting of the will is the handwriting of the accused. That he knew of the will will not be in controversy. In it she left everything to the accused, with a request that he should give a small gift to two friends. The will also stated, " To my son, William Edward Fox, I leave one farthing, and sincerely hope that he will never want his mother." Before that time there were no accident policies. Nine days after the making of that will the accused took out the first of the accident policies, and on 1st May asked the clerk of an insurance company if this policy would cover a case of drowning in a bath. Would it apply, supposing a person was poisoned, let us say, by food at a restaurant? So that you have this : nine days after the will is made you get him going to one of these insurance companies to take out the first of these accident policies, and you get him ask-

Opening Speech for the Crown.

ing that sort of question, indicating, as I suggest to you, the sort of thing he had in his mind on 1st May, 1929. From 1st May, 1929, down to 23rd October last, when this poor old soul died, there are 176 days, and there was a series of policies. These policies covered 167 days out of 176. From 1st May to 23rd October these people had £22 10s. coming in to them by way of their joint pensions of 10s. and 8s. weekly, and the premiums on these policies for the same period of time came to just over £10, so that substantially half the total income is spent on paying premiums, not for an ordinary policy but for an accident policy which covered, and covered only, death from injuries by violent external visible means.

The prosecution present this case as being a case in which there is one possible explanation, and only one possible explanation of the death of Mrs. Fox, and that explanation is that she lay on her bed that night on the 23rd of October refreshed as she had been by a half-bottle of port, sleeping drowsily, perhaps; that there entered room 66 by the communicating door her son, that he went to the bed, that he stretched out his hand and put his hand upon her neck, and possibly with his other hand pressed the pillow down upon her face, and so brought his mother's life to an end. Having done that, constrained as he was to construct some explanation of her death, he then proceeded to make a fire so as to make it appear that her death, which in fact had taken place in the way I have described, was a death as the result of a fire. It is manifest, grave though any crime may be, that the crime with which this man is charged is as grave as it can be in the eyes of the law, and it behoves you to listen well to the evidence. That is the case for the prosecution.

Evidence for the Prosecution.

GLADYS MEADMORE, examined by Sir HENRY CURTIS BENNETT—I am employed at the Grand Hotel, Dover. I remember three separate occasions when the accused and his mother paid visits to the hotel. They were from the 12th to the 14th September, from the 20th to the 23rd September,

Sidney Harry Fox.

Gladys Meadmore

and from the 28th of September to the 3rd of October. An account for £3 5s. 6d. was left unpaid. On no occasion did I see any luggage.

Cross-examination by Mr. CASSELS—Are there any single rooms with communicating doors?—There are no single rooms with communicating doors, but there are rooms where you could have a door between them.

Do you remember on the 23rd of September the accused saying that he was expecting a telegram?—I do not.

Did the accused when he was going to Ostend ask you to rewire a telegram he was expecting to *poste restante*, Ostend?—Yes.

And did a telegram arrive, and was it forwarded to him?—Yes.

After that did the accused come and stay at your hotel?—Yes, five or six days later.

And did he pay?—The first time they left without paying. The second time they came he paid for the first time. The third time they left without paying.

Did they occupy rooms on the same floor?—Yes.

Were they always on the same floor?—They were always on the same floor except for one night, the second night of the first visit.

How long did they stay on the first occasion?—Three nights.

Re-examined by Sir HENRY CURTIS BENNETT—Do you identify the telegram you have referred to as the one I now show you, which states, "Fox buried plot 200 grave eleven British Cemetery five miles north west of Arras"?—Yes.

Miss CROSIER, examined by Mr. ST. JOHN HUTCHINSON—I am a reception clerk at the Royal Pavilion Hotel, Folkestone. I know the accused. He came with an elderly lady on 3rd October and they stayed until 12th October. He owed £15 5s. when he left.

Cross-examined by Mr. CASSELS—Are there communicating rooms in your hotel?—Yes.

Did you receive the accused and his mother when they arrived at the hotel?—No.

78

Evidence for Prosecution.

And, so far as you know, no application was made for communicating rooms?—No.

FLORENCE BROWN, examined by Mr. ST. JOHN HUTCHINSON—I am a chambermaid at the Royal Pavilion Hotel, Folkestone. I remember the accused and his mother arriving at the hotel. They had a room next to each other with no communicating door. They had no luggage or night clothes. On the day they were leaving the accused said he would return on the Friday.

Cross-examined by Mr. CASSELS—Did they go out together?—They went out in the morning after the lady had her breakfast.

And as far as you could see did the accused show every fondness for his mother?—Yes.

Did she require a lot of assistance in getting about?—Yes.

On what floor did they occupy rooms?—On the second floor.

Had they a communicating door?—There are some communicating doors on the second floor.

FRANK MASON, examined by Sir HENRY CURTIS BENNETT—The accused and his mother stayed at the County Hotel, Canterbury, from 12th to 15th October, 1929. They had no luggage. They only had a small parcel when they left. I threatened to communicate with the police. They occupied rooms 29 and 30. There was no door between.

Cross-examined by Mr. CASSELS—Are there any rooms with communicating doors?—There are.

Was any request made by the accused or his mother for communicating doors?—No.

VERA WINIFRED ALWYN HOPPER, examined by Sir HENRY CURTIS BENNETT—I am receptionist at the Hotel Metropole, Margate. The accused came to the office window on the 16th of October and asked for two single rooms for one night. He did not want them overlooking the sea, as it was too cold for his mother. I offered him rooms side by side, and he thanked me. He took rooms 68 and 70. They occupied these rooms for some days. After dinner on the

79

Sidney Harry Fox.

Vera W. A. Hopper

16th the accused told me he had been to France to see the graves of his three brothers who were killed in the war, and he gave me a small packet and asked me to look after it. It was a little, square envelope. He asked me to put it in the safe, and I put it in the safe. He said they had no luggage, that it had been sent on, but he did not say where to. On the 17th of October I saw him in the morning and he asked if he could keep the rooms on for another day. He said he wanted to see somebody in the neighbourhood. I do not remember seeing him on the 18th. On the Friday he said his mother had a headache, that she was not well enough to travel, and he wanted to stay on. I said he could. He asked each day how much the bill was, and I informed him how much it was. On the Saturday he was still there. On the Sunday he wanted the bill, and the manager gave it to him. He told me Dr. Austin was coming. On the afternoon of the Sunday the accused said that the chemist had said he had broken down the prescription, that an overdose might be fatal. I saw the accused again on the Monday. He said his mother was much better. He said he was going to town to cash a cheque. I said if he liked I would put it through the hotel account, but he said there was no need to trouble as he had to go to town anyway. He went to town on Monday evening. He returned on Tuesday evening. I gave him the bill every day. On Tuesday when I gave him his bill to date he asked how much it was, that they were leaving early on the 23rd. It was on the Tuesday night that he said they were leaving early on Wednesday, the 23rd, when he asked me the amount of the bill. It was £10 11s. 8d. He said he was going the next day to a new home—I think in Hampshire. I offered to lend Mrs. Fox a coat for travelling. The accused said that they were not going by car, that he would rather go by train. He said he had left his car in Canterbury. On the morning of the 24th he seemed very much upset about his mother's death, and said he had hoped to have her for twenty years longer. He said he was awakened the previous night by his window rattling, and smelt a smell of smoke. Later he opened his mother's door and found the

Evidence for Prosecution.

Vera W. A. Hopper

smoke was in there. He asked for the envelope back, and he opened it. It contained papers—no money. He left on Friday, the 25th, and asked me to send his account to Mr. Wilson. It is still unpaid. He gave me the address of the Royal Hotel, Norwich.

Cross-examined by Mr. JAMES—Do you agree that it was cold weather in October?—Yes, it was cold on the front at Margate.

And was the first thing the accused did to show great concern as to the room his mother should be put in?—Yes.

He did not want his mother to be cold?—No.

Was he very grateful for the room?—Yes.

Did you ever speak to Mrs. Fox?—No.

Did she seem to be in good health?—She seemed rather feeble. I did not really see her sufficiently well to see what was her condition. She was walking very slowly with a shuffling step.

Did her son assist her?—Yes. He was not always taking hold of her. I did not pay great attention.

Did you see the accused the morning after the fire?—Yes.

And did he seem distressed?—Yes.

Did he appear to be broken-hearted?—I did not take sufficient notice.

May I say that son and mother appeared to be the best of pals during the time?—Yes.

EDWARD COX, examined by Sir HENRY CURTIS BENNETT— I am a photographer. I took the photographs of room 66 which are produced.

Cross-examined by Mr. CASSELS—How often did you go to the room?—I went twice.

And were you each time accompanied by the police?—Yes.

And while you were there was the chair adjusted in position?—Yes.

Was the bed already arranged?—Yes.

You took photographs according to their directions?—Yes.

JACK GODWIN TOMLIN SMITH, examined by Sir HENRY CURTIS BENNETT—I am an engineer in the Burgh Surveyor's

Sidney Harry Fox.

Jack G. T. Smith

Department, Margate. I produce a plan showing rooms 66 and 67. The door opens inwards to 66, and has a bolt on each side. The area of scorched carpet at its widest is 3 ft. 3 ins., the length being 4 ft. 3 ins. The narrowest end was nearest to the gas fire, and that was 12 ins. The mark where the burning had gone right through the carpet was 3 ft. 2 ins. from the gas fire, and it was 1 ft. 9 ins. from the centre of the gas fire to the middle of the scorched carpet. From the nearest point of the fender to the nearest part of the scorched carpet was 6 ins. The chair was in the room and was put in position by a police officer. There were 2 ft. 2 ins. from the right-hand front corner to the middle of the gas fire, and 3 ft. from the fire to the left-hand corner.

Cross-examined by Mr. CASSELS—In measuring distances have you always taken the middle of the gas fire?—Yes.

Can you give the distance from the nearest portion of the gas fire to the nearest portion of signs of burning on the carpet?—I cannot.

Would the distance from the nearest portion of the gas fire to the nearest portion of the chair be slightly less?—Yes.

Was the chair put in position by police officers?—Yes.

Was the chair immediately above the most burned part of the carpet?—Yes.

Was the bottom of the chair very close to the carpet?—Yes.

Have you measured the distance from the burned boards to the middle of the bed?—I have not.

By Mr. JUSTICE ROWLATT—What is the length of the bed?—6 ft. 7 ins.

What kind of a bed is it?—The bedstead is a metal bedstead.

Was there between the bedstead and the scorched part an untouched part of the carpet?—Yes, so far as I could see.

ROWLAND BAIRD, examined by Mr. ST. JOHN HUTCHINSON—I reside at 6 Westbrook Road, Margate. I was page-boy at the Hotel Metropole last October. The accused told me he had just returned from France after visiting three graves.

Evidence for Prosecution.

Rowland Baird

On Sunday, 20th October, I took a prescription to Woolls, the chemists, and I waited and received a bottle from them. I did not pay for it. On the 23rd of October I again went with another prescription. I took the bottle to room 66 and put it on the mantelshelf. I could not be sure of the time, but I believe it was in the morning.

FREDERICK PALMER, examined by Mr. ST. JOHN HUTCHINSON—I am a pharmacist employed by Messrs. V. J. Woolls, Margate, and I live in Cecil Square. I remember on Sunday, 20th October last, getting a prescription from a page-boy. It was a simple tonic for Mrs. Fox, a tablespoonful every four hours. There was sufficient in the bottle to last three days.

JAMES ELGAR FARMER, examined by Sir HENRY CURTIS BENNETT—I reside at College Road, Margate, and I am a pharmacist in the employment of Messrs. Woolls, Cecil Square. I remember cashing a cheque for the accused on the 21st of October last. That cheque came back marked " no account."

Cross-examined by Mr. CASSELS—Do you remember the accused putting an empty bottle on the counter?—No.

MARGARET CATHERINE ALLEN, examined by Sir HENRY CURTIS BENNETT—I am a chemist's assistant. I remember on the 21st October being handed a cheque by the accused. I took it to the cashier and gave the accused £1 16s. change.

Cross-examined by Mr. CASSELS—Did you notice the accused put an empty bottle on the counter?—No.

Has anybody asked you about an empty bottle before?—No.

The Court adjourned.

Sidney Harry Fox.

Second Day—Thursday, 13th March, 1930.

DENNIS F. HAWKES, examined by Sir HENRY CURTIS BENNETT—I am a clerk at the Norwich branch of Lloyds Bank. No. 19 of process is a cheque which was received at my branch. There is no account in the name of Rosaline Fox. The cheque was returned marked " no account."

WALTER F. WILSON, examined by Sir HENRY CURTIS BENNETT—I am a solicitor in practice at Cecil Square, Margate. I know the accused. He consulted me on the 24th of October. In consequence of what passed between us at that interview, on 25th October I advanced him £25, and on 28th or 29th October I advanced a further £15.

Cross-examined by Mr. CASSELS—I suppose you know Dr. Nichol and he knows you?—Yes.

So that it might well be that your name would be in Dr. Nichol's mind if he mentioned a solicitor to any one who required one?—It might be so.

Did the accused come to see you before the inquest?—Yes; he requested me to represent him at the inquest.

And did you attend the inquest?—I did, and so did the accused.

Did the accused hand to you his mother's will and papers? —Yes.

Did you look through the papers?—I certainly looked through them, and I discovered some insurance policies.

Did you express a doubt to him as to whether, seeing that his mother was supposed to have died from shock and suffocation, the policies would be any good and whether they would cover such a death?—I believe I did.

Did you tell him you would write a letter to the insurance companies to make a claim and see what their reply was? —I did. He asked me to communicate with the companies.

I think that on 29th October you wrote a letter to him?— Yes.

[Letter read by Clerk of Assize, starting at fourth paragraph.]

Evidence for Prosecution.

Walter F. Wilson

Do you say there that you had looked through them again and had found that they referred to a holder who " shall sustain bodily injury caused by violent, accidental, external, visible means, which injury, independent of any other cause, shall result in death " ?—Yes.

Does the letter proceed, " I shall, therefore, not be surprised if these two companies dispute the liability on the ground that the death was not caused by means within this description. However, we will see what the reply is. I do not know of anything more that can be done until you have gone down to Lyndhurst and brought back all the papers and securities, as arranged. As desired, I enclose £15 in Treasury notes." From which policy were you quoting?—I could not say.

[Shown Exhibits 62 and 63.]

Do you notice in the Cornhill Company's policy the following, " It is hereby decreed and declared that if at any time during the aforesaid period the assuree shall sustain any accidental bodily injury caused directly and immediately by violent external and visible means whilst travelling or resident within the following limits—London, Dover, and south coast resorts " ?—Yes. It was these words which first made me cast a doubt as to whether in the circumstances I knew of at the time the death was covered by the policy.

Were the policies in favour of the accused?—Yes.

Mrs. GERTRUDE PLATT, examined by Sir HENRY CURTIS BENNETT—I keep an apartments house at 10 Liverpool Street, King's Cross, London. I know the accused. He and his mother stayed at my house on several occasions in August of last year. They had two single rooms on the second floor. They had no luggage. The accused said he was an insurance agent somewhere in the city. On the morning of 22nd October I was given a telephone message by Blake, who is in the employment of my father-in-law, about 11.30. I had a telephone conversation with the accused in the afternoon about 4.30. He said he was coming to London that

Sidney Harry Fox.

night and had I a room. I said I was afraid I had not. I said, " I have a message for you, ' Return home at once, your mother seriously ill.' " He said, " That is funny. She was quite well when I left her this morning." He said, " What am I to do? I haven't money to get home. Do you think, Mrs. Platt, you could lend it to me? " I suggested he could obtain it by having security. I think he said he required 16s. 10d. He said he had not anything of any value except an old watch. I said probably the railway would let him pay at the other end. He said, " That is a good idea. I hadn't thought of that."

Cross-examined by Mr. CASSELS—When was the first time the accused and his mother stayed with you?—I think about 6th and 7th August. They stayed on and off the whole of August.

Can you say whether he was there on the 26th and 27th?—No.

Is No. 10 Liverpool Street a bed and breakfast apartments house?—Yes.

What is the accommodation?—Two rooms on the level, sitting-room and back-bedroom; four apartments on first floor, all bedrooms; and three rooms on second floor, all bedrooms.

What were the two rooms on the second floor occupied by the accused and his mother?—One is at the back and the other is at the front. A large room has been turned into two rooms by a partition.

Is there a landing between the two rooms that were occupied by the accused and his mother?—Yes, there is a landing between them of a pace or two.

Did you observe that the accused and his mother were very affectionate?—Yes; the son was very affectionate to his mother.

Did she require a great deal of attention?—Yes.

And was he constantly in her company?—Yes.

Between the 10th of August and the 31st of August did the accused and his mother come backwards and forwards? —I cannot say exactly. I had my holidays in the meantime, but they were there then, as far as I know.

86

Evidence for Prosecution.

Mrs. G. Platt

How long were you away?—I was away for ten days—not the last ten days.

Then they went away and came back again?—Yes.

And were they with you all the time of the last week in August?—No. That was when he went home.

When did you next hear from him?—We next heard from him from France. I have heard no more from him since. I have a lot of people staying in my house.

Had you other people by the name of Fox or Cox at your house?—We had some one by the name of Cox, but not at that time (22nd October).

Is Mr. Blake an office boy at the builder's next door?—Yes, my father-in-law's. Blake gave me the message.

Did not the message received relate to some one not at Margate but at Norwich?—Yes. That is what I understood. I thought it referred to accused and his mother.

Was the accused surprised to receive the message you gave him?—Yes, he seemed to be, and said he had left his mother quite well.

Re-examined by Sir HENRY CURTIS BENNETT—Can you say when Cox stayed at your house?—No.

It might have been in 1928?—Yes.

Was it a Mr. and Mrs. Cox?—I think it was.

Do you remember a Mr. Cox and his mother staying with you?—No.

Were you given to understand that the accused and his mother had gone home?—The accused had told us they were going home. He told us where his home was when he first came. The address he gave was Cathedral Close, Norwich.

Did he invite you down some time in August?—Yes.

Did he tell you he was going home some time towards the end of August?—Yes.

What did he tell you about Margate?—He only told me he had got a nice place at Margate.

Did you receive a card from him from France?—Yes, some time in September. It came from Arras.

WILLIAM HENRY SMITH, examined by Sir HENRY CURTIS BENNETT—I am hall porter at the Hotel Metropole, Margate.

Sidney Harry Fox.

William H. Smith

I was away on holiday in August last from the 16th to the 20th, and I came back to work on the 22nd of August. I knew the accused as a visitor. On Tuesday, 22nd October, about 12.30 in the morning, I received a telephone call. As far as I could understand it was from the accused. It was inquiring for Mrs. Fox. The next day I was requested to collect a bottle of medicine about 6 p.m. It was collected, and I directed the page-boy to take it up to room 66. On the alarm of fire that night I went to the first floor and saw a number of people in the corridor. There were several people in the doorway of No. 66. I did not see the accused at that time. Next morning he said it was unfortunate he had lost his mother, that he was the last of his family. He left on the Friday. There is a gas fire in No. 66, the gas being obtained by a penny-in-the-slot meter.

Cross-examined by Mr. CASSELS—At what time did you arrive on the scene on the evening of the fire?—About 11.50.

How many persons were there when you arrived?—About six persons.

How many were in the doorway?—Two.

Did you subsequently go into the room that night?—Yes, along with several others.

By Mr. JUSTICE ROWLATT—How long would a penny in the slot allow the stove to burn?—About two hours.

HAROLD FREDERICK MORGAN, examined by Sir HENRY CURTIS BENNETT—I am the manager of the Hoy Hotel, Margate. I saw the accused in the bar about 9.30 p.m. on the evening of Wednesday, 23rd October. He purchased half a bottle of port for 3s. I wrapped it in a " Johnnie Walker " wrapper. Exhibit No. 21 is a bottle similar to the one I sold to the accused. I identify Exhibit No. 22. Exhibit No. 23 is a similar wrapper to the one I put on the bottle. That was the only time I saw the accused.

Cross-examined by Mr. CASSELS—Are your premises opposite the Metropole?—They are not very far away.

GWENDOLINE BUGG, examined by Sir HENRY CURTIS BENNETT—I am a waitress at the Hotel Metropole, Margate. I knew the accused as a visitor in October last. The accused

88

Evidence for Prosecution.

Gwendoline Bugg

and his mother sat at one of my tables. The accused did not take breakfast; he only had coffee. His mother did not come down to breakfast. Mrs. Fox was sometimes upstairs and sometimes downstairs alone when the accused was out. On one or two occasions only they lunched together. In the evening as a rule they dined together when he was there. On the Sunday Mrs. Fox did not come down. The accused was away. I do not remember whether they both dined together on the Tuesday. I remember the 23rd. They did not lunch together that day, but they dined together. Mrs. Fox had a kind of a wobbly walk; she was very shaky on her feet, and required assistance in walking. When she was left alone downstairs I assisted her; I just took her arm and helped her to sit down. On Wednesday, the 23rd, she appeared quite normal. She had a mixed grill, and half a pint of bitter for dinner at about 7.30. She left the dining-room at about 8.30 or 8.45. That was the last I saw of her. On the 24th I had some conversation with the accused. I said how sorry I was to hear of his mother's death. " What are you going to do? " I said. " You will have to get married." He said he was going abroad to Australia. He also said he had only one aunt and some cousins in Norwich. He handed me 2s. 6d. and said, " Here you are; you know how I stand now, but I shall be coming back next week." The accused also told me that £24 had been burned in his mother's handbag.

Cross-examined by Mr. Cassels—Was the accused very devoted to his mother?—Very devoted indeed.

Elizabeth Wager, examined by Mr. St. John Hutchinson—I reside at 18 Dane Park Road, Margate, and I am a barmaid in the saloon lounge of the Hotel Metropole. I knew the accused as a customer. On Sunday, 20th October, between 2.30 and 3, he asked me if I knew the doctor who came, and I said yes, but not as a patient. He asked me if I knew that he drank, and I said I heard so, but I had not seen him. The accused said, " He was drunk when he saw my mother," and he added that the doctor went to her and said, " You're all right, old lady. Bogey, bogey! " [The

Sidney Harry Fox.

Elizabeth Wager

witness illustrated the action with which the accused had accompanied the words by placing her hands to the sides of her head and waving them.] The accused said he had been to get the medicine, but they had had to break it down, as Dr. Austin was not responsible for his actions. On Wednesday evening, about 6 p.m., the accused came in and said he had been to Dover with his mother. He came into the bar between 6.30 and 7 p.m. He paid for drinks. He said he was going down to Lyndhurst when he left Margate. He also said he had a car; it was up in the Norfolk Garage at Margate. The accused was there until 10.20 or 10.25 when I had warning for time about 10.30. He borrowed the *Evening Standard* about 9.45.

On the morning after the fire I asked him how he came to find out about the fire. He told me he had always been in the habit of going to see his mother in bed. I asked him why he had not that night. He said he had been up to see her with a paper at 9.45 and asked her whether he should come in as usual and put the light out. She said, " There's no need," that she would put out the light herself and get into bed. He said when he went up he did not go in to see her because she would be fast asleep, and as they were going away the next day he did not want to disturb her. He said that about 11.30 the window was rattling and he got out of bed to plug it, and then he smelt the fire. He added that he went back to bed, and a few minutes after he could smell cloth burning. He then got out of bed and could not smell anything in the corridor, so he opened his mother's room, which was full of smoke. He then shut the door and came down for help. To my recollection he left the bar about 9.45. I had never lent him an evening paper before, and he had never asked me before. On 23rd October he told me his mother was much better, that they had been playing; they had had a sham fight, which they sometimes did when she felt well.

Cross-examined by Mr. CASSELS—This fire had created a good deal of interest, and everybody was talking about it, were not they?—Yes.

And you had a conversation about the fire with the accused

Evidence for Prosecution.

Louise Bickmore

of stockings, one pair of shoes, a hat, coat, and fur. She left her clothes rather untidily on the chair by the fire at night. I had not noticed her teeth before the Sunday. When she moved into No. 66 I noticed her teeth in a glass on the wash-hand stand. On another occasion I noticed that they were down by the bedside. Two mornings out of three the teeth were in the glass. The accused asked me for a piece of rag on Sunday morning to clean his mother's coat. I cleaned Mrs. Fox's coat and he cleaned his own. The petrol was brought into the vacant room by me and we both used some of it. The bottle was taken back to room 70. I do not remember taking it to room 67. Mrs. Fox never came down on the Monday; she stayed in her room. I think I saw the accused once that morning. Nothing took place except that I just took in tea. He asked me to look after his mother, and he gave me 7s. 6d. just after lunch. He took his mother a bunch of grapes at the same time. I saw him again about 5 p.m. before he went to London. He was away that evening.

The next morning, Tuesday, I took Mrs. Fox tea at 7 a.m. She was up about eleven. I took her down to the drawing-room about 12.30. That day she required help. I left her in the drawing-room and she stayed there. The accused got back soon after seven. I saw him. I do not remember what time Mrs. Fox went up to bed that night. I was off duty from seven o'clock. The accused was just coming from the station as I went out of the hotel. Some one else would put the bottles in the beds. I used the communicating door on the Wednesday morning. The door was bolted on room 66 side. That had not happened before. I noticed nothing else. The teeth were by the bedside on the Wednesday morning. They were on the floor by the pedestal. I picked them up and rinsed them and gave them to Mrs. Fox. She had dropped them in the night. She had breakfast as usual in the morning. The accused went down for his breakfast. Mrs. Fox was dressed at 11 a.m. She did not have lunch in her bedroom. I saw her again in the afternoon in the drawing-room, and later on I saw her at seven o'clock sitting by the fire in her bedroom—in an armchair by the gas fire.

93

Sidney Harry Fox.

Louise Bickmore

She was talking to the accused. She was reading a news-paper. The accused was wiping his hands on a towel. The only basin with running water was in Mrs. Fox's room. They went down for dinner together. At 8.15 I entered the room and it was empty. There was no fire on. I put a hot-water bottle in the bed. I did not go into the room again that night. I never saw Mrs. Fox alive again.

I went into the room on the 24th of October, Thursday morning, after I knew of the tragedy. I only had a peep into the room for curiosity. I did not notice anything about the dresses till the Friday. I spoke to the accused again about 3 p.m. on the Thursday. I asked him if his mother's clothes were any use. He said no, nor the teeth, so I took them. There were two dresses, one pair of stockings, a coat, a fur, a hat, a pair of shoes, and the teeth. I gave them to one of the maids. I kept the coat and the little fur. I identify them, and also the teeth. One tooth was gone. I saw the accused on the Friday and he asked if I had found a little necklace of his mother's. The teeth were there on the Friday. I never saw the petrol bottle then. I identify the petrol bottle now shown me. I do not remember seeing it in No. 66 at all. I identify the two medicine bottles. They were there during the Monday, Tuesday, and Wednesday. I did not see a bottle of aspirin once in room No. 66. I identify the corsets as being very similar. I cannot identify the stock-ings, production No. 9, as the pair I gave to Miss West. The other pair might have been the ones (referring to Pro-duction No. 25). The black dress was generally worn outside. The navy blue was worn as a petticoat. The handbag was a black one. I only saw it open once. It had an inner pocket. The handbag exhibited to me looks like it. As regards the bedclothes in room 66, there was only a bolster and one pillow. When I called Mrs. Fox I always found her lying on the pillow. I had never before seen the pillow put on one side. She lay on the side of the bed nearest the door. I took the things upstairs on the Friday. I have not made the bed since. I stripped the bed on the Friday and noticed the stain. I emptied the chamber every morning,

Evidence for Prosecution.

Louise Bickmore

and I emptied it again on the Friday. The accused had no pyjamas.

Cross-examined by Mr. CASSELS—When was the first time you went into the room after the tragedy?—Friday. I did not touch the room on the Thursday.

Can you remember where Mrs. Fox usually left her clothes at night?—On one occasion her combinations were lying over a cane-seated chair in front of the fire. Her other clothes were then lying on the armchair.

What other articles had Mrs. Fox?—She had a toothbrush and tooth paste, a comb, and a little handkerchief she used as a face flannel. She did not have a hairbrush.

What did the accused have?—The accused had a comb, but I did not notice any shaving material. I did not take much notice of him to see if he had been shaved.

With regard to the petrol bottle, what was its state as regards the contents?—Its present state is about the state it was in as regards contents when it was left in room 70 before the fire. (About an inch from the top.)

As regards Mrs. Fox's teeth, what was your practice in the morning?—Each morning when I went in and took her a cup of tea I gave Mrs. Fox her teeth from out of the wash basin.

On Monday night, 21st October, was room 67 occupied?— The accused was away and I had no occasion to go through the communicating door into the room with tea the next morning.

Do you agree that if the door was not bolted there would be free access to Mrs. Fox's room through room 67?—Yes.

Have you not made a mistake, and that it was on 22nd October that you found the door was bolted?—No, it was Wednesday morning.

Are you perfectly certain?—Yes. I put the tray of tea on my knee when I undid the door.

Were you ever in the room when Mrs. Fox was dressing?— On one occasion I was in the room when she dressed and washed. That was on the Tuesday morning.

Do you remember her being ill on the Sunday?—Yes. Mr. Harding went up to see her. She went to No. 66 and

Sidney Harry Fox.

Louise Bickmore

went straight into bed. I took two hot-water bottles and put them close to her feet. She was very cold. On that day she had nothing solid for lunch.

When were you off duty on that Sunday?—I was off duty at 2.30. The accused was with Mrs. Fox in the room when I left.

Did the accused seem very worried about his mother?— Yes, very worried. He asked me to look after her when he was away. He gave me a tip of 7s. 6d.

Did you see the accused on the Tuesday evening?—Yes, between 6.30 and 7 I saw the accused getting off a tram from the station. I was getting on the same tram. I told him his mother would be pleased to see him, that she was anxious. I had been looking after her while he was away and she was anxious about her son.

Can you remember when the accused got up on Wednesday? —No. I remember him taking Mrs. Fox downstairs about 12.30.

Did you see the accused about tea time?—No.

As a rule were Mrs. Fox's clothes untidily thrown on the chair?—Yes.

Have you ever seen her stockings on the floor?—No, but I have seen them on the arm of the chair. They were on the floor on the Friday when I picked them up.

Of course, a very large number of people had been in the room since the Wednesday?—Yes.

Where did you pick them up from?—By the bottom of the bed.

Did you see her bag and corsets?—No, just the stockings and shoes. The shoes were under the bed rail close to the stockings. The stockings I saw were not burned. I only saw the one pair.

Did you see any article of burned clothing in the room? —No.

Have you been asked to arrange the room in any way since the 23rd of October?—No.

Was the bed a double bed, and was there only one pillow?—Yes.

Where did you generally find that pillow?—I generally

The burned carpet

Evidence for Prosecution.

Louise Bickmore

found the pillow on the left of the bed when I made the bed, and I put it in the centre. Mrs. Fox always slept near the door and moved the pillow to the left.

Is the pedestal very close to the top of the bed?—Yes, it is parallel with the mattress.

Re-examined by the ATTORNEY-GENERAL—When did you see Mrs. Fox's teeth after the tragedy?—On the Friday.

Were they broken then?—No.

When you went into the room on the Friday, where was the cane chair?—By the window.

Had the accused bought half a bottle of port on the night of the 23rd?—Yes.

Had there been any other occasion on which Mrs. Fox had had a drink in her room except a drink with her meal on Monday night?—No.

By Mr. JUSTICE ROWLATT—You say the door was bolted on Mrs. Fox's side on Wednesday morning. Can you tell me also whether it was bolted on Tuesday morning?—It was not, my lord.

How do you know it was not?—It never is.

Had you any reason to go from one room to the other on Tuesday?—No, I do not think I had.

If it had been bolted the night her son was away and you did not notice it, was there any reason why it should still be bolted on Wednesday morning, so far as you were concerned?—No.

It occurred to me it might possibly have been bolted the night her son was away and never opened again until Wednesday morning?—It may have been that, but I do not think it was. I feel so sure about it.

Further cross-examined by Mr. CASSELS—Have you, after guests have gone away, found empty bottles in their rooms?—Yes.

Was there a glass in the accused's room and also in Mrs. Fox's room?—Yes. One was an ordinary tumbler, the other a water bottle and glass.

How many rooms had you under your charge at that time?—Seventeen.

Sidney Harry Fox.

And how many of them had communicating doors?—
Four.

By a JUROR—Were there any articles made of celluloid in
the room?—No.

By Mr. CASSELS—What became of her comb?—I took the
comb to the accused downstairs when he was leaving.

By the ATTORNEY-GENERAL—You saw the comb after the
tragedy?—Yes.

JOSEPH HENRY HARDING, examined by Sir HENRY CURTIS
BENNETT—I am manager of the Hotel Metropole, Margate.
The accused stayed from the 16th to the 25th of October of
last year. He arrived on the 15th along with Mrs. Fox.
I did not see them until the 17th. On the 17th I received
a sealed envelope from the accused to put in the safe. I
knew that neither of them had any luggage. On the
18th I spoke to the accused about 10 p.m. He asked
me to recommend him to a solicitor as he wished to
consult one for insurance purposes. I gave him the
name of a firm of solicitors. I said I would be
pleased to cash a cheque for him or get it passed. He
said he would cash it at Lloyds, Threadneedle Street.
He said his baggage had been sent on to Lyndhurst,
Hampshire, to a new house his mother had bought,
and they were going there on Saturday. I only saw him
to pass the time of day.

On Sunday, 20th October, about 11 a.m., he said his
mother was in a faint, and I gave him some sal volatile
and sent for Dr. Austin. I suggested that he and his mother
should occupy rooms Nos. 66 and 67, which had fires in
them. In the afternoon he came and told me the doctor had
been and could he send a boy to the chemist's. Later he told
me his mother was better and told us to tell Dr. Austin not to
come on Monday. On Monday he inquired regarding trains
to go to London. He did not tell me why he was going to
London. I saw him again on the Tuesday evening about
seven o'clock.

I did not see the accused on Wednesday, the 23rd, during the day, but I saw him about 10.30 p.m. in the lower
bar. As I went in, he left. I went to bed about 11.25.

Evidence for Prosecution.

Joseph H. Harding

Shortly after that I was aroused by an alarm of fire. I walked to the end of the corridor to No. 66. There was then very little smoke in the corridor. Some of the guests had arrived before me. I saw the body of Mrs. Fox pass me in the corridor. It appeared to me that she was being drawn along by two guests. She was in her undervest only. I saw the accused a few minutes later. He was on the landing of the first floor, a little away from the room. The accused was attired only in a vest. I went to the door of No. 66, which was open, and I saw two men in the room. I saw a chair burning. There were no flames. Mr. Reid was bringing out the chair. He was taking it towards the communicating door, and I told him to bring it out into the corridor. He did so, and I assisted him. I saw him moving the armchair. There was a cane chair in the room. I could not see the cane chair at the time the other chair was being dragged out. I identify the chair now produced. As the chair came along I caught hold of the left front leg and it broke away. The chair was still smouldering, but not very much. There was practically no burning afterwards. I have noticed how the chair underneath has been burned. The front and sides are about equally burned, and more so than the back. I noticed that the charring on the front and the two sides was about the same. I also noticed that round the back of the chair was scorched almost to the top. When the chair was brought out of the room there was a great deal of smoke. The chair was afterwards taken out into the street. As far as I noticed there was nothing on the chair when it was brought out except a spectacle case. It was on the seat of the chair, and I put it on a chest of drawers in the room. The smoke in the room was very general. A few embers on the floor were being stamped out.

By Mr. JUSTICE ROWLATT—When the chair was brought out the body was lying close to the door. It did not come near the body as it came out.

Examination continued—I identify the piece of carpet produced as the carpet that was running down the side of the room in front of the gas fire. It shows where I saw

Sidney Harry Fox.

Joseph H. Harding

embers burning. It would be to the right of the gas fire. I identify the place on the carpet where the fender was, and I also identify the felt as being the felt that was underneath the carpet. Where the burns went through the felt the floor boards were scorched. I know that tests have been made by the fire brigade on other pieces of carpet. It was when I was looking through the door that I saw the embers burning. Water was obtained and put on the fire.

I was present when the body was taken downstairs. Dr. Austin examined the body downstairs, and it was then put into No. 126 and locked up by the police. I went up to the room at about 1 a.m. with Dr. Nichol. The door was unlocked by the police and then locked up again by the police. It remained locked until the body was removed on the 24th by the undertakers.

I went into No. 66 after the smoke cleared. I saw a set of false teeth in the wash basin. I left them there. I also saw a magazine on the floor between the window and the armchair. I noticed sundry pieces of charred newspaper, but I did not actually examine the paper. The charred paper was in front of where the chair stood. I saw the position of the chair before it was actually moved; it was immediately over the hole which was burned in the carpet. The fire had not reached the bed by a very considerable space. The clothing on the bed was drawn back from the pillow to the right, from the door side towards the window. There was rather a deep impression on the bolster and a light impression on the bed. There was a wet patch on the under sheet. I saw some clothing lying behind the door, and a pair of stockings on the floor. The clothing behind the door consisted of one dress and one coat, as far as I saw. I am quite clear that there was a dress there. The stockings were between the chair and the bed. I identify Exhibit No. 102 as the cane chair which was in room No. 66. This chair was in front of the window and close to the wardrobe —not near the fire at all. The right-hand back leg was burned on the back, and more particularly on the inside. It was not burned on the outside right. There was no other leg burned. It looked as though it had certainly been alight. I went into room No. 66, I think some twenty

100

Evidence for Prosecution.

Joseph H. Harding

minutes after the alarm of fire. I am quite clear as to the place where I found the cane chair. I was present at the inquest. The accused and I discussed things in general. When the accused left the hotel on the 25th of October he said he was going to fetch his motor car, which had been repaired at Canterbury, and was then going to a hotel at Norwich. He never told me his mother was insured against accidents.

Cross-examined by Mr. CASSELS—It was on the Sunday he said his mother was in a faint?—Yes.

And did you go up to see her?—I did. I said I knew something about ailments.

What did you find when you went up?—She certainly looked as though she had recently been in a faint and was extremely cold.

And was it you who suggested that they should have different rooms where they would have a gas fire?—Yes.

Is it quite clear and definite that the idea of Mrs. Fox having a room with a gas fire was in your mind and was not suggested by either Mrs. Fox or her son?—That is quite true.

When was she removed to No. 66?—I do not know exactly.

Did you follow downstairs when Mrs. Fox's body was carried downstairs?—Yes.

Were there many people in the corridor when you arrived? —There were some four or five persons already there. Mr. Reed was at the armchair when I got there, and I told him to bring it out, and he brought it out of No. 66.

Either you or Mr. Reed must be making a mistake as to the door it was brought out by?—Yes. I am certain it was not the communicating door.

Was there a good deal of smoke in the room by that time? —Yes.

Who was it that was stamping out the embers?—I believe it was Mr. French.

Where were the embers?—The embers were on the outer edge of the lower part of the burning. You could see the embers beneath the smoke.

101

Sidney Harry Fox.

Joseph H. Harding

Had water already been put on the burning?—Yes. It was as the chair was pulled away that a gentleman stamped out the embers.

How far was the chair from the bed?—I think the chair cleared the bed by quite ten inches.

If there had been a cane chair in front of the chair and between it and the communicating door would it have been easily seen?—Yes. If a cane chair had been there it would have been knocked over.

Was the electric light on when the chair was being brought out?—Yes, and even with smoke you will find you can discern opaque objects quite plainly. I have my own experience of fire smoke.

Was the stamping done all over the burned area?—No.

Has the chair produced ordinarily a canvas bottom, then coarse wool, and then more canvas?—Yes.

I think you found some springs?—Yes, I found the springs in the corridor. I took it they were from the chair.

A great point has been made in this case of the burned portion of carpet under the armchair. I suggest, for your consideration, that when the bottom of the chair caught fire the material was released and fell on to the carpet and provided fuel for the fire?—There was no debris under the chair.

What I am suggesting to you is that the bottom of that chair, or part of it, fell on to the carpet, thus creating an intensity of burning which was much greater than the burning anywhere else?—To my mind some of that stuffing has disappeared, probably by carting it about.

I do not want too many of your probabilities. Was there any debris beneath the chair that night?—There was no debris on the floor when I walked in.

The flames beneath the chair must have lapped round the front and sides and gone round the arms?—Yes.

Did you see the top canvas of that chair when you looked at the bottom of the chair that night?—No. There appeared to be more of the horsehair at the bottom of the chair that night. There was some cottonwool out.

102

Evidence for Prosecution.

Joseph H. Harding

As nearly as possible, is the chair now very identical to what it was that night?—Yes.

With regard to the cane chair, the right back leg of which is charred, does it not look as if it had been burned whilst standing over something?—I think it may have been used to poke the fire.

Is it not the case that at the very bottom of the leg, and for half an inch up the leg, there is no burning?—Yes, it might not be burned because it is not varnished. It might not have caught.

If there had been a pair of woman's combinations hanging on the back of the chair and they had caught fire, would you have expected any other marks than those you see on the chair? Look at them as I look at them?—Yes, I notice that.

By Mr. JUSTICE ROWLATT—Is your answer that, so far as the round rails at the bottom and the flat rails at the top are concerned, it might be so if a woman's combinations caught fire whilst hanging over them, but the leg could not?—That is what I thought.

Cross-examination continued—The leg may have been burned by being on a portion of carpet which was burning?—It might have been.

About the impression on the bolster, that is a matter which has been mentioned to-day for the first time?—Yes.

It was such as would have been made by any one sleeping normally on it?—Yes.

Nothing was said at the inquest or the Police Court?—I was not asked about it at the Police Court. A remark was made on the night that a head had rested on the pillow.

Where was the impression?—It was towards the door.

With regard to the impression, was it such as would have been made by any one sleeping normally on it?—Yes.

Were the bedclothes flung on one side as if some one had got out of bed quickly?—No; the bedclothes had been flung back, but I could not say that they looked as if some one had got out quickly.

Re-examined by Sir HENRY CURTIS BENNETT—[Shown photograph of carpet contained in book of photographs.]

103

Sidney Harry Fox.

Can you say what the little black mark on the carpet is?—
No, I cannot.

When the photograph was taken had the carpet been
touched?—No.

[Shown No. 5.] What does that photograph show?—This
photograph represents the carpet and fender as they were
on the day of the tragedy.

Was the light over the bed on when you arrived?—No,
but the other light was on.

The atmosphere in the room would be thicker at the top
than the bottom?—Yes.

Did you see the cane chair?—I did not.

And if it had been there would you have seen it?—Yes.

Louise Bickmore (recalled), examined by Mr. Justice
Rowlatt—I suppose the gas fire will run for some time for
a penny?—Yes.

And is there a tap which can be turned off and leave
gas to your credit?—Yes.

Did you notice in the morning, as part of your duty, that
the tap was turned off?—Yes. I never turned it off on
any of these mornings, so that it must have been turned off.

Samuel Francis Douglas Hopkins, examined by Sir
Henry Curtis Bennett—I am a commercial traveller, and
I reside at Walthamstow. I was staying at the Hotel Metropole, Margate, on the night of 23rd October. I had never
stayed there before. I arrived about 5.30 on the 23rd. I left
the hotel at 8 p.m. and got back about 11.15 or 11.20. I
entered the lounge. There were two or three travellers and
three seamen there. I stayed in the lounge for some little
time, about twenty or twenty-five minutes. About 11.40 I saw
the accused running downstairs clad in a shirt of some
description. The accused said, " Where is the boots? I
think there's a fire. There is a fire. Where is the boots? "
I gave the alarm and followed the accused upstairs. I
don't know who followed me. We went along the corridor
and the accused went straight to room No. 67. The door
was closed. There was just a small quantity of smoke in
the corridor. When the accused opened the door of No. 67

Evidence for Prosecution.

Samuel F. D. Hopkins

and went in I followed him. There was smoke in the room and there was no light on. I retired to the corridor and the accused followed me and pointed to No. 66 and said, " My mother's in there." I did not notice the communicating door. I opened the door of No. 66. Up till this it had been closed. I was beaten back by the smoke. I walked in upright a few feet. I made a second attempt with a handkerchief over my mouth, but I did not get much farther. I did not see the accused after I had left him in the corridor. I again went in on my hands and knees and came into contact with Mrs. Fox's legs hanging over the bed. I felt her foot. I caught her under the arms and pulled her off the bed. I think her back was towards me. She had a vest on.

By Mr. JUSTICE ROWLATT—Was she under the clothes on the bed ?—I cannot remember.

Examination continued—I laid her down about three yards from the door. I noticed, I think, Mr. Reed through the glare while I was in the room. He must have been going through the communicating door. I remember the chair being brought out, but I do not remember through which door it was brought. I appealed to the people round me to get her out of the smoke. I was feeling very bad. The accused played no part in helping to remove his mother. I was ill for three weeks afterwards.

We are all agreed you did a very plucky action. You are all right now, I hope?—Yes. I am still a little nervous and my legs give me a little pain if I am on them too much.

Cross-examined by Mr. CASSELS—When you went into the room on your hands and knees in what direction did you go?—I made a little left incline. I did not know the position of the bed.

On which part of the bed did you get hold of Mrs. Fox? —I could not say. I pulled her off as rapidly as possible. As far as I can recollect she was lying on her back. I came to that conclusion from the position I held her in.

In what position was she lying on the bed?—She would be lying aslant on the bed—not lying across the centre, but with her head to the top and her feet towards the bottom in a slant.

105

Sidney Harry Fox.

Henry Miller

HENRY MILLER, examined by Mr. ST. JOHN HUTCHINSON—
I am a commercial traveller, of Brighton, and I was staying at the Hotel Metropole, Margate, on the night of 23rd
October last. At about 11.40 I heard a cry of " Fire! " and
some one shouting for the boots. I said to some friends,
" We had better go up and put it out." I ran upstairs into
the corridor and saw slight smoke in the corridor. There
was smoke coming out of Nos. 66 and 67. Several people
rushed up with me. We entered room 67 and I heard a voice
say, " My mother's in there." I then saw the communicating door of room 66, and I opened it. I was driven back
by the smoke. I backed out of the room, and Reed, who
had crawled in on his hands and knees, pushed a chair
through the communicating door into No. 67 and then out
into the corridor. I heard a voice say, " Mind, you are
burning her feet." Mrs. Fox was lying a few feet from
the door. Hopkins was just inside the room. I helped to
carry Mrs. Fox along the corridor. I then went back to
see if Reed was all right. After that I came back and saw
Mrs. Fox's face, and I thought she was dead. Her mouth
was open and there were no teeth in her mouth. She struck
me as being rather pallid. I did not touch the pillow or
the bed in No. 66. She was then carried carefully downstairs.

Cross-examined by Mr. CASSELS—How far did you get
into the room?—Only about one or two feet. The smoke
was very thick and prevented me going farther.

Did the smoke fill up the corridor and did the atmosphere get thicker?—Yes.

Could you say definitely whether the door of 67 was open
or not when you got there?—No.

Do you recollect a chair being pulled through the communicating door?—Yes, it was the easy chair. It did not
come through room 66 on to the corridor; it came through
room 67.

Had Reed to go in on his hands and knees?—Yes.

Could you see anything in the room?—I could see absolutely nothing.

Was the accused close to you all the time?—I could not
say. I had my back towards him.

106

Evidence for Prosecution.

Henry Miller

You assisted Mr. Hopkins?—Yes; when I first assisted, the body was just outside the door—a foot or two.

In what position was Mrs. Fox when you first saw her?—She was on her stomach.

Have you seen a person die?—Yes.

And do you agree that the mouth falls?—Yes. Mrs. Fox's mouth was open as though she had no control of her muscles.

Did you notice, as the body was carried downstairs, the head flop about?—No.

Do you not remember the accused saying, " Be careful. Look at her head "?—No, I do not remember that.

Did you notice whether the mouth was closed going downstairs?—No.

Was her face pale?—Yes, her face was very pale.

Did you see artificial respiration being applied?—Yes. In the first instance it was done with her lying on her stomach, the police constable kneeling by her side.

Did you notice whether the accused was standing by?—No.

Was it the Schäfer method of respiration which was being used?—Yes.

How was the face lying at that time?—I cannot say where her face was at that time.

Did you touch the fender in the room?—No, nor did I kick anything in the room.

Were you in the room when water was thrown down?—No.

How many were in the room when you were in?—There were about four or five in addition to myself.

The Court adjourned.

Sidney Harry Fox.

Third Day—Friday, 14th March, 1930.

REGINALD LEONARD REED, examined by Sir HENRY CURTIS
BENNETT—I am a commercial traveller, and I live at Odessa
Road, Harlesden. I travel for a Clerkenwell firm. I was
staying in the Hotel Metropole, Margate, on the night
of 23rd October. At 11.40 p.m. I was in the billiard room
when I heard a cry of fire. I rushed upstairs to the first
floor corridor. I saw the witness Miller. We went into
room 67. From there I went into room 66 by the communicating door, which had been closed. I saw no light in
room 67. Miller opened the communicating door. I crawled
into room No. 66, which was pretty thick with smoke, and
I saw a burning chair. The flames were coming up from
the side nearest me and from the seat of the chair and also
from the back. I identify the chair produced as the chair
I refer to. There was no other chair between the communicating door and that chair. I attempted to move the chair
from the room. I caught the back of the chair somewhere.
I noticed the carpet was alight immediately under the chair.
I got the chair out into room No. 67 and then into the
corridor. I did not notice anything on the chair when I
took it out. Some burning material was dropping from the
chair. I went back into the room and tried to stamp out
the burning material, but I did not succeed. I then picked
up a fender near the gas stove and used it to beat out the
flames. I did not see any other chair. I did not see anything of the removal of Mrs. Fox. I did not see the body
until I returned downstairs. When stamping out the flames
I tried to pull up the carpet and I tore the carpet. It was a
short tear; the split would be about eight inches from the
fender. The next day I replaced the chair in the position
it was the night before.

On Friday, 25th October, I returned to the hotel with a
copy of the *Isle of Thanet Gazette* which contained a full
report of the inquest held on the previous day, and, seeing
the accused, I said to him, " Fox, have you seen this? "

Evidence for Prosecution.

Reginald L. Reed

He replied, " No. What is it? " Upon being told, he said he would like to read it. Having read it, he said, " It is all right. I certainly did not say, ' Mummy is in there.' I am not a baby." I said, " Are you sure, Fox, your mother was in bed when the fire occurred? " He said, yes, because either the doctor or the coroner told him the bed had been wetted. He told me he was in the insurance line. He mentioned the names of various hotels, but he did not mention where he had been recently. On the 24th or the 25th of October I saw the accused in a telephone box at the hotel, and I could hear part of his conversation. I heard him make an appointment with some one at the Strand Palace Hotel for eight o'clock that night, and I also heard him say, " This is very important." I believe it was eight o'clock that was mentioned. No more was said —simply that it was important. The accused had a sort of pin-striped suit with him. He purchased a new coat on Friday, the 25th, while I was with him. I asked him if he was positive that there had been £24 in his mother's bag, and he said, " Yes, because mother only recently cashed a cheque."

Cross-examined by Mr. Cassels—How many people went to the room when the alarm was given?—I think at least four.

When you first arrived at the door of No. 66 are you satisfied it was full of smoke?—Yes. I had to go in on my hands and knees. I thought it better to go like that.

How far could you see?—I could not see farther than the burning chair. I could see it all right.

Did you notice whether the gas fire was alight?—No. I was most anxious to deal with the situation.

The chair was alight, the carpet was alight, and the room was full of smoke?—Yes, and I took no longer time than necessary to put it out.

How did you pull the chair out?—I was standing up when I pulled the chair out.

Was the smoke pretty thick?—Yes.

Was it fairly thick in the corridor when you pulled the chair out?—Yes. I could not see the ground in the corridor.

Sidney Harry Fox.

Reginald L. Reed

Could you see clearly up to the burning chair in the room?—Yes.

Did any of the burning stuff come off the chair in the corridor?—I am not certain of that, but some of the burning embers fell off the chair in the room.

What did you do after you got the chair out?—When I got the chair out I went back pretty quickly to the room.

And what was the condition then?—There were very short flames on the carpet. The carpet was burning, so much so that I tried to smother it, if I could, by pulling a portion of the carpet over the flames. In doing that I tore the carpet.

Was the room then full of smoke?—It was not quite so full of smoke. I had not waited long before I went in again.

Was some water handed in to you while bringing out the chair?—Yes, and there was some more handed to me on my second trip.

When you picked up the fender did you burn your hand? —Yes. I dropped it pretty quickly. I only touched the fender in one place.

What were the relative positions of the chair and the fender?—The chair was on my right and the fender was on my left.

Mr. JUSTICE ROWLATT (after examining the burned carpet and the position of the tear in it)—Could this carpet be relaid in exactly the same position as it was found on the night of the fire?

Sir HENRY CURTIS BENNETT—It can be done, because I saw it on Saturday last myself.

Mr. JUSTICE ROWLATT—I think a plan should be prepared showing the exact position of the carpet.

The ATTORNEY-GENERAL—That will be done.

Mr. JUSTICE ROWLATT—I would also suggest that the oil-cloth and the gas fire from the room be brought into Court to-day so that the exact position of the stove in relation to the oilcloth can be seen.

Sir HENRY CURTIS BENNETT—I have arranged for that, my lord.

By Mr. JUSTICE ROWLATT—Have you a good recollection of how you found the chair on the night in question?—I

Evidence for Prosecution.

Reginald L. Reed

had a vivid recollection next morning of how I found the chair on the previous night, and I replaced it in that position.

Does the photograph produced show the correct position? —To the best of my knowledge, it does.

When did you put the chair in position?—It was about 10.30 or 11 a.m. the next morning when I put it in position.

Who were there at the time?—Inspector Palmer and several others. I do not know who the others were.

Did you take any particular notice of the gas stove the next morning?—No.

Are you quite certain you did not knock anything over in the room?—Yes.

Did anybody go into the room after you had brought out the burning chair?—No; not before I ran into the room again.

FREDERICK FRENCH, examined by Mr. ST. JOHN HUTCHINSON—I am a commercial traveller, and I reside at St. James's Road, Tunbridge Wells. On the 23rd of October last I was staying at the Hotel Metropole, Margate. I heard a cry of " Boots, fire," between 11.30 and 12 at night. I did nothing at first because I thought it was a false alarm. I then got up and saw two people disappearing upstairs. Mr. Underwood was with me. I ran upstairs and turned into a short corridor which was fairly full of smoke. I found a gentleman bending over a body. There was another gentleman by the side of the body. These two men were Mr. Hopkins and Mr. Miller. I did not know whether the body was that of a lady or a gentleman. Mr. Hopkins was bending over the head with his arms under the armpits. The other man was bending over, but he was not touching the body. I then saw the witness Reed with a smouldering armchair outside No. 66. The door of No. 66 was open, but I am not certain about No. 67. I looked into room No. 66 and it was full of smoke. I could see very indistinctly into the room. I then went into the room. I was standing upright. It was too thick to breathe properly. I went towards the glow and found the carpet to be smouldering,

111

Sidney Harry Fox.

Frederick French

and in some places there were short flames, so I stamped them out. I noticed the gas fire was three parts on and alight, so I turned it out. As soon as the fire was out I went over and threw the window open. That caused a draught into the room and it blew the smoke out of the doorway. I then came out of the room and pulled the door of No. 66 behind me. I did not notice any difference in the smoke in No. 66 when I went out. The photograph No. 3 shows how I went in. I went across to the fire and then to the window and came back by the same route. I never in my route came across a small chair. I knocked the corner of the bed. When I saw the chair, part of the seat underneath and at the side was burning. Other people were pouring glasses of water on the chair and beating it. Mr. Underwood and I carried the chair downstairs and took it out of the hotel. I saw no springs whatever. I saw nothing on the chair until I got it downstairs. I found stockings similar to the burned ones on the arm near the back. There was also a bag on the seat near the back, and a pair of stockings.

Cross-examined by Mr. Cassels—The chair was not in the room at that time?—No. I could not see what was on the chair in the corridor because of the smoke.

And so far as you know, that was how the chair came out?—Yes.

So far as you can say, nobody had put the things on the chair after it was brought out?—No.

Was the smoke in No. 66 uncomfortable?—Yes, it was most difficult to breathe.

Was the carpet alight when you were in the room?—Yes, for an area of about a square yard. That part would be about two feet from the gas fire.

Have you seen the carpet since?—No.

You think it would be about two feet from the fire where the burning began?—Yes.

Would a distance of about a yard take you to the centre of the burning patch?—Yes.

Can you say definitely whether the door of No. 66 was open when you arrived?—Yes. I went into room No. 66.

112

The burned chair in position

Evidence for Prosecution.

Frederick French

Could you say through which door the chair had been taken?—No.

Do you know where the chair had been?—No; I could not say.

When you were in the room were the fumes very pungent? —Yes; they made one cough.

When were you first asked if you saw a small chair in the room?—Yesterday, or the day before.

Would it be correct to say that you only saw indistinctly into the room?—Yes.

You would do what you did do as quickly as possible, and you would remain in the room for as short a time as possible?—Yes.

Did you say at the inquest that the chair was badly burned above the side?—Yes.

Re-examined by Mr. ST. JOHN HUTCHINSON—Are you quite sure you did not see the chair?—Yes.

Could you say whether the flames on the carpet were burning to or from the centre?—I could not.

WILLIAM A. B. UNDERWOOD, examined by Mr. ST. JOHN HUTCHINSON—I am a commercial traveller. On the 23rd of October last I was staying at the Hotel Metropole, Margate. I was in the lounge with Mr. French when we heard the alarm, and we went upstairs and down a corridor. There was some slight smoke in the corridor. We found a body with two men near it. Mr. French and I entered the door of room No. 66. I noticed a glow to the left of us as we entered the room. We moved towards the gas fire and Mr. French turned it out. I then went across the room to the farther side and along with Mr. French opened a window. I then turned back and went out of the room. The door was open behind us. I do not think the door was closed. I never came across a small chair, to my recollection. When I came out the armchair was in the passage still smouldering, and Exhibits Nos. 24, 25, and 26 were on the chair. When we had the chair outside I took the bag up in my hand and shook it. I could not feel anything in it. I handed the things over to the police constable.

H   113

Sidney Harry Fox.

William A. B. Underwood

Cross-examined by Mr. CASSELS—It is five months ago since all this happened. When were you first asked whether you had come across a small chair in that room?—Since arriving here.

GEORGE EDWARD BRAY, examined by Sir HENRY CURTIS BENNETT—I am a police constable in the Margate Borough Police. On the 23rd of October I went to the Hotel Metropole at 11.50 p.m. and went up to the first floor. I there saw the body of a woman on her back. There was nobody touching her at that time. I went to room No. 66. The door was open. The smoke was dispersing from the room. I opened another window. I then left the room and went to the woman. She was still lying in the same position. I called for assistance to carry her downstairs. She was carried downstairs by me with the help of four others. When we got downstairs she was placed at the foot of the stairs and I tried artificial respiration. She was placed face up. I rolled her gently over on her right side and then on to her stomach. I commenced artificial respiration, using the Schäfer method. I carried that on for about five minutes. I then had her removed to near the door because of the smoke. I noticed no sign of life. As she was carried downstairs her face was uppermost. Nobody touched her head as she was carried downstairs. She had no teeth in her mouth. Nobody touched her tongue during that time. When we got her down near the door she was placed on her back again and the same procedure took place as before— the same respiration method was applied. I never saw any signs of life. Dr. Austin then arrived on the scene and said that life was extinct. I then went with Dr. Austin and Dr. Nichol to room No. 66 and had handed to me Exhibits 24, 25, and 26.

I gave evidence at the inquest on the 24th of October. On the 11th of November I went to the refuse dump and found Exhibits Nos. 24, 25, and 26. They were scattered in close proximity to each other. They were no longer in a parcel. I was also handed part of an *Evening Standard* on the night of the 23rd October which had been found close to the front

114

Sidney Harry Fox.

George E. Bray

of the armchair. It was on the left-hand side of the burning. I saw it picked up from the floor. It was in my possession at the time of the inquest, and was placed by me in the dustbin after the inquest. It was done up in the same parcel. I found it on the 11th of November. I saw the bag, Exhibit No. 24, opened by Dr. Nichol on the night of the 23rd. Inspector Palmer was present. There was a mourning card inside about six inches by four inches. There was no writing or printing on it. It was not burned or scorched. It came from the centre portion of the bag. It was put back into the bag as far as I can remember. I heard the accused at the inquest identify the comb.

Cross-examined by Mr. CASSELS—Where is the mourning card?—It was in the possession of some one and is now missing.

How many people carried the woman downstairs?—Five people, including myself.

Do you remember the accused saying, " Be careful," or something to that effect?—No. I did not in fact notice the accused.

Was her head all wobbly and flopping about?—No.

Was her mouth open?—Yes.

Did she seem to be dead?—Yes.

How was the body placed on the floor for artificial respiration?—She was gently turned over and artificial respiration was started by me. It was the Schäfer method I adopted. I knelt beside the patient and placed the palms of my hands on the lower ribs with the fingers well apart and slowly applied pressure, thus driving out air and producing expiration. Each movement occupied three seconds. We then produced inspiration for two seconds. About seventy-five movements of that character were administered. The body was then carried to the door for more air, the head being turned so as to get the benefit of the air.

Otherwise the face was inclined to one side?—Yes. Police Constable Fleet kept up the same method for another five minutes. Dr. Austin then pronounced life extinct.

Re-examined by Sir HENRY CURTIS BENNETT—Was the body first put down on the back and then turned over?—Yes.

115

Sidney Harry Fox.

Arthur W. Kemp

ARTHUR WILLIAM KEMP, examined by Sir HENRY CURTIS BENNETT—I am a police constable in the Margate Borough Police. On the night of 23rd October I went to the Hotel Metropole about twelve o'clock. I saw the body and saw artificial respiration being applied by Police Constable Fleet. The mouth was open and there were no teeth in it. I put my fingers into the woman's mouth and caught hold of the tip of the tongue and withdrew it. When I released the tongue it stayed where I had put it.

Cross-examined by Mr. CASSELS—When you saw Mrs. Fox, in what position was she lying?—She was lying face downwards, and I knelt down beside her. I put my right hand under her right cheek and slightly inclined her to the left. Her mouth was then sideways, slightly open, sufficient to allow me to get my fingers into her mouth. I found the tongue and drew it out so that the tip of the tongue was outside the lips. It did not go back when I let go.

HERBERT FLEET, examined by Mr. ST. JOHN HUTCHINSON—I am a police sergeant in the Margate Borough Police. On the 23rd of October last, before midnight, I went with Inspector Palmer to the Hotel Metropole and saw the body of a woman lying partly on her right side. Her mouth was open and there were no teeth in it. She was receiving attention from Police Constable Bray. We moved her to the door. She was placed on her back and rolled on to her right side, and we commenced artificial respiration by the Schäfer method. Dr. Austin and Dr. Nichol both arrived on the scene. Dr. Austin arrived first. I went up to the room with Inspector Palmer and found the teeth intact; they were in the wash-hand basin. They were not particularly clean. There was no water in the basin. There was a considerable quantity of charred newspaper about. Some of it was a French newspaper. I did not see it on the carpet. The French newspaper was all burned through, but there was enough to tell that it was a French newspaper. The body was then removed to room 126 by Bray, Norris, Galer, Mr. Ryan, and myself. The body was first of all placed on a carrying sheet, then on to a stretcher. It was rolled over

116

Evidence for Prosecution.

Herbert Fleet

on to the bed and the carrying sheet was taken away. It was all done gently.

I was present on the 24th of October when the coroner spoke to the accused. The coroner asked, " Now, tell me, Fox, what condition was your mother in last night? Was she cheerful? " The accused replied, " Oh, yes, quite well. Just before she went to bed we had a sham fight—you know, a boxing match." The coroner was surprised, and said, " What! A boxing match? " and the accused said, " Only in fun, of course."

Cross-examined by Mr. CASSELS—When you tried the method of artificial respiration did you put your finger in the woman's mouth?—Yes, just to the back of the tongue. That was before Kemp pulled out the tongue.

Did you get right to the back of the tongue?—Yes, as far as I can say. I did it to make sure her teeth had not fallen into the back of the throat. I used the first finger of my left hand.

Did you press down the tongue?—No. I was satisfied there was no obstruction of the air passage.

How was she lying at that time?—She was lying on her stomach, with her head inclined to the left side.

What happened after that?—Bray then followed me and carried on respiration until Dr. Austin arrived.

What was done when the doctor arrived?—She was turned over on to her back so that she could be examined.

What did you do then?—I went to room No. 66.

Were you asked about the French newspaper at the police court?—No.

What sort of a paper was it?—It was a paper similar to the remains of the *Evening Standard*. There were French words printed on it.

Were there any illustrations?—No.

Is it in existence now?—No; it has not been found. Pieces of the *Evening Standard* were all that could be found.

By Mr. JUSTICE ROWLATT—With regard to the stockings, handbag, corsets, charred newspaper, &c., which were wrapped in a parcel and deposited on a refuse heap after the inquest, how were they found?—They were buried in a dump for about fifteen days, and it is estimated that 502

117

Sidney Harry Fox.

loads were afterwards placed on the dump. The parcel was found about three feet from the surface, but had become open, and the fragments of the newspaper and an undergarment were missing.

A JUROR—Can we be told whether Mrs. Fox or the accused could speak French?

Mr. JUSTICE ROWLATT—We do not know, and cannot ask yet.

Mr. CASSELS—I shall not answer the question now, but it will be dealt with.

Cross-examination continued—In what condition was the parcel when you found it?—It was slightly damp.

And what was done with the things you found?—They were all folded up and put in a large piece of paper.

At the inquest you said, " I formed the opinion that deceased took off her underclothing and placed it on the arm of the chair, from which it fell and caught fire "?— That was the only opinion I could come to at the time, and I was guided then by the view of the chief officer of the fire brigade. It was his opinion.

Re-examined by Mr. ST. JOHN HUTCHINSON—Were you asked to say how they fell?—No.

Previous to the Police Court had you made a statement in which you dealt with the question of the French newspaper?—Yes.

By Mr. JUSTICE ROWLATT—Did you ascertain what quantity of gas was left in the meter?—Yes, by the indicator.

Dr. CECIL C. AUSTIN, examined by the ATTORNEY-GENERAL —I am a medical practitioner, and I am in practice at Hawley Street, Margate. I was called to see Mrs. Fox at the Hotel Metropole on 20th October. I got there between 1.30 and 2 p.m. I had never seen Mrs. Fox before. She was lying in a bed on the first floor. As far as I can recollect, she wore a nightgown, but I am not absolutely certain. I examined her. She was not very ill, a little run down, and stomach trouble. I prescribed a simple tonic, which included chloroform water. There was nothing dangerous in the mixture. If one drank the whole bottle it might make one sick, but that would be all. There was

118

Evidence for Prosecution.

not the slightest need to break it down. I said I would call and see her again on Monday, but I did not go, as I got a telephone message telling me not to call. There is not the slightest truth in the suggestion that I said to Mrs. Fox, " You are all right, old lady. Bogey, bogey."

I was summoned to the Hotel Metropole by the police on Wednesday, 23rd October. I got there about midnight. When I arrived I found that artificial respiration was being applied. I found that Mrs. Fox was dead and I told them to stop respiration, that it was no good. The body was still warm. Dr. Nichol also arrived on the scene. I made no post-mortem examination. I certified the death as being due to shock and suffocation. I went up to room 66, but I only made a casual examination. I noticed the chair was burned. It was in the room. I also noted that there was an impression on the bed as though some one had lain across it and not in the ordinary way, lengthwise. That was all I really noticed.

Cross-examined by Mr. CASSELS—What examination did you make on the Sunday?—I only examined her pulse, not her heart or lungs.

Do you remember being told that she had been in a faint? —No.

Was the tonic a perfectly harmless one?—Yes.

How did you come to the conclusion that she was dead?— As the result of my observation.

Did you see any signs of death by asphyxia?—No, except that the face was very flushed, which you would find in a case of asphyxia.

Mr. JUSTICE ROWLATT—What do you mean by asphyxia, Mr. Cassels?

Mr. CASSELS—I mean as to whether this doctor, observing that body, would have said, " This is the body of a person who has died from asphyxia."

Mr. JUSTICE ROWLATT—I perfectly understand that, but what is asphyxia? Does it mean suffocation by smoke? Is that asphyxia?

Cross-examination continued—Does asphyxia embrace all methods of depriving the lungs of oxygen?—Of oxygen, yes.

119

Sidney Harry Fox.

Mr. JUSTICE ROWLATT—That is what we wanted to get at.

Cross-examination continued—Persons who are throttled die from asphyxia?—Yes.

And throttling is one word for manual strangulation?—Yes.

Did you see any signs of death from asphyxia?—No, because there would be no signs to see apart from the redness of the face.

Did you see any marks of violence?—No.

Or appearances consistent with death by heart failure?—Well, I should hardly think so.

By Mr. JUSTICE ROWLATT—Why not? What would you expect to find in heart failure that you did not see here?—In heart failure there is a history attached to begin with.

Cross-examination continued—Did you say, in examination at the Police Court, " I saw no signs of death from asphyxiation and no marks of violence. As far as I was able to see, the appearances were consistent with heart failure "?—If I am reported to have done so, I must have done. It is five months ago. If you have a case of asphyxia, and it is prolonged, the heart gives out, thereupon the real cause is heart failure caused by asphyxia.

Did you say further, " I saw no sign of froth or blood stain at the mouth or nose "?—I did say that.

Did you observe the hands of the deceased?—Yes, they were colder than the other parts of the body.

And her eyes?—They were bleary.

What about her ears?—I cannot say I observed her ears.

Were they cold?—Yes.

Did you examine the mouth?—Yes, I examined the face generally.

Were the lips open?—The lips were parted.

Did you observe the tongue?—No.

There was nothing unnatural about the tongue to draw your attention to it?—Nothing at all.

When you went up to room 66 did you notice that the clothes of the bed were thrown off in part, and that there was an impression on the bed as if somebody had been lying there?—Yes.

Evidence for Prosecution.

Where was the position of the impression?—It was about the centre of the bed, crossways.

Was it parallel to the head and foot of the bed?—As far as I can remember, the impression was in the centre and was parallel with the head and foot of the bed; it was in the centre and across it.

Can you say how long it was?—No.

Was that the only impression you noticed on any part of the bed?—Yes.

Re-examined by the ATTORNEY-GENERAL—Is your memory good?—Well, I think it is normal.

By Mr. JUSTICE ROWLATT—You did not see anything remarkable about the lady at all. She was simply dead, and that was the long and the short of it?—Yes.

A JURYMAN—Will it be possible, my lord, to examine room 66 at the Hotel Metropole?

Mr. JUSTICE ROWLATT—It will not. I will not expound the reason. I have no jurisdiction outside this county.

Dr. ROBERT WILLIAM NICHOL, examined by the ATTORNEY-GENERAL—I am a medical practitioner practising in Margate. I was called to the Hotel Metropole on the night of the 23rd October and I viewed the body of Mrs. Fox. It would be about 11.45. Dr. Austin had got there before me. Dr. Austin said she was dead. I did not examine the body at all. I went upstairs to No. 66 along with Dr. Austin, Inspector Palmer, I think, Mr. Hammond, Sergeant Fleet, and others. The window had been opened. The room was fairly full of smoke and there was a strong smell of fire. The photograph No. 6 does not represent what I saw. The armchair was not in the room, and I don't think the patch on the floor was as big as it is shown in the photograph. My impression is that the hole through the carpet was not more than about one foot. I paid particular attention to the space between the fire and the fender. There seemed to be no connection between the obvious source of the fire and the site of the fire itself. I noticed a considerable quantity of charred paper—enough to associate in my mind the cause of the fire. Somebody seemed to say that one of them was a French paper. The bed had not been touched by fire;

Sidney Harry Fox.

Dr. Nichol

it seemed very much stripped of bedclothes. I have the impression that the bedclothes were farther off than is shown in that photograph No. 2. I had the general impression that the bed had been lain on by some heavy person. There was a large wet patch about eighteen inches to two feet in circumference about the centre of the bed—a patch of urine. It was towards the left-hand side of the bed about equidistant from the top and bottom. I paid particular attention to the gas stove. The gas was turned off. We looked to see if any of the asbestos '' candles '' from the gas stove, or parts of them, had flicked on to the carpet, but we saw none. The stove seemed to be in good working order.

The policeman brought me three bottles, and I tested them. The first one contained a bitter tonic, the second one the same, and the third was petrol. One tonic bottle was almost full and the other had some out of it. The armchair was brought back into the room while we were in it, and some one put it in position, nearly over the burned patch. I have the impression that I saw teeth lying in the basin, but I cannot swear to it. My attention was not specifically called to a cane chair.

I then went downstairs and saw the accused. He was in a private room of the manager's. He was sitting in a chair, and the manager's wife was trying to steady him. He was very upset. I later took him to see his mother's body. I tried to tell him rather slowly that his mother was dead. I asked him several leading questions as to how old his mother was and if she had had an illness. I mentioned that the coroner would have to hold an inquiry. I do not know exactly what he said, but he was very upset. He did not collapse at the word '' coroner,'' but he collapsed at about that part of the story. The body was placed in room 126. The accused asked if he might see his mother again, and Inspector Palmer produced keys and we went up to the room where the body was. The accused walked up to his mother, looked at her, and touched her. I stood back to give him as much privacy as possible. He was there a few moments, and then came out. He behaved quite normally,

122

Evidence for Prosecution.

Dr. Nichol

I thought. The colour of the deceased's face was the normal colour one would expect to find in death. In cases of carbon monoxide poisoning the body is usually rosy coloured and the lips fresh. There were no symptoms of that kind in this case. As we went downstairs the accused seemed a bit more collected, and I advised him that he should get a legal representative to attend at the inquest. I did so because I knew if any insurance policies were involved there would be difficulties and he should be represented. He did not tell me that there were any insurance policies involved. I may have mentioned the name of a solicitor. He said very little coming downstairs. We went along to his room, and I tried to talk him into a more comfortable frame of mind. He told me he had been to France recently with his mother to see some war graves. He spoke of how he was the only son left and what a good mother she had been. He said what a curious thing it was that his mother should have died in the same way as Walburga, Lady Paget, as his mother had heard from her not long before her death. According to the newspapers, Lady Paget died as the result of her dress catching fire. The accused also told me that his mother had £24 in her handbag. He said she had changed a cheque a day or two before. He told me he had been in to see his mother early in the evening, and that he had left her sitting reading a paper in front of the fire. He added that he wished he had gone back later as he usually did, for he might have found out the trouble before it was too late. I then told him to get into bed, and after he got into bed I gave him an injection of morphia. Then Inspector Palmer came in to see him. After he had told the story about the £24 in the handbag we looked for it at once. The bottom of the bag was burned out, but the top and sides were not burned. The inner pocket was unharmed and there was nothing in it. I believe there was a visiting card in it.

Cross-examined by Mr. CASSELS—What was the first thing you observed when you arrived at the hotel?—The first thing I observed was the body on the floor. I came to the conclusion there was somebody ill. Dr. Austin told me she was dead.

Sidney Harry Fox.

Dr. Nichol

Would it be right to say that Mrs. Fox's face was composed, pale, and presented no special significance?—It would.

There were no signs of death from suffocation, nor were there any marks of violence?—I did not see any.

By Mr. JUSTICE ROWLATT—What did she die from?—I cannot say. I did not examine her.

Cross-examination continued—What is the colour from carbon monoxide poisoning?—It depends on the quantity inhaled.

In order to get that rosy colour in the face which the learned Attorney-General has asked you about the blood has almost to be saturated with carbon monoxide?—I do not agree. Such a little carbon monoxide is required to cause death very quickly that it is not of much importance how much is present. Most cases I have seen have been looking very life-like. The colour depends on the gases in combination with it.

By Mr. JUSTICE ROWLATT—As soon as the last breath is taken no more carbon monoxide is inhaled?—Yes.

Cross-examination continued—Are you an expert on carbon monoxide poisoning?—No.

Did you observe the hands?—No.

What about the tongue?—The tongue was sufficiently forward to be satisfactory. It had not fallen far enough back to be an obstruction to breathing.

Was the mouth slightly open?—Yes.

Where was she when you saw her?—When I got there she was lying on her back and Dr. Austin was on her right side touching her. Her head was resting on the ground. I do not recollect anything being under it. There may have been a folded coat.

Did you see any evidence of death from asphyxiation?—No.

By Mr. JUSTICE ROWLATT—Would being choked by fumes from the burning carpet be asphyxia?—Yes. If a person has been garrotted or choked to death, or by inhaling poisonous gas, or being smothered, or killed by having a cord tied round the neck, or drowning, the face would be

Evidence for Prosecution.

congested. I saw no marks of violence of any kind. Throttling need not cause death by asphyxia.

All these are asphyxia?—Asphyxiation means not breathing. In such cases as I have mentioned the face would be congested, probably swollen, the eyelids would be puffy, and the whole face would look as if the person had been strangled. The eyes usually look protruding and strained, and the tongue is swollen.

Cross-examination continued—Those are the things you would expect if a person had been strangled?—If a person had died from asphyxia.

By Mr. JUSTICE ROWLATT—In any form?—I would rather not say in any form.

Cross-examination continued—You noticed none of these things on Mrs. Fox's face that night?—The woman did not give me the impression of having died from asphyxia.

By Mr. JUSTICE ROWLATT—What did you think she had died of?—I had no particular idea then.

Cross-examination continued—When you went up to room 66 did you see any indication of any struggle?—No more indication than would have been given by a body being pulled out of the bed.

Was the impression in the bed the impression of a heavy body?—Yes.

And was Mrs. Fox's body the body of an average woman? —Yes. Her body was covered with coats when I saw it, of course. She appeared to be a good-sized woman.

With regard to the patch of urine, that may indicate many things, may it not?—Yes.

It might occur as the result of fright?—Yes.

And the ejection of urine is a frequent accompaniment of death?—Yes.

Would it suggest that the patient was dead before being taken off the bed?—Yes.

Have you told us all that you observed about room No. 66?—I think so.

I think you then went down to see the accused?—Yes.

He was very much distressed, was he not, by the circumstances of that night?—He struck me as needing morphia,

Sidney Harry Fox.

which he would not have done if he had been depressed. He was extremely agitated.

You talked to him?—Before I gave him the injection I talked to him. Then he saw his mother, and I had another conversation with him.

Were you the first to mention legal aid?—I do not know. I talked about the solicitor first. He did not ask me.

Re-examined by the ATTORNEY-GENERAL—Do you pretend to be an expert on the topic of asphyxia?—I do not.

As to the cause of death, you said you did not know what it was?—No. I was not satisfied with the cause of death.

If the matter had been left in your hands you would have had a post-mortem examination?—Yes.

A sudden blow on, or squeezing of, the larynx might cause death?—Yes.

Such a death would not be from asphyxia?—No; but I do not know why. Throttling need not cause death by asphyxia. Asphyxia is a word which comes from the Greek and means " no breath."

Were the symptoms you saw that night consistent with death resulting from throttling and not asphyxia?—Yes, in so far as sudden death has no special features.

In addition, then, to the forms of death where the cause is the stoppage of oxygen, there is another cause of death. How would you describe it?—I can only describe it from what I have been taught. A blow on the larynx, or Adam's apple, or sudden squeezing might be sufficient to cause death in an apparently healthy person.

By shock?—That is not a good word.

[Mr. Cassels objected to the word " shock " being put into the witness's mouth by the Attorney-General.]

By Mr. JUSTICE ROWLATT—Why it would cause death you do not know?—No, but it is definitely laid down in the textbooks.

Mr. JUSTICE ROWLATT—That is very candid.

Re-examination continued—Is it called asphyxia?—No. It is immediate death.

Further cross-examined by Mr. CASSELS—You said you were not an expert upon these matters upon which you have

126

Evidence for Prosecution.

been examined?—I think a doctor is more an expert than a member of the laity. I am not an expert among doctors.

By Mr. JUSTICE ROWLATT—You have not made a special study of this?—No, but I have seen people gassed, and half-throttled, and properly throttled.

Further cross-examination continued—You do not need to be an expert to say whether a face is pale or congested?—I do not think a lay person would be able to say.

You would regard yourself sufficiently an expert to say whether the face was pale or congested?—I think most experts place great reliance upon their textbooks and precedents.

That is not an answer to my question?—I was answering out of the book.

You were not answering out of the book when you said that the face was pale, composed, and presented no special significance?—I think you would get that answer from anybody who saw the body.

Further re-examined by the ATTORNEY-GENERAL—You get that from throttling, which is not asphyxia?—Yes, with no special features.

Police Constables GALER and E. NORRIS, of the Margate Police, who helped to move Mrs. Fox's body, gave evidence to the effect that neither they nor any one in their presence touched the woman's head or neck.

WILLIAM PALMER, examined by Sir HENRY CURTIS BENNETT—I am an inspector in the Margate Borough Police. I went to the Hotel Metropole shortly after midnight on the night of 23rd October, and I there saw the body of Mrs. Fox at the foot of the stairs. I went to room No. 66. There was nobody inside the room when I arrived, but there were a number of people outside. There was more smoke in the corridor than in the room. I returned to the hall and found that they were still applying artificial respiration to the body. The face was blue; the lips and cheek were inclined to purple. The mouth was open; there were no teeth in the mouth. She was later carried upstairs. I was given the key of room No. 126 by Sergeant Fleet. I saw

Sidney Harry Fox.

the accused when I first arrived kneeling at the head of his
mother. When I returned he appeared to be distressed.
I returned to room No. 66. I noticed the carpet. I found
a quantity of burned paper and unburned newspaper, and a
quantity of charred carpet. Mr. Harding, Drs. Austin and
Nichol, and Mr. Hammond were with me. Subsequently on
taking up a newspaper it appeared to be a portion of a
French newspaper. The chair was brought back into the
room and Mr. Reed put it into the position in which it
was ultimately photographed. I noticed that a strip of
carpet in front of the fender approximately six inches wide
was unburned and unscorched. The top cover of the bed was
thrown back from the left to the right. The pillow was on
a pedestal at the head of the bed near a chest of drawers.
I found a lady's coat and fur necklet hanging behind the
door, also two stockinette dresses. I found the shoes (Exhibit No. 8) under the left side of the bed, the side nearest
the door. I found the stockings (Exhibit No. 9) on the
bedpost at the left foot of the bed. I found the bottle (Exhibit No. 13) on the chest of drawers. There were two bottles
of medicine on the mantelpiece. There was also a bottle
of cascara and three or four unspent matches and a booklet
of matches on the mantelpiece. I saw a set of false teeth
in the wash-hand basin. The spring of the teeth was not
then broken. All the teeth were there then. There were
dirty particles of food adhering to them. I found a telegram on the dressing-table (Exhibit No. 28) dated 23rd
September, 1929, relating to the position of a grave at Arras,
also a railway excursion handbill, and a beret hat.

Later that night I saw the accused in room No. 42. He
was wearing a singlet. As coroner's officer, I told him it
would be necessary to take a statement for the coroner. He
said he felt able to make a statement, which I took down in
a notebook. I took down his answers at the time. [State-
ment put in and read.] He gives the full name of Mrs.
Fox as Rosaline Fox, aged sixty-three, a widow, and his
father's name as William Fox. [In the statement
the accused said his address had formerly been 19
Cathedral Close, but that his mother had bought a

Evidence for Prosecution.

house at Lyndhurst, called " End View," to which their luggage had been sent on. He said his father, who died in
1913, had been proprietor of Fox's Flour Mills, East Dereham, Norfolk, and that he was educated at Framlingham
College.] The accused said, " Have you found my mother's
bag which contained a lot of money," and I said that the
bag had been found partly burned by fire. He said, " There
is £24 in notes in it." He added, " I went to London yesterday to change a cheque for £24 at Lloyds, 39 Threadneedle Street." He also said they were going to Lyndhurst
the next day. I said I would make inquiries about the
money and let him know. The bag was examined by me
in the presence of Dr. Nichol. There was nothing in the
handbag except a scorched mourning card. The inner part
of the bag was apparently unscorched.

On the 24th of October I again saw the accused at the
hotel along with Sergeant Fleet. Mr. Hammond was also
there. I said we had not found any notes. He said he was
sure she had them, and added, " I went to London on
Tuesday to change a cheque at Lloyds, 39 Threadneedle
Street." I asked him if his mother had any jewellery or
odd change. He said he expected she had packed it in the
luggage. He said that she had no odd change as she never
carried money about herself. I questioned him about luggage, and he said that he had no luggage. " We only came
here for a day, but mother was not well enough to travel,
so we stayed on from day to day." I said, " Your mother
had no night attire," and he said, " No; she has worn none
for some time." The accused said his mother was of independent means and had an income. He said he was the
only one left of the family, three having been killed in the
war. He also added that he never had to work. The
accused gave evidence at the inquest. I produce his deposi-
tion. He did not mention that his mother was insured.

On the 7th of November I visited room No. 66 of the
Hotel Metropole with Detectives Hambrook and Ayto. Exhibit No. 22 was found in the fireplace of room No. 66 behind
the gas fire. Exhibit No. 23 was found in the same place.
Exhibit No. 67, an empty half-bottle of port, was found in

Sidney Harry Fox.

the cupboard of the wash-hand stand. On the 9th of November I received the teeth, which were subsequently handed to Sir Bernard Spilsbury. On the 17th of November tests were made with the carpet by Mr. Hammond. On the 9th of January I saw the accused detained at the police station at Margate, when he was charged with the murder of Mrs. Fox, to which he replied, " It is absolutely untrue. I deny every word of it. I have nothing further to say until I have consulted my solicitor, Mr. George Hindle, of London." I examined the gas fire to see if it was intact. All the candles were whole.

Cross-examined by Mr. CASSELS—Who were present when you arrived on the night of the 23rd?—When I got there there were Police Constable Bray, a taxi driver, Mr. Harding, and a number of commercial travellers.

How long after you arrived was it before Dr. Austin arrived?—I should say ten minutes. Dr. Nichol arrived about a minute after Dr. Austin.

Where were you when Dr. Nichol arrived?—I was downstairs, but I had been upstairs.

Was the body in the same condition when Dr. Nichol arrived as when you arrived?—Yes. I saw the body again the next morning. There were post-mortem stains round the neck, otherwise I noticed no change.

How many candles has the gas stove?—I do not know.

I show you photograph No. 4. Can you see how many there are from that photograph? Do you not agree it looks as if one is missing?—No.

Do you know that there is a burner beneath each candle and if one burner is out then a naked flame goes up?—Yes.

When you went into the room had the fender been removed?—Yes.

Was there burned debris in the grate on the night of the 23rd?—Yes.

Do you know everybody who was in the room before you? —I know some of those who had been in the room before. I went alone first.

Was the armchair there then?—No.

Was the fender there on your subsequent visit?—Yes. I

130

Evidence for Prosecution.

saw it standing up by the water basin. Somebody had done that before I got into the room.

You do not know what had been shifted in its position before you got there?—No.

Did you find some matches on the mantelpiece in room No. 66, some petrol in a bottle, and a magazine on the floor, which was unburned?—Yes.

You did not find other paper unburned, except a telegram and a railway bill?—Yes.

Was the accused in bed when you saw him?—Yes.

Did you know he had had an injection?—Yes.

Was his statement in part volunteered and in part in answer to questions?—Yes.

Did you make a thorough search for everything that might apply to the case that night?—Yes.

Did you come across any pawn tickets in your search of the room?—No.

Did you subsequently have any given to you which related to Mrs. Fox's rings?—They were in the accused's possession when he was arrested.

Were they all dated prior to the 23rd October, 1929?—Yes.

After the 23rd of October did the carpet remain until it was partly removed on the 17th of January?—Yes.

And has the room not since been used for visitors?—No.

On the 17th of January was the carpet taken to the police station?—Yes.

Was it rolled up?—Yes.

And were tests made with pieces of the same carpet?—Yes. [At this stage the following particulars of the pawn tickets were given:—30th March, 1929, at Portsea, Portsmouth, gold watch, 2s. 3d.; 3rd June, 1929, at Colchester, diamond ring, £2, Mrs. R. Fox, 19 Cathedral Street, Norwich; 3rd June, 1929, at Colchester, nine-carat gold wrist watch, 8s. 6d., Sidney Fox, 19 Cathedral Street, Norwich; 20th June, 1929, leather case, 15s., Sidney Fox, 19 Cathedral Street, Norwich; 25th June, 1929, at Gray's Inn Road, W.C., pair of trousers, 5s., John Fox, Cathedral Street, Norwich; 8th July, 1929, at Chatham, safety razor, 1s. 3d., Mr. Fox; 7th

131

Sidney Harry Fox.

October, rain coat, 8s. 6d., Mr. Fox, Camden Gardens, Dover.] Among the other papers in the accused's possession were two declarations for pawn tickets lost and one blank cheque.

Re-examined by Sir HENRY CURTIS BENNETT—On the night of the 23rd October was the gas fire intact?—Yes.

And the photograph was taken on the 7th of November?—Yes.

On the 17th of January the carpet was taken for production at the Court?—Yes.

Did Mr. Hindle inspect it before removal?—Yes.

The Court adjourned.

Evidence for Prosecution.

Fourth Day—Saturday, 15th March, 1930.

Detective Sergeant AMBROSE AYTO, examined by Sir HENRY
CURTIS BENNETT—I am a detective sergeant attached to New
Scotland Yard. On 5th November last I went to Margate
with Chief Detective Inspector Hambrook. I was present
when the photographs were taken and the plans made. I
was also present when the tests were made by Hammond.
On the last day of the Police Court hearing I received from
Mr. G. Hindle a document purporting to be the last will
of Mrs. Fox. It is Exhibit No. 101.

[The document which was read nominated Sidney Harry
Fox as the sole executor, and left everything to him with a
desire that a gift from the testatrix's belongings should be
given " to my dear friends Louise Baxter and Emma Young
in token of their kindness and friendship." It further
stated, " To my son, William Edward Fox, I leave the sum
of one farthing, and sincerely hope that he will never want
his mother; the remainder to my son, Sidney Harry Fox,
for his own use and benefit absolutely." The document was
dated 21st April, 1929, and was purported to be signed by
Rosaline Fox. The name was signed twice.]

I cut out the piece of carpet, Exhibit No. 14. A test was
made by Mr. Hammond. The under felt was similarly
treated. Exhibits 30, 31, 32, 33, and 104 were also similarly
treated. I produce eleven pieces of a burned evening paper
which I found on the floor of room No. 66 on the 23rd of
October. They were from an irregularly folded paper. I
produce a duplicate copy of the paper—the *Evening
Standard*.

[The duplicate copy of the paper was closely compared
with the burned fragments by Mr. Cassels, at whose request
the witness took the duplicate paper and folded it as he
suggested it must have been folded in order to produce the
eleven fragments. In its folded state the paper was then
examined by Mr. Justice Rowlatt.]

[At this stage the depositions of a number of witnesses
were read to the jury by the Clerk of Court to the effect that

133

Sidney Harry Fox.

Ambrose Ayto

there was no account at Lloyds Bank, Threadneedle Street, E.C., in the name of Rosaline Fox; that there had been no student at Framlingham College of the name of Fox during the last twenty-five years; that there were no Fox's Flour Mills at East Dereham; that there was no house named End View at Lyndhurst; and that no luggage had arrived at Lyndhurst Station for a person named Fox.]

THOMAS WILLIAM GRIFFIN, examined by Sir HENRY CURTIS BENNETT—I am a claims clerk in the employment of the Wesleyan and General Insurance Company. A policy for ten guineas was taken out by Reginald M. Fox on the life of Mrs. Fox on 10th November, 1913, and the premiums were kept up until August, 1928. Subsequently the arrears were paid up by Mrs. Fox, and on 4th October last Mrs. Fox wrote enclosing 2s. arrears, and saying in future she would pay the premiums to her own agent. Under Mrs. Fox's signature were the initials " H. F." We received a claim for the amount after the death of Mrs. Fox.

HENRY GARLAND SHEPHERD, examined by Sir HENRY CURTIS BENNETT—I was the Norwich district superintendent of the Wesleyan and General Insurance Company. In May, 1929, I went to 19 Cathedral Street, Norwich. The next day the accused called and said his mother was down at Cathedral Street and I could see her. I said I would require a medical examination, the arrears of 12s. 6d. paid up, and a new book issued.

Cross-examined by Mr. CASSELS—As far as you could see, did Mrs. Fox understand that the policy was being renewed and the arrears paid up?—Yes.

Was the accused with her when she was examined?—I would not say that he was there when she was examined, but he went to the doctor's with her.

STUART KENNEDY DUNFORD, examined by Sir HENRY CURTIS BENNETT—I am a clerk employed by the Norwich branch of the Eagle Star and British Dominions Insurance Company, Limited. I had a conversation with the accused when he was discussing a policy for himself. He came to our office

134

Evidence for Prosecution.

one day and spoke about a £1000 accident policy on the life of his mother. He asked what was meant by an accident and several other questions. One was that if the assured, his mother, was drowned in the bath, would that be an accident within the meaning of the policy, and the other question was, that if she were poisoned by food in a restaurant would that be an accident. I said I presumed if she were taken ill in the bath and consequently drowned, that would not be an accident. I also said that poisoning by food in a restaurant would not be regarded as an accident.

Cross-examined by Mr. CASSELS—Did the policy provide for other benefits than payment of £1000 in the event of death under certain circumstances?—It did.

And I daresay the accused is not the only individual who has asked you the meaning of the words, " Death from any accidental, external, invisible means "?—I cannot recollect that any one else has asked me that.

Did you ever have any claim under this policy?—No.

ARTHUR ALBERT BAXTER, examined by Sir HENRY CURTIS BENNETT—I am employed in the accident department of the Eagle Star and British Dominions Insurance Company, Limited. The accused called on the 24th of July and asked for a policy on behalf of his mother for one month, from the 27th of July to the 27th of August. The policy was issued, and was not called for, and was not taken up. Another policy was issued at the request of the accused from 8th August to 20th August, and that policy was extended from the 20th of August to the 27th on payment of another 3s.

Cross-examined by Mr. CASSELS—The policy came into existence on the 8th of August and ceased on 27th August? —Yes.

And if Mrs. Fox had met her death on the 26th or 27th of August the company would have been liable for £1000? —Yes.

ARCHIBALD WALTER CAMPBELL SEYMOUR, examined by Sir HENRY CURTIS BENNETT—I am an insurance clerk employed in the head office of the Royal Insurance Company, Lombard

135

Sidney Harry Fox.

Archibald W. C. Seymour

Street, London. The accused had a monthly accident policy in respect of himself with my company for £1000. An accident policy was taken out in respect of Mrs. Fox on the 26th of June last year. That policy was subsequently cancelled.

Cross-examined by Mr. CASSELS—Was the accused's policy originally taken out from 17th May to 17th June of last year and extended?—Yes.

In such cases there is a further premium required?—Yes.

Had your company any policy in respect of Mrs. Fox from 17th May to 17th June?—No.

A. R. CAMERON, examined by Sir HENRY CURTIS BENNETT—I am a deputy underwriter in the employment of the Cornhill Insurance Company, Limited. Exhibit No. 61 is a proposal form which was accepted and a policy issued with a premium of £1 5s. The benefits are as follows :—In the event of death within ninety days of occurrence of accident, £1000; two limbs or two eyes, £1000; one limb or eye, £500. The policy was framed in the ordinary form.

NORMAN H. THOMPSON, examined by Sir HENRY CURTIS BENNETT—I am a clerk in the accident department of the Cornhill Insurance Company, Limited, at their head office in London. I received the proposal form, Exhibit No. 61, and issued the policy accepted, No. 62, in pursuance of that proposal form. It is dated from the 10th of August to noon of the 24th of August. Shortly before the 24th of August the accused telephoned and asked that the policy should be extended for eight days as he and his mother had not returned. The policy was extended and an additional payment of 12s. 6d. made. It was extended to noon on 1st September, 1929. I received the letter exhibited, No. 68, from the accused, written from the Strand Palace Hotel, London, saying that the policy should be kept in force until 13th September. There was no further premium paid after 14th September.

Cross-examined by Mr. CASSELS—Is it the fact that if Mrs. Fox had died on the 26th or 27th of August in the circumstances set out in your policy your company would have been liable for £2000?—That is so.

136

Evidence for Prosecution.

David D. Beaton

DAVID DEWAR BEATON, examined by Sir HENRY CURTIS
BENNETT—I am employed in the renewal department of the
Cornhill Insurance Company's head office in London. An
accident policy was issued by us for Mrs. Fox to the amount
of £2000 on 24th September of last year, which lapsed on
the 8th of October, 1929. On that day I received a telegram
from Folkestone from the accused, saying, " Hold cover till
noon to-morrow." I did so, and eventually the policy was
extended to noon 13th October, and then to noon on the
20th of October. The last time it was extended it was
extended, not as previously to noon, but to midnight on 23rd
October.

Cross-examined by Mr. CASSELS—Have you issued other
policies which have expired at midnight?—Very seldom. I
expect I have. Our usual policy is noon.

Have you sometimes done it?—Oh, it can be arranged if
a policy is required to cover a particular period, perhaps for
a journey.

ERNEST BERTRAM CRUSE, examined by Sir HENRY CURTIS
BENNETT—I am a clerk in the renewal department of the
Cornhill Insurance Company, Limited. [Shown Exhibit
No. 63.] The accused called between twelve and one o'clock
on the 22nd of October and asked for an extension of the
policy. He said he wanted it extended to midnight on the
23rd. He mentioned his mother and said she was very
nervous and would not go in a railway train without being
insured.

BRYAN JOYCE, examined by Sir HENRY CURTIS BENNETT—
I am a clerk employed by the Sun Insurance Company.
Exhibit No. 85, the proposal form, was filled in in my
presence on the 26th of August. Five shillings was paid on
the 28th of August and a policy issued. The policy insured
the deceased against death by accident by violent, external,
and visible means. The policy was allowed to lapse.

ROBERT HAWKINS, examined by Sir HENRY CURTIS BENNETT
—I am claims assessor of the Ocean Accident and Guarantee
Corporation, Limited. There were a number of one-day
policies taken out on the life of the deceased, Mrs. Rosaline

137

Sidney Harry Fox.

Robert Hawkins

Fox, the last of which expired at midnight on 23rd October. A claim was received. Inquiries were made, and the claim is still outstanding.

HERBERT CHARLES HEWSON, examined by Sir HENRY CURTIS BENNETT—I am employed by Pickfords. Exhibit No. 59 was filled in by the accused on the 22nd of October. He said he wanted the policy to cover the 23rd of October. I handed the ticket of the policy to the accused. There was no writing on it at all when I handed it to him. The premium of 2s. was paid by the accused.

Cross-examined by Mr. CASSELS—Has the policy to be signed by the person assured before you are on the risk?—Yes.

You would not be on risk unless the policy was signed by the assured?—No.

ARTHUR JONAS WATTS, examined by Sir HENRY CURTIS BENNETT—I am principal clerk at the Ministry of Pensions. The deceased Mrs. Fox received a pension of 4s. per week in 1917 in respect of the death of a son in the war. After being increased to 5s., this was abolished in June, 1923, and a pecuniary need pension of 10s. a week substituted. This was continued until her death. The accused received a pension of 5s. a week in February, 1929. After being increased to 12s. it was made a life pension of 8s. a week in February, 1923. The pension was granted in respect of epilepsy, aggravated by military service confined to this country.

[At this stage evidence given before the magistrates that Fox was adjudged a bankrupt in March, 1928, with a deficiency of £267 and was still undischarged, was read by the Clerk of Assize.]

GEORGE ARTHUR IRVINE, examined by Sir HENRY CURTIS BENNETT—I am a relieving officer at Portsmouth. The deceased Mrs. Fox was an inmate of St. Mary's Infirmary, Portsmouth, from 20th February, 1928, to 27th March, 1929. She was admitted as a destitute person.

Cross-examined by Mr. CASSELS—Was the deceased in the

Evidence for Prosecution.

first instance admitted to the workhouse from a house in Neville Road, Copnor, Portsmouth, and was she transferred to the infirmary immediately?—Yes.

Was she very feeble on her feet?—Yes, she was.

Did she fall about?—She shuffled about.

Was it necessary that she should be helped to make a journey?—I should think it was necessary.

Mr. JUSTICE ROWLATT—I thought that was established.

WILLIAM EDWARD FOX, examined by Sir HENRY CURTIS BENNETT—I am a monitor at Queen Alexandra's Hospital, Cosham, near Portsmouth. I am the eldest son of the deceased Mrs. Fox. The accused is my youngest brother. One of my brothers was killed at Woolwich Arsenal in 1919, and the other was killed in France during the war. I last saw my mother alive on 28th January, 1928, when she visited me at my quarters with the accused, who took her away. I first heard of her death on 5th November by seeing it in a newspaper. The accused was educated at the parish school at Fransham, Norfolk. [At this stage witness was shown a number of documents, including a letter, a cheque for £2, purported to have been signed by Rosaline Fox, and insurance policy forms.] I identify the signature on the cheque as being in the accused's handwriting. The signatures in the proposal forms are also in the accused's handwriting. I do not think that the signature in the daily insurance ticket issued by Pickfords is in my mother's handwriting. Her handwriting in recent years was very, very shaky. She could not keep her hand still. With regard to the will, which is now shown to me, the body of that document is in the handwriting of the accused. My father lived at Great Fransham, Norfolk, at the time my mother was married to him. My brothers and myself were brought up together as boys. Our father was a railway signalman on what used to be the Great Eastern Railway. As far as I know, my mother had no knowledge of the French language.

Mr. CASSELS—I have several questions to ask the witness to-morrow.

The Court adjourned.

Sidney Harry Fox.

Fifth Day—Monday, 17th March, 1930.

When the question of the position of the fender and carpet in room 66 in relation to the fireplace and oilcloth was referred to on Friday, Mr. Justice Rowlatt suggested that some plan or display might be made in Court, and in consequence a Scotland Yard expert, Mr. Harding (the hotel manager), and others immediately went to Margate and visited room No. 66 at the Hotel Metropole. They returned with a gas stove, meter, and oilcloth, and also certain measurements, and then reconstructed room No. 66 in a room adjoining the Court. The gas stove, meter, oilcloth, fender, carpet, and armchair were placed in the positions they were in on the night of the fire, whilst the bed, washstand, and drawers were marked on the floor in chalk, the intention being that, as the jury could not go to the hotel and see the room they should see a reconstruction of it, but this was not permitted by the judge in that way.

Mr. Justice Rowlatt said it might be possible to arrange some reconstruction in the juryroom when they retired, but he could not allow the jury to be attended by any one. It was, after all, only a question of having the gas stove in its place in relation to the marks on the oilcloth and carpet. He could not move towards a reconstruction of the crime. He thought that they had better get on as best they could, and he would have the things taken into the juryroom in bits, and the jury could put them as they pleased when they were consulting among themselves.

The ATTORNEY-GENERAL—I will fall in with that course.

Mr. CASSELS—I am willing to co-operate in that course.

Mr. JUSTICE ROWLATT—I shall tell the jury that if, by reason of anything being in the nature of a fixture in another place, something is not clear, any doubt must be taken in favour of the accused. If it is not made clear by evidence it must remain unproved.

Mr. CASSELS—The effect of your lordship's ruling is that these objects are at the disposal of the jury?

Mr. JUSTICE ROWLATT—Quite.

140

Evidence for Prosecution.

Evidence for the Prosecution—continued.

WILLIAM EDWARD FOX, cross-examined by Mr. CASSELS— How old are you?—Forty-one.

When did you last live in the same house as your mother? —I have not lived in the same house since 1908.

Had there been some family differences?—In what way do you mean?

That there had been differences between your part of the family on the one hand and your mother on the other?— Not my mother.

Whilst your mother was with you at Christmas, 1927, and January, 1928, did you notice her health was such that she frequently fell?—Yes.

By Mr. JUSTICE ROWLATT—Do you mean she fell because she could not walk or because of a faint?—She appeared to fall backwards.

Cross-examination continued—Had she a peculiar shuffling of her feet in walking?—Yes.

Did you notice that she found a good deal of difficulty in rising from a seat?—She did.

The same thing would happen if lying in bed. She would not be able to rise as easily as a more active person?—I cannot say.

She could eat well?—Very well indeed.

Did she seem strong in her arms—able to pull herself up with a little assistance?—No, she could not.

Was she cheerful?—She was more or less depressed the latter part of the time I saw her in January, 1928, and Christmas, 1927.

When she was not depressed was she inclined to be playful? —No, I do not think so.

Did you notice at all that if you gave your arm to help your mother she seemed to be quite strong in the arm?—No.

Did you ever see your brother, the accused, holding her arms in play, as if they were—perhaps sham fighting is scarcely the term to give it—but more or less moving their arms about?—No.

Sidney Harry Fox.

William E. Fox

In January, 1928, did you visit your brother, the accused, at the office where he was employed—the Portsmouth office of the Gresham Insurance Company—in reference to your mother?—I went to the office, but not to see him.

Your mother was getting rather difficult to manage owing to her falling about?—Yes.

What I am suggesting is that you saw your brother and suggested that he should make arrangements for her to be moved to some place where she could be better looked after? —No.

Did you know where your brother was going to take your mother when he took her out of your house?—No, but I found she had gone to a Mrs. Taylor in Neville Road, Copnor, Portsmouth.

And was she then in a very feeble condition?—Yes.

Do you know that your mother was an inmate of an institution at Portsmouth?—Yes.

And did you visit her there?—No.

Have you had any letters from her since she was in that institution?—No.

She did not communicate with you much?—No, very little.

Before this happening you had not heard from her for a considerable time?—I last heard from her when she was going into the institution at Portsmouth.

Did you have a cousin named Cecil Fox who was killed in France?—I am practically certain he is still alive.

Was there not a cousin called Cecil Fox who, as a boy, was very often at your mother's home when the accused was a boy?—No.

Did you have any cousin killed in the war?—I think there was one, but I do not know his Christian name.

Where was your mother staying between the years 1916 and 1922?—At Cavendish Mansions, Hampstead. She had a flat there.

Do you know how much she paid for that flat?—£60 a year.

Previous to that she had a house in Haslemere Road, Thornton Heath?—Yes.

[At this stage Sergeant Edward Shelah, of the Metropolitan Police, gave evidence with regard to removing the

Evidence for Prosecution.

William E. Fox

gas stove and oilcloth near it from room 66, and when the various articles had been brought into Court he arranged them in position. Mr. Harding was then recalled and said the articles were in their correct positions.]

GEORGE WILLIAM MILLBANK, examined by the ATTORNEY-GENERAL—I am manager of the Norwich branch of the Cornhill Insurance Company, Limited. On 29th October last the accused called at my office and told me that his mother had met with her death in a fire at Margate. He said he was attending her funeral that afternoon, and he thought he would call about the tour and travel policy which she had taken out with our office. He told me about the fire and the death of his mother. I asked him about the origin of the fire, and he said that apparently his mother had left some wearing apparel on a chair near the gas fire. Some of this had become scorched, caught fire, set the chair alight, and the fumes had suffocated his mother. He asked me whether in the circumstances of her death there would be a claim under the policy his mother had with us. I looked up a specimen copy of the policy and told him that the circumstances were rather peculiar, and it was difficult for me to express an opinion. He said that he himself had some doubt on the point, and I understand that he had handed the policy with other policies to a Margate solicitor for the purpose of making a claim. Four days later I met him at the Royal Hotel, Norwich, and I asked him what his profession was. He told me he was a farmer at Lyndhurst, Hampshire, and that he had a very capable steward looking after the farm in his absence. He asked me how soon my company paid out claims, and I said immediately liability was admitted. I said in his case there might be some delay because of probate. He produced a letter from a solicitor at Margate and pointed out the fifth paragraph. [Reads.] He said he had an appointment at Dereham; he was going to see a lady about dogs; that he was interested in breeding dogs.

Detective Inspector HERBERT WILLIAM BALL, examined by the ATTORNEY-GENERAL—I am a detective inspector in the

Sidney Harry Fox.

Herbert William Ball

Norwich City Police. I saw the accused at the Royal Hotel, Norwich, on 2nd November, and took him to the police station. He packed his bag before leaving the hotel and took it away with him, also an envelope which he got from the cashier. He took fifteen £1 notes from the envelope and paid his hotel bill of £1 4s. 7d. He handed the balance to me at the police station. I know No. 19 Cathedral Close. It is a large house—a very good house. It is occupied by Miss Johnstone. I have known her for twenty years, and she has occupied it for the past forty years. I know No. 19 Cathedral Street. It is a six-room apartments house occupied by Miss Bacon. I ascertained that the accused and his mother stayed at 19 Cathedral Street in May and June last.

Cross-examined by Mr. CASSELS—Did you make inquiries regarding the will?—I interviewed two persons—a Mr. Cubbit and Miss Bacon in regard to the signatures.

[Mr. Cassels intimated that he proposed asking a question in regard to these interviews.

The Attorney-General raised an objection, and Mr. Justice Rowlatt pointed out that no evidence had been called in connection with the signatures on the will, and, therefore, he would tell the jury when summing up that there should be no suggestion that they were forged signatures.]

ALFRED CLARK WILLIAMS, examined by the ATTORNEY-GENERAL—I am assistant official receiver for Southampton. I produce Exhibit No. 97. I identify the accused as the bankrupt. The deficiency was £750 1s. 1d. He is still undischarged.

Cross-examined by Mr. CASSELS—Was the bankruptcy brought about by a debt on his part to a defendant in proceedings which he had brought, unsuccessfully, in respect of personal injuries?—The receiving order was made on a moneylenders' petition.

Did you understand that the money had been borrowed for the purpose of a claim in regard to a personal injuries case? —No. The money was borrowed for the purpose of discharging a liability he had incurred for the costs of the case.

144

Sir.

The point has been very much stressed at this trial regarding my Mother's physical disabilities. I think it should be made plain, that although she certainly did suffer from attacks of giddiness & fainting & did walk with a shuffle, she was in other ways quite in normal health for her age.

It is strongly suggested that on account of her weakness, she could not if attacked have put up any resistance. it would be wrong to say this, & I think in view of the fact that as recent as May 6 months before death she was examined by a Norwich doctor* who certified she was in a normal state of health for her years, then considering the fact, that as recent as 3 weeks before her death she travelled over a good portion of Belgium & France, went all over the Battlefields, had to walk of course.

I am afraid the Jury may think that in the words of the Attorney General "this poor old woman infirm, lying in bed if attacked would not be able to put up any fight at all

Please forgive me for offering this information.

<the left margin note:>
* for
Woolseys
of Genl
Insurance

Letter written by the Accused in Court

Evidence for Prosecution.

Albert C. Williams

He had been involved in a case?—He said so, but it was never confirmed.

HARRY HAMMOND, examined by the ATTORNEY-GENERAL—I am chief officer of the Margate Fire Brigade. I am a member of the Institute of Fire Engineers, and have had twenty-nine years' experience. On 23rd October at 11.54 p.m. we received a call to a fire at the Hotel Metropole. The fire was in room No. 66. There was a great deal of smoke about both in the corridor and in room No. 66. I made an examination of the room. In my opinion the fire had unquestionably originated directly underneath the armchair in room No. 66, because the sides and top of the chair were scarcely damaged, except by heat, and the underneath part was burned away. The carpet was very badly burned, the felt beneath it was also burned, and the edges of the floor boards were charred. There could not possibly have been a great deal of flame or the upper part of the chair would have been damaged far more than it was. My conclusion was that it was more or less an incandescent fire; the material had smouldered more than flamed. At first I thought the fire had been caused by the deceased woman bringing some portion of her clothing into contact with the gas fire and then dropping it on the floor by the chair, but I have since considered the matter further and made certain tests. In my opinion, the fire was burning for certainly less than half an hour. My first tests were made with pieces cut from the carpet belonging to room No. 66. [Witness showed how the pieces had been scorched or burned in different ways, and described the tests he made by burning stuff on the top of the portions of carpet taken from room No. 66.] I tried newspaper, a merino vest, horsehair, and newspapers, and horsehair and cotton wool together, but in each case only the pile of the carpet was burned. I then placed a merino vest, cotton wool, and horsehair in a heap on a piece of carpet, and saturated them with half a pint of petrol. The heap burned for seventeen minutes, and then only ashes were left. The result was that the carpet was burned through in three or four places. I should think it would be almost

K   145

Sidney Harry Fox.

Harry Hammond

impossible to burn that carpet when lying flat on the floor. I also made tests with underclothing hanging over a cane chair, and in that case the highest part, the top rail, was almost burned away. The cane chair which I was shown as being the cane chair from room No. 66 was burned mostly on one back leg. The bottom rails at the back were scorched and the slats at the top were blistered by heat. I also carried out an experiment on a chair of the same style by placing a pair of combinations over the back and setting a light to them. Most damage was done to the top of the chair. By lighting the article a little distance from the bottom the lower portion would drop to the floor as the flames rose, but it would not be sufficient to set light to the carpet. If a pair of combinations was touching the fender in front of a gas stove the heat would not be sufficient to ignite it. More smoke was produced by using petrol when carrying out the tests, but even then it was not very dense.

Fully conscious of the seriousness of this question and the responsibility of the answer, I want you to tell the jury what conclusions your experiments have led you to with regard to the origin of the fire. Do you or do you not think this fire could have been an accidental fire?—My answer is that I cannot find any means of it being an accidental fire.

Cross-examined by Mr. CASSELS—How many years' experience have you had of fires?—Twenty-nine years' experience. I have attended many fires, and my experience enables me to gather in things very rapidly when I go to a fire.

Did you see the room on the night of the 23rd October and the morning of the 24th?—Yes; I saw the chair, the extent of burning of the carpet, and the position of the stove.

Have you made any experiment by lighting paper beneath a chair like the armchair that was in the room?—No.

Did you not try the effect of cotton wool and horsehair burning whilst suspended about six inches over something else burning, such as a carpet?—No.

By Mr. JUSTICE ROWLATT—What sort of a carpet is it?—I believe it is a Wilton carpet.

146

Evidence for Prosecution.

Cross-examination continued—Do you know whether the carpet with which you experimented was as worn as that near the gas stove?—I did not compare the thread of the carpet so I do not know if the parts I experimented with were more worn than the part which was burned.

Can you suggest how the cane chair was burned?—No.

The only suggestion made up to the moment is that the leg was used to poke a fire?—Impossible. If it was, the bottom of the leg must have been burned, and it is not. I cannot make any suggestion whatsoever.

By Mr. JUSTICE ROWLATT—It must have been in some flame?—Yes.

Cross-examination continued—Supposing a fire was started with half a pint of petrol to create or help the fire, do you think it would still be possible after twenty minutes or half an hour to trace a smell of the petrol?—I do not think so.

Is it not the case that when using petrol a great deal of smoke is caused?—Not dense smoke.

You know that Hopkins, Reed, and others had to crawl on their hands and knees, and they described is as very, very thick?—Yes, but my experiments have not helped me with regard to that. My experiments have shown me that there is more smoke without petrol.

Have you experimented with a gas fire and a fender like the one shown in an ordinary room?—No.

Why do you consider that a chair like this would not burn readily?—Because horsehair is padded so tightly into the chair. Also that horsehair would have to have air under and around it before it would do so.

Mr. CASSELS—I suggest that you take a handful of horsehair from the chair and burn it in Court.

Mr. JUSTICE ROWLATT—I do not think that should be done, Mr. Cassels. It may affect the air of the Court.

Mr. CASSELS—I think it is important, my lord.

Mr. JUSTICE ROWLATT—Then I give my consent.

[Witness demonstrated with a handful of horsehair from the armchair. He first held some upwards and lit it on the side. That went out before it had completely burned. Then

Sidney Harry Fox.

he held a piece downwards and put a match underneath. It flared up, and he had to drop it in the fender to burn out. It gave off a thick, pungent smoke.]

Cross-examination continued—Suppose petrol had been used on the carpet, you would have had a good deal of burning through the carpet?—I do not think it would burn through the carpet with petrol alone.

Have you, in your experience, ever known a fire, the origin of which could not be ascertained?—Oh yes, many.

Re-examined by the ATTORNEY-GENERAL—The carpet won't burn by itself?—No.

Would it make a difference if you had horsehair lying on it?—I do not think it would. If the horsehair was packed comparatively tight it would not burn as the piece did in Court. You must have oxygen for a fire.

Lieutenant-Colonel C. J. Fox, formerly of the London Salvage Corps, was then called into the witness-box.

Mr. CASSELS—I object to Lieutenant-Colonel Fox giving evidence. I submit he should not be allowed to give his opinion on what is a matter for the jury.

The ATTORNEY-GENERAL—I asked Lieutenant-Colonel Fox personally to come, as I think it is desirable that we should have an expert. I will, however, waive the matter if it is pressed.

Mr. CASSELS—I repeat my objection, my lord.

Mr. JUSTICE ROWLATT—Then I think the witness might kindly withdraw.

HERBERT WILLIAM LAW, examined by the ATTORNEY-GENERAL—I am an undertaker at Margate. On the 24th of October the accused called on me and requested me to make arrangements for the burial of his mother at Great Fransham. He said he was alone now; that he had recently returned from France, where he had been visiting his brother's grave. I placed the body of the woman in our mortuary, where it remained until the 29th of October, when it was taken to Great Fransham. I accompanied the body. I was present on 9th November at the exhumation which was conducted by Sir Bernard Spilsbury and others.

148

Evidence for Prosecution.

Herbert W. Law

I opened the coffin and identified the body. The funeral expenses amounted to £47 10s. The condition of the body when the coffin was opened showed no signs of decomposition or putrefaction.

ARTHUR WILLIAM CROSS, examined by Sir HENRY CURTIS BENNETT—I live at Great Fransham, and I am sexton of the Parish Church there. I knew the deceased Rosaline Fox for some time. I identify the photograph, Exhibit No. 18, as that of the deceased. I knew her father; he was a farm labourer. The deceased was a native of Great Fransham. I also knew her husband. He was a signalman at Great Fransham Station. The accused went to Great Fransham School. I was present at the funeral of Mrs. Fox on 29th October. I was also present on the 9th of November when the coffin was removed from the grave, and I identified the body as that of Mrs. Fox.

WALTER HAMBROOK, examined by Sir HENRY CURTIS BENNETT—I am chief inspector of police at New Scotland Yard. I had charge of this case. On 7th November I went to room No. 66 and certain measurements were taken under my directions. I found the lead capsule, Exhibit No. 22, behind the gas stove. I also found the wrapper and the port wine bottle. I was present when certain tests were made.

Cross-examined by Mr. CASSELS—When was the first time you visited the room?—On the 5th of November. The photographs were taken on the 7th of November after the room was put in exactly the same position as I had found it.

You cannot say what happened to the room between the 23rd of October and the date when you first saw it?—No, but the room had been locked. I was taken up by Inspector Palmer, and the photographs were taken of the room exactly as I found it.

Dr. GERALD ROCHE LYNCH, examined by Sir HENRY CURTIS BENNETT—I am senior official analyst to the Home Office. I examined the stomach, the stomach contents, and other organs taken from the deceased's body, which I received from

Sidney Harry Fox.

Dr. G. R. Lynch

Sir Bernard Spilsbury. I did not find any poisonous or noxious substances, but I found a very small quantity of alcohol in the stomach contents. It was probably ethyl alcohol, which is present in beers, wines, and spirits. If the deceased had had half a pint of beer between 7 p.m. and 8.15 p.m. on 23rd October, and had died between 11 p.m. and 11.20 p.m. I would not expect to find any trace of it in the body. If, however, she had had some of half a bottle of port about 9 p.m. or 9.30 p.m. I would expect to find a small amount in the stomach. What I did find was consistent with about a quarter of a bottle having been taken.

Cross-examined by Mr. CASSELS—Were you looking for anything particular?—I was looking for poison as a whole, but Sir Bernard Spilsbury raised the possibility of there being a trace of alcohol in the stomach.

How much alcohol did you find?—About a minim.

That is about a drop?—Yes.

If she had taken a wineglassful of port it would no doubt have disappeared from the stomach in the time which elapsed?—Yes.

By Mr. JUSTICE ROWLATT—Is it fair to put it this way, that what you found shows that if it were taken two hours before death there must have been a good deal more?—Yes.

Sir BERNARD SPILSBURY, examined by the ATTORNEY-GENERAL—I am a Bachelor of Medicine and Surgery of the University of Oxford, and a Member of the Royal College of Physicians. I hold the position of honorary pathologist to the Home Office. I attended the exhumation of Mrs. Fox's body at Great Fransham Churchyard on 9th November. The body was identified in my presence. I took samples of the soil surrounding the coffin. There was no smell when the lid was raised other than that of sawdust, which was clean and dry. The body was removed from the coffin. It was that of a short, stout woman, rather heavy. Slight putrefactive changes had taken place externally. The wall of the abdomen was tight and its colour in the lower part was green. On the back of the trunk there were blisters containing a red fluid. The lower part of the face,

150

Evidence for Prosecution.

Sir Bernard Spilsbury

neck, and shoulders were a dark red colour. The rest of the face, whites of the eyes, arms and forearms and flanks were a bright red colour. Post-mortem changes generally appear a few hours after death. There were no external marks or signs of violence. I found slight disease of the arteries of the brain, but the brain appeared to have been sufficiently nourished. There was evidence of very common senile changes. The spinal column and cord were healthy. The heart was moderately enlarged. The cavities were healthy, dilated, and almost empty. There is no significance in that. I found a patch of fibrosis on the wall of the heart and slight disease of the aorta and the left coronary artery of the heart. A patch of fibrosis is most commonly associated with disease of the arteries of the heart, and is the result usually of a poor blood supply. When the heart suffers seriously in its blood supply from disease of its arteries there is always a risk of sudden death; that is one of the commonest causes of sudden death in old people. The end is more likely to come in times of exertion—much more frequently when a great strain is thrown on the heart by physical exertion than when leading a quiet life. I thought the disease which I found in the heart of the deceased was insufficient to account for sudden death from heart failure.

By Mr. JUSTICE ROWLATT—That means that you do not think she could have died from heart failure pure and simple?—No, my lord.

Examination continued—The blood of the deceased was thick and dark red, quite distinct from the colour of blood in carbon monoxide poisoning, which is of a much brighter colour. I examined the air passages. The lungs were congested at the back. The air passages were clear. The lungs were of a deep red colour which might have been due to post-mortem changes. Usually the lungs would be at that time a dull slatey colour. That, in my opinion, showed that the putrefactive changes were slower than usual.

I produce a model of the human mouth showing part of the air passages, the jaw, and the tongue. Knowing what I did of this case I paid special attention to the air passages.

151

Sidney Harry Fox.

Sir Bernard Spilsbury

I found the air passages clear, and there was no trace of soot on the linings of the passages, either visibly or microscopically. By soot I mean fine particles of carbon which are to be found in smoke. At the back of the larynx, lying between it and the upper part of the gullet, I found a large, recent bruise about the size of half a crown which, in my opinion, was caused by some mechanical violence, a breaking or tearing of small blood vessels. It was then that I had the first indication of the conclusions to which I finally came, that death was due to strangulation.

To what do you attribute that bruise at the back of the larynx?—My first suspicion when I saw that was that the bruise was the result of some handling of the larynx, such as is found in manual strangulation, but I did not finally decide until I had made a more thorough search and dissection of all that part, and excluded all other possible causes. I found no injury to the cartilages or bones of the larynx at that time, and I subsequently examined the larynx in greater detail the following day and found no injury either to the cartilages or to the bones. I also examined the tongue. The thyroid gland was a deep red colour. The contents of the abdomen were healthy. There was some gas as the result of putrefaction. The liver was small and congested, but that at this stage is of no importance. The spleen was also small, firm, and congested. The kidneys were small and congested. The bladder was healthy, but empty. The coffin was dry inside. There was no escape of urine after burial. I also examined the tongue and I found a recent bruise in the substance of the tongue, on the left margin, about midway between the tip and the back base of the tongue, just behind the left wisdom tooth. The bruise was not visible to the naked eye, and was only found by making transverse cuts across the tongue. It was a quarter of an inch in diameter and was very close to the surface. I later took certain portions of the organs to my own laboratory.

Did you at any time find any traces of soot?—Under microscopical examination I found no trace of soot.

How much carbon monoxide would have caused death in

Evidence for Prosecution.

Sir Bernard Spilsbury

this case?—As little as one part of carbon monoxide in 500 parts of air in a room would produce serious effects, and three or four parts in 500 would be rapidly fatal. There should be no carbon monoxide in the blood of a normal, healthy person.

Did you find any carbon monoxide in Mrs. Fox's blood? —No.

Supposing a dead body was in a room containing a great deal of carbon monoxide, would any of it find its way into the blood?—No. Experiments have been made with dead bodies and dead animals, and it has been found that whilst a certain amount of carbon monoxide could get through the skin, and possibly into the blood vessels under the skin, the body, generally speaking, would show no sign. It would require a long exposure to the atmosphere—probably ten or twelve hours—to produce even that.

Having regard to the absence of any soot and the failure of your tests to reveal any carbon monoxide, have you reached a point when you can eliminate certain causes?— Yes. I can eliminate the effects of the fire in that room.

By Mr. JUSTICE ROWLATT—That is to say, that in your judgment the fire was not the cause of the death of that woman?—That is so, my lord.

The Court adjourned.

153

Sidney Harry Fox.

Sixth Day—Tuesday, 18th March, 1930.

Sir BERNARD SPILSBURY, examination continued by the ATTORNEY-GENERAL—I examined the body for carbon monoxide at the time of the post-mortem examination. I tested the blood at my laboratory for carbon monoxide. My tests would have revealed anything over 20 per cent. The lowest amount I have ever known to cause death is 45. The usual amount which would cause death would be nearer 70. I found none. I examined the throat and the air passages at the post-mortem to see if there was any smoke or soot. I placed scrapings under the microscope to see if there were any minute particles of smoke, but I found none.

If the person had been alive when there was any appreciable quantity of smoke in that room, must you have found minute particles of smoke or soot?—Yes.

Are you able, then, to say whether Mrs. Fox had died before there was any appreciable quantity of smoke in that room?—Yes.

Is there any possible room for doubt?—In my opinion, none at all.

By Mr. JUSTICE ROWLATT—As I understand it, you can have a great deal of smoke reaching you if you are lying in bed in these circumstances without reaching the stage of getting any carbon monoxide?—That is so.

What happens to a person lying asleep, apart from carbon monoxide, if the room fills with smoke?—The choking effect of the smoke would be certain to rouse him.

You think it would—before any poisoning would arise?—There would be violent coughing, and the person would wake up.

The person would wake up before any question of carbon monoxide poisoning arose?—Yes.

Examination continued—Could the positive symptoms you found possibly have been accounted for by any disease of the heart?—No.

154

Evidence for Prosecution.

Sir Bernard Spilsbury

Did you form any opinion about the bruise on the tongue?
—It was a bruise which showed infiltration of the tissues
with blood, which means crushing of the surface of the
tongue, rupture of the tissues, and escape of blood. The
size of the bruise was about a quarter of an inch in diameter, approximately. It was spherical in shape. It was
like a small pea. It was a bruise that had been inflicted
during life, or within a minute or so after the heart had
stopped beating, probably by artificial teeth being in the
mouth.

Are you able to say whether, when the bruise was caused,
the teeth were in the mouth?—In my opinion they were.

We have heard that when the body was lying in the hall
of the hotel one policeman put his fingers in the mouth
and pulled out the tongue, whilst another policeman pressed
down the tongue to see that there was no obstruction to
breathing. Is it conceivable that a bruise of the dimensions
you found in that place on the tongue could have been
caused then?—No, not even if she was alive.

Can you tell me how long before death you think that
bruise could have been caused?—It was certainly only a
short time before death. I think probably within half an
hour, but the very outside one could allow would be two
hours before death.

Is it consistent with that bruise that it was caused a
couple of minutes before the heart ceased to beat?—Quite;
it is more likely to have been before the heart ceased to
beat than after.

Look at those artificial teeth which were taken from the
mouth of the deceased. Could these teeth if they came together with some violence have caused that bruise?—Yes.
The back or crushing teeth, as distinct from the front or
cutting teeth, could easily produce such a bruise by forcible
contact.

In cases of manual strangulation do you usually find
some bruise on the tongue?—Well, sometimes, but not always.

But investigation of the tongue is very important where
manual strangulation has to be considered?—Yes.

When you find a bruise like that how does it come about?

155

Sidney Harry Fox.

Sir Bernard Spilsbury

—Either by placing a hand on the throat and pushing upwards so that the jaws come together, or by placing a hand over the mouth to prevent crying out, which would also force the jaws together.

We have all had the experience of biting our tongue. Is the bruise on the tongue in a position which would result from biting the tongue while having dinner?—No, it is not. When eating it is the tip which is generally caught by the front teeth.

By Mr. JUSTICE ROWLATT—In other words, you do not bite your tongue with your back teeth?—No.

Examination continued—Are you able to account for that bruise in any other way than that of some pressure being applied to the throat or jaws before her death?—No other way.

And at a time when the teeth were in her mouth?—Yes. Immediately death takes place the jaw drops. Mrs. Fox's teeth would be kept in position by a spring on each side which tended to force the two plates apart and keep them firm against the gums.

With regard to the bruise at the back of the larynx, which has been termed the half-crown bruise, do you think it could have been caused after death?—No, not in this case. This was an unusual sort of bruise, and I have only found it in certain types of injuries, such as injury to the spinal column or a severe blow with the fist on the frontal side of the neck.

Assuming some kind of strangulation, how would such a bruise be caused?—By the wind-box, or larynx, being either pressed firmly back against the spine or, more probably, I think, by some upward movement pushing the larynx up towards the mouth and so throwing a strain on the tissue of the larynx.

Would that same action also possibly cause the biting of the tongue?—Yes, it would force the jaws together.

Have you ever seen such a bruise in a case of natural death?—No, never.

What inferences do you draw from the fact that the epiglottis was congested and had some small marks indicat-

156

Evidence for Prosecution.

Sir Bernard Spilsbury

ing bleeding?—These two conditions are very characteristic of death from strangulation.

Can this condition be caused by any natural disease?—I know that a condition resembling that is produced by certain natural diseases, but I did not find any of the diseases which might have caused this condition present in the case of the deceased.

In this case, then, are you able to account for that condition by any assumption other than that of strangulation? —No.

Does that observation also apply to the bruise on the larynx?—Yes.

And to the bruise on the tongue?—Yes.

And with much greater force to the three symptoms added together?—Yes.

You had the thyroid gland under microscopical examination?—Yes. I found a small dark area just on the surface which I thought might be a bruise. I made microscopical preparations of it which in my view confirmed the presence of a little bruising. I showed the preparations to Dr. Weir, Professor Smith, and Dr. Brontë, who, however, did not take the same view, and for that reason I prefer that the bruise shall not be considered as a possible injury caused at that time.

Apart from the thyroid gland, are we, in your view, outside the region of doubt?—Yes.

Was there any visible sign of bruising on the neck?— There was no outward sign. In cases of strangulation there generally is such a sign—even separate marks of finger nails can be seen on the neck.

What do you say as to the possibility of this bruise being caused to the subcutaneous tissues without there being any mark on the neck?—It has been shown by experiments that this part of the wind-box can be compressed between finger and thumb sufficiently to close the larynx where the vocal cords are by a slight degree of pressure, only to such a degree as might be inadequate to bruise the skin over this part of the neck. Further, if the force employed is sufficient to crush the tissues, and if the fingers and thumb are kept

157

Sidney Harry Fox.

Sir Bernard Spilsbury

accurately to the same areas throughout the period of strangling, and for a brief period after the heart has ceased to beat, there might be no escape of blood into the tissues at all.

By Mr. JUSTICE ROWLATT—In death by strangling you simply die for want of breath? The air passages are closed? —That is the theory, but in practice the victim in many cases loses consciousness extremely rapidly.

Why?—Because of some effect upon the lining of the larynx.

It is very unpleasant to have your throat squeezed?—Very.

When persons have their throat squeezed can they put up a vigorous fight?—In some cases the victim drops immediately, and in others they struggle for a short time, but it is a very brief struggle. The effect of any struggle on the part of the victim necessitates a firmer grip by the assailant if he is to retain his hold. That is why one usually finds marks or injury on the skin of the neck.

Examination continued—Having heard the symptoms of Mrs. Fox, what do you think she was suffering from?— Paralysis agitans, or shaking palsy.

Do you think such a woman as Mrs. Fox, possibly sleeping, would be able to put up much of a resistance?—No.

With no resistance, or wholly inadequate resistance, do you think the absence of external marks might be accounted for?—Yes.

Would it be much easier to strangle a person with the head thrown back or the head forward?—With the head thrown back. The head thrown forward may cover the Adam's apple.

Would it be easier to strangle a person sleeping in bed with the head on a pillow or without a pillow?—It would be easier without a pillow.

Supposing you had a case of strangulation by a pillow placed with one hand upon the face obstructing the mouth and nostrils—the air passages—and the neck held in position as it were, would you get the symptoms you have found here?—It might well be so. In those conditions it would be impossible for the victim to move her neck.

Evidence for Prosecution.

Sir Bernard Spilsbury

You know the gravity of this case and the responsibility that rests upon you?—I do.

Have you, or have you not, any doubt as to the cause of this woman's death?—No, after weighing all the facts carefully I can come to no other conclusion.

Cross-examined by Mr. CASSELS—What, in your opinion, was the cause of death?—I repeat that the cause was asphyxia due to manual strangulation.

Did you change that opinion in any way after your microscopical examinations?—No, I did not.

Is it right outside the region of doubt?—It is, in my opinion.

Assuming Mrs. Fox died just after seeing the room was on fire, would you expect to find much carbon monoxide in the blood?—I should expect to find none.

With regard to the presence of soot, what was the nature of your examination?—I took a microscopical scraping of the greater part of the inner formation of the throat. That was done on the day following the post-mortem examination.

Would not the method you used for testing for soot in the air passages tend to press the particles into the throat rather than remove them?—I do not agree.

Did you examine the mucous lining of the nose?—No, because every person has a deposit of soot in the nose, and therefore you cannot say whether a person died in a smoky atmosphere because of soot found in the nose.

Did you find disease of the coronary artery of the heart? —I found that among other conditions. In the arteries of the brain the disease was moderate; in the arteries of the kidneys it was more marked; and in the main artery, the aorta, it was slight, except in the lower part of the abdomen.

Supposing Mrs. Fox had dropped dead in the street and at the post-mortem examination you had found these conditions, would you not have found sufficient to have caused sudden death?—No, not in my opinion.

Would it alter your opinion if, three days before her death, she had fainted, and her extremities were very cold? —No. I should have decided upon what I found.

159

Sidney Harry Fox.

Sir Bernard Spilsbury

The history would not make any difference?—Not as to the cause of death.

Have you considered the effect of fright, exertion, or a fit of coughing?—Yes.

If a woman such as Mrs. Fox suddenly attempted by exertion to get out of bed, would it not be likely to bring about a sudden collapse, especially if accompanying that exertion there was fright?—Such exertion as she could make would play no part.

You mean she could not make any exertion which was capable of having any effect upon her heart?—That is what I think. Paralysis agitans develops slowly and gradually weakens the person, and by reason of the fact that it renders the person unable to move quickly it helps to protect the person from sudden death from exertion. I think myself the deceased was rather helpless. The paralysis was not in an advanced stage. She could get out of bed, but she could not do it quickly.

Had the condition of the heart which you found in this case any part in the death of Mrs. Fox?—I do not think it had any part.

Do you mean you would be astonished if you found Mrs. Fox dead in a street or in some circumstances above suspicion, and the condition of the heart was as you found it here?—And nothing else? Yes. I do not think I should be satisfied with the cause of death.

Have you considered the effect of a fit of coughing produced by smoke?—Yes, but I do not think it can be taken into account with the heart disease found in Mrs. Fox in the case of sudden death.

Do you not think the fact of her throwing her legs over the side of the bed in order to get out quickly, combined with fright, would have an effect of a serious character?—No.

Surely an experience of that kind would give extra work to the heart?—Of course it would, but the heart is capable of far more work than it is doing when at rest.

How many bodies have you exhumed in cases of death from manual strangulation?—I think this is the only exhumation I have done in a case of manual strangulation.

160

Evidence for Prosecution.

Sir Bernard Spilsbury

I want to ask you about that bruise which you say you found on the thyroid gland, but about which the other experts did not agree with you. Is your opinion upon this part of the case as definite as it is on the other parts of the case?—Yes.

By Mr. JUSTICE ROWLATT—Your opinion is still that the thyroid gland was bruised?—That is so.

Cross-examination continued—Not only bruised, but such a bruise as you would expect from firm pressure of the thumb and finger applied to the larynx?—Yes.

What was it you saw that made you express that opinion? Was it anything which was larger than a pin's head?—Yes.

How much?—It is difficult to estimate the size. It is a very tiny area.

Is it something which requires a microscope?—Of course, to define it advantageously, but it is something I thought I saw before.

Something which might occur from a fit of coughing?—Not in these circumstances.

Was there anything you found about the deceased's neck to suggest a blow?—Yes, the bruise upon the back of the larynx.

I mean a blow as distinct from manual strangulation?—I am sorry, no.

With the exception of the chief constable of Norfolk, who was present at the post-mortem examination, has any other person seen that bruise on the back of the larynx?—No.

Is it available for inspection now?—No.

When you got to your laboratory the next day could you see it?—No, I could not. The bruise could not then be seen because of putrefaction which had set in after the exhumation.

Have you ever suggested that there should be a final exhumation?—That would not help, because decomposition is particularly rapid after a body has been once exhumed.

The bruise at the back of the larynx might easily be a mark of putrefaction?—It was a bruise, and nothing else. There are no two opinions about it. If it had been putrefaction the mark would not have been red in colour, but green.

Sidney Harry Fox.

Sir Bernard Spilsbury

What I put to you is that if that mark had been produced by pressure it would not have disappeared between the time of your examination in the schoolroom and your examination in your laboratory the next day?—It did not disappear; it became obscure by the uniform green colour which appeared afterwards.

[At this stage Mr. Cassels referred the witness to the hyoid bone—one of the bones of the larynx.] Do you agree that the hyoid bone becomes ossified in old people, and might easily be broken?—Yes, but in the case of Mrs. Fox it was not broken at all.

When you were examining this bone, which was taken from Mrs. Fox's mouth, did you in handling it actually break it twice?—I broke it twice, but not actually in handling it. I first of all dissected sufficiently to uncover it to ascertain that it was not damaged, and then I dissected other parts of the larynx. I leaned on the bone and first it cracked on one side and then on the other. I had first of all ascertained that there was no injury.

It was very brittle?—Yes, it was. It does not require a great deal of force to break it.

It is very important in this case, is it not, the absence of any fracture or damage to this brittle hyoid bone?—Oh, yes, certainly.

Would it have strengthened your opinion if the hyoid bone had been broken?—It would have made it more evident.

Was the cricoid cartilage in the neck broken?—No.

It is very easily broken, is it not?—Yes.

And especially so in the case of manual strangulation?—Yes.

If you had found this cricoid cartilage and the hyoid bone both broken that would have strengthened your opinion of manual strangulation?—Yes.

And, as a matter of fact, neither of these was broken in this case?—That is true.

How many cases of manual strangulation have you had in your experience without the hyoid bone being fractured?—I cannot give the exact figures, but I have the abstracts here

162

Evidence for Prosecution.

Sir Bernard Spilsbury

of six cases, and in those cases the hyoid bone was broken in one.

What were the ages of the other five persons?—16, 27, 33, 37, and 56.

Have you propounded a theory that this woman was attacked while she was asleep?—I certainly think that is probable.

Now, about the tongue and the bruise which you say you found there, do you go so far as to say that you cannot involuntarily bite upon that part of the tongue?—Try to bite the back of your tongue. It is most difficult to get it between the teeth.

Supposing anybody were to pull out the tongue after death, might not a few fibres of the muscles be ruptured, and you might get before the blood accumulates a small quantity of blood into the ruptured fibres?—If you pulled the tongue out after death, you might, if you used sufficient force, pinch the tongue between the thumb and the finger and crush it in that way. I do not think that death makes any difference on the question of injury.

What was the size of the bruise on the tongue?—A quarter of an inch.

Is that not a very small bruise?—Not for a tongue bruise.

The bruise is on no part of the surface?—In my opinion it was caused by the forcing up of the lower denture on to the upper denture. If you examine the teeth you will see that they have smooth, flat surfaces, and between them the tongue might be bruised without being torn on the surface.

Did you find any damage to the gums?—No.

Or any damage to the plates?—No damage other than the loss of a tooth and a broken spring.

With those teeth kept in juxtaposition could a person go to sleep without them falling back?—It is a little hard to say. It is just a question whether a spring on one side would keep them up, or whether they would sag. I should have thought they would be too uncomfortable to wear with only one spring.

What I have in my mind is your suggestion of the teeth being in the mouth when the manual strangulation took

Sidney Harry Fox.

Sir Bernard Spilsbury

place. You, of course, say it would be so by reason of the bruise upon the tongue. Have you propounded a theory at all in this case that this woman was attacked when she was asleep?—I do not know whether that theory originated from me, but I certainly think it is probable.

The word " probable " arises a very great deal in your evidence?—With regard to what actually happened, it must.

What are some of the external marks and signs one might expect to find in a case of asphyxia by strangulation?—If I saw the body of a person who died from asphyxia by strangulation, say, a quarter of an hour after death, I should expect to find marks where pressure had been applied to the neck—depressions, I mean—with or without bruises beneath, and often with marks of finger nails in these areas. Those marks might extend right down to the windpipe. In most cases the other external injuries consist of cutting of the lips, bruises about the wrists, arms, and abdomen—signs of a struggle. There would also be changes in appearance. In some cases the surface of the face and neck is purple, almost black, with tiny pinpoint hæmorrhages. The eyes might be congested, and there might also be tiny hæmorrhages. The lips would be discoloured and the finger nails are often livid. Sometimes the tongue is protruding, and the tip of the tongue between the teeth may be bitten and bruised. There might possibly be traces of froth at the nose and mouth.

And all these signs were absent in this case?—Yes. The whites of the eyes were red when I saw the body. All I heard was that the face was pale.

You will agree that the sooner you have a post-mortem after death the better?—Yes.

The more putrefaction there is the more difficult it becomes?—Yes.

What would you expect to find on making a post-mortem examination of a person who had died from asphyxia by strangulation?—If on post-mortem examination you find the right side turgid with blood and the left side empty it is a sign of death by asphyxia. You would expect to find the veins of the neck full of blood.

164

Evidence for Prosecution.

Sir Bernard Spilsbury

And what did you find in this case?—I found the heart cavities empty and the right side was not turgid with blood. The large vein of the chest and neck was nearly empty. In asphyxia it is nearly always full immediately after death. Blood after death tends to find its way into the lower parts of the body. That is why you get post-mortem stains.

Have you done many exhumations connected with crimes of violence?—Yes, but I cannot recall having done an asphyxia one. I have examined bodies which have not been buried in asphyxia cases.

In your experience of strangulation cases have you ever known of a case with fewer signs than this?—No, I have not.

Re-examined by the ATTORNEY-GENERAL—Have you ever had a case of an old woman suffering from paralysis agitans strangled in bed?—No.

And do appearances vary according to the degree and point of application of pressure?—Yes. If the fingers were placed on each side you might get the ordinary signs of death from asphyxia without little more than a livid colour of the face, and if death occurred very quickly the face might be pale.

You have conducted many hundreds of post-mortem examinations?—Many thousands.

Did you observe that the coffin in this case had putty round the lid, which would make it airtight?—Yes.

That would help to prevent putrefaction?—Yes.

Was there any evidence of putrefaction in the tissues round the bruise?—No.

Is it possible for you to have made a mistake and to have mistaken a post-mortem change for a bruise?—No, quite impossible.

This was a bruise?—Yes.

Do you think the bruising of the tongue could possibly be accounted for by the tearing of the fibres of the tongue?—No, certainly not.

By Mr. JUSTICE ROWLATT—Even in life?—No, my lord.

Re-examination continued—Have you ever had a similar

Sidney Harry Fox.

Sir Bernard Spilsbury

case to this?—I once had a case of a woman of fifty-one who died in bed from carbon monoxide poisoning. She was a cripple and bedridden, and was taken from her bedroom one night when the room was full of smoke, and found to be dead. She had smoke in the air passages, and even a smell of smoke in the stomach. She had a patch of fibrosis and disease of the coronary artery. In spite of that disease of the heart, she survived in the smoke long enough to take in carbon monoxide.

If you were asleep and the atmosphere became smoky, what would happen?—The effect of the smoke would be to make the person cough and wake up from an ordinary sleep.

What have you to say about the fainting attack which Mrs. Fox is supposed to have had on the Sunday before her death?—I know very little of the position, but I am satisfied that the attack was not of the nature of angina following the disease of the coronary artery.

Nothing leads you to think that that was consequent upon the heart condition?—Nothing at all.

By Mr. JUSTICE ROWLATT—Several times a pillow has been mentioned in this case as having possibly something to do with the killing of this old lady by asphyxia. Have you any views on that? You saw nothing to show whether the pillow had been used?—No. Of course, it would leave no mark if it was used. It is only supposition, but if the head was resting on the pillow the neck might be so bent as to make it difficult to strangle with the hand.

There was nothing to throw any light upon the question of whether the pillow could have been used to suffocate?—No, except that suffocation by a pillow could not have produced the changes I found.

Dr. HENRY D. WEIR examined by the ATTORNEY-GENERAL—I am Pathologist to the National Hospital for Diseases of the Heart. I had consultations with Sir Bernard Spilsbury on 6th and 7th of March concerning this case, and I considered carefully with him the post-mortem findings he came to. It was not possible for me to see the half-crown bruise at the back of the larynx, but the description of it was not

Evidence for Prosecution.

consistent with post-mortem changes. It would be caused during life or within a few moments of death. If the bruise on the tongue had been brought about the day before death I do not think it would have remained below the surface. In my opinion the deceased did not die as the result of the fire. Considering the condition of the heart, it is possible the woman might have died from heart failure, but not likely. There is no natural cause of death which would account for the bruise on the larynx, the bruise on the tongue, and the hæmorrhage on the epiglottis.

Have you ever had to deal with any similar case? I mean where there were inward bruises, but no external marks of violence?—Only once. That was in the case of an infant, one year old.

Supposing the victim is a broad, big, strong man standing up, or is a frail woman lying down?—You would not expect such severe injuries in a frail woman as in a strong man who puts up a resistance.

Cross-examined by Mr. CASSELS—Was there sufficient disease to account for sudden death if there had been just before a fright on the part of the deceased or a fit of coughing, or anything to throw extra strain upon the heart? —In my opinion, except for the bruises, there was sufficient disease in the heart to account for death from natural causes.

Would you be prepared to say what you saw in the microscopical slide was, and must be, due to violence?—In my opinion, yes. Supposing this woman had suddenly seen the fire and tried to get out of bed, I think it possible, in combination with seeing the smoke and beginning to inhale it, that it might be a cause of natural death, but for the bruises.

Re-examined by the ATTORNEY-GENERAL—In your answer about there being evidence of a natural death apart from the bruises, what had you in mind?—I had in mind that, assuming Mrs. Fox had seen the fire and tried to get out of bed, that, in combination with the emotion of seeing the smoke, perhaps beginning to inhale smoke, might have been sufficient to cause death.

That, of course, is not your considered opinion of the cause

167

Dr. Weir

of this death. I want you to repeat that opinion?—In my opinion death was due to heart failure due to partial strangulation, to commencing strangulation. In other words, that the strangulation in itself did not cause death, but brought on heart failure.

By a JUROR—I am anxious to know whether, when Mrs. Fox's body was brought out of the room by the witness Hopkins, the jaws might not have come together on the tongue when Hopkins lifted her up and so caused the bruising of the throat and tongue?—In my opinion, no.

Sir BERNARD SPILSBURY—In my opinion the bruises could not have been caused in that way. As a matter of fact, the teeth were not in the mouth then.

A JUROR—The jaws would come together.

Sir BERNARD SPILSBURY—The smooth jaws could not have produced the bruise on the tongue. Only if the teeth were in the mouth could it have been caused.

Evidence for the Prosecution closed.

Opening Speech for the Defence.

Mr. J. D. CASSELS—Ladies and gentlemen of the jury, the question which you have to answer is this—the only question is, was Mrs. Fox murdered? Throughout this day you have been listening to the arguments, one way and the other, of two eminent doctors called for the prosecution. You will not lose sight of the fact that these two have their differences. It is at least a tribute to the fairness of the prosecution that in a case of this kind in this country, notwithstanding that difference of opinion, both views are presented to you by the prosecution for your consideration. It is a profoundly difficult case. You will be told—and I ask you to bear it in your mind right through—that where there is a doubt you must lean to the side of the accused. The accused is probably the youngest person actively concerned in the investigation of this case, and the charge against him is that he murdered his mother. You may build round a

Mr. J. D. Cassels, K.C.

Opening Speech for the Defence.

Mr. Cassels

case of this kind a mountain of motive and surround it with suspicion, but if you do not prove that the person whose death you are investigating was murdered your mountain of motive and your suspicion are without value.

The accused was brought up by his mother, a widow, and from his youth up he has known no other companion than the mother, for whose death, it is said, he is to be held responsible. The accused did some military service, and afterwards obtained some employment. In 1926 he lived with his mother in a boarding-house at Southsea, and obtained employment in an insurance office. In 1927 his mother's health began to fail, and at Christmas that year they both went to the accused's brother. The mother's health became beyond the attention of the eldest son in his house, and she was removed by the accused to a house in the neighbourhood to be looked after, and afterwards she was taken to the Infirmary, where she remained for a year. In March, 1929, when he was able, the accused removed her from there, and was afterwards her constant companion. They went to Norwich, staying with Miss Bacon at 19 Cathedral Street, for several weeks, and, making Norwich their headquarters, they were wanderers to the extent that, every day they were able, they spent in visiting relatives and friends in the neighbourhood, of whom they had many. Sometimes they stayed in hotels.

Now, let me come at once to incidents which must naturally loom large in your mind, but which, in my submission, are a long way from the real charge which you are trying. I am not going to present to you this young man as being a man who tells the truth. I present him to you as one who, over and over again, has stayed with his mother in hotels and has left without paying. I present him to you as a liar. I present him to you as a man who, from the experience he had had, was able to go to hotels, and by his plausibility and by his falsity to obtain for his mother and for himself comfort and attention which neither of them could afford, which neither of them was entitled to, and which, in its surroundings, was altogether beyond their circumstances. I present him to you as the

Sidney Harry Fox.

Mr. Cassels

liar he was bound to be. He could not have conducted himself in these surroundings without representing himself to
be something far better than he really was. You may well
reflect that that old woman must have had many difficult and
awkward moments in the course of the life she was spending
with her son at that time. He lied about his position
financially, future and past, but you are a long way, are
you not, from finding murder proved because you find that
a man has gone from hotel to hotel without being able
to afford it, or because, being an undischarged bankrupt
for a sum of £267, he is to be regarded as an individual
likely to have a motive to murder?

With regard to the point made by the prosecution that
just before midnight on 23rd October the accused had a
bill for £10 or £11 which he could not pay, do you think
that would have worried him after the success which had
attended his efforts at other hotels, when the only luggage
he had was a brown paper parcel, when his mother had
practically no change of clothes and he himself had only
what he stood up in? Do you think it would have worried
him to murder because his financial position was such that
he knew he could not pay? I present him to you as an
individual of that type who had provided for his mother
at but little cost to himself, entertainment and maintenance
in circumstances which to them must have been lucky. He
must have had some money, and with that money he was
able to gratify the desire of his mother to go to France to
see the grave of her son who had been killed in the war.
They went there and came back, and then visited the hotels
of which you have heard.

A great deal has been put before you about an hour and
twenty minutes before midnight—about the fire not being
accidental, and a man going upstairs at twenty minutes to
eleven intent on murder. Are you going to say that that
must have been the case, when the motive which has been
put forward—the motive of insurance—had been in existence
ever since the 4th day of May? Let those insurances have
from you every consideration, but do not look at them from
one point of view and say, " Oh, there was £1000 for death

Opening Speech for the Defence.

Mr. Cassels

by accident,'' and ignore all the features of the policies. I ask you to reflect that if the accused is the kind of person suggested by the prosecution he had, in order to carry out his intention, every hour from midnight on 22nd October. In my submission too much has been made of the insurance policies. The reason for taking out these policies was that, in the event of his mother meeting with an accident, they would provide a weekly maintenance which would have given her medical attention and comfort very different from that which she had had during the thirteen months in the poor law institution. I ask you not to lose sight of the fact that the accused, who is supposed to have set the room on fire in order to carry out his crime, was the first person to give the alarm. He was unable to get further than a yard or two into the room, and that was the experience of those who went to his aid. No person who set eyes upon that body that night saw any sign which would lead them to suppose that it was the body of a person dying from manual strangulation. There were no marks upon the neck for even the observant Dr. Nichol to see, though it might have escaped the unobservant Dr. Austin. The fire in room No. 66, too, deceived policemen and firemen alike, according to the prosecution.

Now when you get into the dangerous realm of reconstruction it may lead you to the most dangerous results. I shall call before you medical evidence—witnesses in as good a position to express an opinion as was Dr. Weir, for what Dr. Weir saw those two medical witnesses also saw. I shall call before you Professor Smith, whose experience in cases concerning crimes of violence is unparalleled, and who will be able to deal with the structures of the throat and the significance attached to the marks which have been found. What a remarkable piece of circumstance attaches to whatever this young man did, if murderer he be, if, in course of the strangulation, he should have produced no marks upon the outside. What he produced, it is alleged, is a bruise mark, so called and so described, which only one trained person has ever seen and no human person can confirm. One would almost imagine that he had the

171

Sidney Harry Fox.

knowledge of a well-trained doctor. You recall how Dr. Weir said that the condition of the heart and the other organs, apart from this so-called bruise, was sufficient, in his opinion, to account for sudden death arising from sudden exertion or fright. Sir Bernard Spilsbury would not agree. If Dr. Weir's view is presented to you by Professor Smith and Dr. Brontë you are trying this case upon this mark, from a medical point of view at any rate. Evidence will be given that the deceased never slept with her teeth in her mouth. According to the case for the prosecution, the one and only night that she went to sleep with them in was the night when her son had made up his mind to throttle her.

Let me just add that the accused and his mother were the best of friends. They often played together, hand in hand, in a form which might well be described as just an ordinary sham fight. Whatever were the accused's qualities as a man, it is a fact that every one who knew him regarded him— and rightly so in my opinion—as a thoughtful and loving son. The accused will go into the witness-box and he will be cross-examined, which is only right. But, observe this : that it will not be in the nature of a legal battle. He is bound to put himself before you as one who has not always been truthful. One can even put it higher and say he is bound to appear before you as one who has rarely been truthful, who has exaggerated in all circumstances, who has told lie after lie. But, bear in mind, when you hear him cross-examined, that he is giving evidence in his own case in which he is charged, not with obtaining something from a hotel for nothing or with deceiving people, but with the murder of his mother. If you are not satisfied by the prosecution that that has been made out, you can wipe away from this case everything else.

The Court adjourned.

Evidence for Defence.

Evidence for the Defence.

SIDNEY HARRY FOX (accused, on oath), examined by Mr. CASSELS—I am a son of the deceased, and I was born at Great Fransham, Norfolk. I was thirty-one years of age in January last. I had three brothers older than myself, two of whom were killed in the war, in which I saw some military service. A cousin named Cecil Reginald Fox was also killed in the war. I was brought up at home until 1914. After the war my mother lived at Cavendish Mansions, Hampstead, and previous to that she had a house at Thornton Heath. On leaving Cavendish Mansions she took a house at Southsea and took in boarders. That was about 1925 or 1926. I was there part of the time; I was employed at the Gresham Insurance Office at Portsmouth. Up till 1926 my mother was fairly well, but after that her health began to fail. She used to have attacks of giddiness, and fall backwards. She would be shaky and nervous for a few minutes after, but would soon recover. About Christmas, 1927, I took my mother to stay with my brother, whom I had not seen for quite three years, with the exception of once, when I passed him on the front but did not speak. In January, 1928, I went to my brother's house, but my brother was out. His wife told me he had gone to the office to see me to request me to remove my mother, as, on account of her falls, they did not care to take the responsibility for her safety. I therefore made arrangements and took her to the house of a Mrs. Taylor in Vevill Road, Portsmouth. She afterwards went into the poor law institution, and was there until 27th March, 1929. When I went to take her out she was very much grieved that her eldest son had never been to see her. We went to Lowestoft and then to Norwich, where we stayed with a Miss Bacon, at 19 Cathedral Street. I was with my mother from then onwards until the day she died. I looked after her.

What was the state of her health when at Cathedral

Sidney Harry Fox.

Street ?—She walked about quite comfortably by taking hold of my arm. I do not think she ever went out alone.

What was the feeling between you and your mother ?— Well, excellent—the ordinary feeling between mother and son.

While at Norwich did your mother suggest that she should make a will ?—She desired to add something to a previous will, but it could not be found, so she said she would make another one. With that object in view I purchased a will form from a stationer. One evening she said she would make it, and I got a pen and ink. She told me what to put down, and I wrote it word for word as she told me. The question of witnesses then arose.

I show you exhibit No. 101. In whose handwriting is that document ?—The words are my mother's and the handwriting my own. It is my mother's signature in two places.

Did the witnesses witness it in your presence ?—No, I was in London when the will was signed.

Why did you go to Norwich ?—We really went there with the object of visiting friends and relatives in Norfolk. We generally returned to Norwich each evening, but at some places we stayed at an hotel.

In September, 1929, did your mother want to go to France to visit your brother's grave ?—It was always mother's one desire to go to France to visit the grave, and we were able to do so in September, 1929. I knew Dover. We went to the Grand Hotel and stayed there from the 12th to the 14th. We were in France from the 23rd to the 28th of September. We returned to Dover.

While you were in France did you make Ostend your headquarters ?—Yes ; we went from there each day, travelling by coach and train. We visited the graves of my brother and cousin.

When you returned to Dover did you go to the Grand Hotel ?—Yes. From there we went to the Royal Pavilion Hotel, Folkestone, on the Monday.

Tell me this, Fox, did you sometimes leave hotels without paying ?—Yes.

Did you find that at all difficult to do ?—No.

174

Evidence for Defence.

Sidney H. Fox

You had no luggage?—No.

Did you ask for communicating rooms at any hotel?—Never.

With regard to the Grand Hotel at Dover, did you pay on your first visit?—No, but I paid the second time for both. I did not pay the third time.

Were you staying at the County Hotel, Canterbury, on 3rd October?—Yes. I paid part of it.

On 16th October you arrived at the Hotel Metropole, Margate. Did you intend to stay long there?—No, we intended to stay there only one night.

Why was your visit prolonged?—Because mother contracted a chill, and after the 16th was more or less confined to her room. After the 17th she did not go out at all.

When you arrived at the Hotel Metropole what rooms did you ask for?—I asked Miss Hopper for rooms for my mother and myself.

Did you ever ask for communicating rooms at any hotel?—No, never.

You had rooms Nos. 68 and 70 until the Sunday morning?—Yes.

Your mother had the clothes which have been described, and you had just the clothes you stood up in?—That is correct. I had the usual toilet articles, toothbrush, flannel, razor and shaving things.

To those people who have been called—people from the hotel—did you make many statements which were untrue?—I did.

Why?—To impress them.

Were you financially in a position to stay at these hotels, and particularly at the Hotel Metropole?—No.

What was the state of your mother's health while you were at the Hotel Metropole?—The chill which I have told you about rather aggravated a previous attack of bronchitis, and she was unwell.

She was very bad on the Sunday morning?—Yes. When she rose she said she was very, very tired, but would dress. When I went upstairs to fetch her down I opened the door leading to the passage, and she fell down in a faint. It was

175

Sidney Harry Fox.

some while before I could get her up, but I lifted her up
to the best of my ability, and got her on to the bed. After
that I went to the hotel manager and asked him if he knew
a doctor.

Did Mr. Harding, the hotel manager, go up to the room
with you, and was it his suggestion that you should give
her some sal volatile?—Yes.

Did you telephone for a doctor?—Yes.

Before the doctor arrived did Mr. Harding suggest that
as there was no gas fire in room No. 68 your mother should
go to room No. 66?—Yes.

And the transfer was accordingly made?—Yes.

She was put to bed there?—Yes. She got much better in
the afternoon.

Dr. Austin saw your mother and wrote a prescription for
her. Did you take that prescription to Woolls, the chemist?
—Yes, the next day.

Did you pay the chemist a cheque which was not valid
and receive £1 16s. in change?—Yes.

What did you do with that money?—I gave some to Miss
Bickmore to look after my mother; I gave her half-a-crown.
I also bought some grapes and newspapers. I went to London
to try to borrow money from a friend with which to pay the
hotel bill.

When did you go to London?—I went to London on the
Monday evening by the 5.30 train.

Where did you stay?—I stayed in a boarding-house in
Liverpool Street, King's Cross, almost opposite Mrs. Platt's
house.

Were you anxious about your mother while you were away?
—Yes, I telephoned twice to inquire about her.

Did you succeed in borrowing a pound while you were
there?—Yes.

When did you return to Margate?—On the Tuesday
evening. I met Miss Bickmore when I arrived and she
said she was glad I had returned as my mother was worrying
about me, but when I got to the hotel I found her apparently
quite cheerful. I went upstairs with her later and then
came down to the dining-room for dinner. After dinner
I took her upstairs to her room and sat with her for a

176

Evidence for Defence.

Sidney H. Fox

quarter of an hour to twenty minutes before she went to bed.

When did she go to bed?—She went to bed about 9.30 in the evening.

When did you intend to leave the hotel? On the Wednesday?—Yes.

And why did you not?—At one time I broke my leg, and on the Tuesday night it gave me a considerable amount of pain. I was kept awake with it most of the Tuesday night. On the Wednesday I could hardly walk, but I massaged the leg myself and afterwards it got better.

Was the communicating door bolted?—It was bolted on the Monday night, but I could not say whether it was bolted on the Tuesday night or not.

Coming now to Wednesday, 23rd October, just tell us what you did that day?—By the time I got up on the Wednesday morning mother had got up and she came into my room. About 2.30 that day I went to Dover and got back about 5.30. I took my mother up to her room about 6.15 and she sat in front of the fire a little while. I think I put some pennies in the meter and lit the fire.

What did you do next?—I took her downstairs and we had dinner in the dining-room when I think she had half a pint of bitter. I think I had the same.

What did you do after dinner?—We spent about a quarter of an hour in the drawing-room and then I took my mother upstairs to her room. It would be about nine o'clock then. I lit the gas fire and my mother, who sat in the armchair in front of the fire, asked for an evening paper, which I fetched for her. I asked her if she would like a glass of port and she said she would, so I immediately went over the road to an off-licence place and purchased a half-bottle of port.

Had you ever done that before?—I had done it on many previous occasions, but not in Margate.

How much port did your mother drink?—About a quarter of the half-bottle, maybe a little more. I had the remainder.

When did you leave her?—A little after ten o'clock. I placed the cane chair near her in front of the fire to act as a table, the grapes and newspaper being upon it.

Sidney Harry Fox.

Sidney H. Fox

What was she doing when you left?—She was not in bed then. She was sitting by the fire eating grapes and reading either the *Evening Standard* or the *Evening News*.

Before you left did you help your mother to undress?—Yes, I took her dress off for her. I nearly always did that. I then took the eider-down from the bed and just wrapped it round her shoulders and left her reading the paper. I kissed her good-night and asked her if I should come in again and turn the light off but she said, " No, it is quite all right. I shall be getting into bed very shortly and I shall turn it out myself."

The half-bottle of port was finished before you left the room?—Yes. I placed the bottle in the cupboard in my room and I then went downstairs. I had a small glass of beer and read a newspaper in the bar. I had one glass of beer in one bar and one in the other. I went upstairs again after the lower bar was closed about 10.40 and went straight to my room and went to bed.

Did you go into your mother's room at all?—No, I did not.

What were your intentions with regard to the next day?—We had arranged to get up early and leave the hotel to go to London. My mother said she would get up early and have breakfast sitting up dressed in her room.

Did you inquire about your bill?—Yes, on the Tuesday night I inquired about the bill. It was not given to me. It was given to me on the Sunday and I returned it for some corrections.

How much was it?—About £16.

Well, you had no money to pay?—Quite.

Was it part of the pretence you were keeping up?—Yes.

Did you go to bed and to sleep?—Yes.

What was it that wakened you?—I heard a rattling noise. The wind was blowing very strongly, and I attributed the noise to the wind. I thought it was my window. I heard it rattle. I got out of bed and pushed it up. I smelt some burning, which I thought at the time had probably blown in, because overlooking my window were some chimneys from, I think, the Ship Hotel. I got back to bed, but I could still smell this smoke, which seemed even more pronounced. I got up and opened the corridor door and looked

178

Evidence for Defence.

Sidney H. Fox

out, but could not see anything. Then I suddenly remembered that I had left my mother sitting by the fire, and wondered whether she had turned the fire out or whether something was scorching. I opened the communicating door, and a volume of smoke met me, and I could not get into the room. The smoke was very, very thick. The room appeared to be in darkness, but there was just a glimmer where the gas stove was. You could not get into the room at all.

What was its effect upon you?—It knocked me out—made me choke.

What did you do?—I dashed downstairs as that was the quickest way to get help, and raised the alarm for every one else concerned, because, obviously, there was a fire, and I wanted help.

Did you get help?—I was choking and all that, and, being lame, I made the best effort I could. I ran downstairs, which I think I did very quickly. I dashed down in my vest exactly as I had got out of bed. It seemed some time before I could get them to realise what was wrong, but, probably, it was only a matter of a minute or a few seconds.

Can you remember what you did with the door when you rushed off?—I don't remember.

Did you go with the other people upstairs?—Yes. I think I went in front. They did not seem to understand. I thought they thought I was joking or was in my sleep. I thought they were not going to help me, and that I should have to go alone, but they realised then that there was something happening, and came up behind me. I went into the door I had come out of—the door of my room—and when I got in that was also full of smoke. I turned back, and then I thought the best way to get in would be through the corridor door, as it was close to the bed, and that we could get my mother from there.

Do you remember Mr. Hopkins trying to get in and being driven back?—I hardly remember. I remember seeing him drag my mother out.

Where were you then?—Just inside the door of No. 66. I had been trying to get in myself.

Sidney Harry Fox.

Was she being carried or dragged?—She was being held under the shoulders and dragged.

Did they move her along the corridor?—I was then in a state of collapse. The smoke was getting very thick in the corridor, making it difficult to see.

Do you remember her being carried downstairs?—Yes, I do.

Where about were you in relation to her?—I was walking exactly beside her.

Did you notice her head?—Her head was flopping about, and she looked unconscious.

Do you remember saying anything to the people who were carrying her?—Yes. There seemed to be rather a difficulty in carrying her, and I told them to be careful and not to drop her. If I remember rightly, I put my arm under her, but, of course, I was not much good. In the hall I knelt down on the floor beside her to see if I could be of any help. Someone asked who she was, and I said she was my mother. I was taken to the manager's room, and Dr. Nichol came and told me she was dead. I could not believe it and asked if I could see her. The doctor took me up to room No. 126. I was then taken to another room and Dr. Nichol gave me an injection. He mentioned that in cases of this kind it was generally necessary to have someone to represent you at the inquest. He mentioned a solicitor in Margate and gave me the name of Mr. Wilson.

Did you tell Dr. Nichol some things about your mother which were untrue—matters about her independency?—Yes, I am afraid I did.

Did you ask about some money in your mother's handbag?—Yes.

There was, of course, no money in her bag?—Not the amount I mentioned.

Why did you raise that question?—Because I did not want any one to think we were staying at the hotel without money.

Your statements about the house at Lyndhurst and Fox's Flour Mills in Norfolk were lies?—Yes.

Was it all part of your general conduct?—Yes.

You went to see Mr. Wilson in the morning, and you gave evidence at the inquest?—Yes.

Evidence for Defence.

Sidney H. Fox

You left the hotel on the Friday evening and went to the Royal Hotel?—Yes.

The burial was on Tuesday, 29th October?—Yes.

And you were arrested on the following Saturday, 2nd November, at Norwich, at an address which you had left with the police at Margate?—Yes.

Had your mother worn false teeth for a considerable time? —Since 1916.

Had she trouble with them?—She was always breaking them, and one of the springs broke the day before we left Belgium.

Was it ever repaired?—No.

Did she ever sleep with her teeth in?—No.

Why were the springs put on?—Because they were not comfortable, and after the spring broke they were not comfortable. She was more comfortable with them out than in.

When was the first insurance policy taken out for accidents in regard to your mother?—On the 2nd or 3rd of May. I took it out on her own instructions.

Why upon her instructions?—She had mentioned before that she had had similar accident policies. She wished to have her policy really in case she met with an accident in a bus smash or rail smash, or slipped in the street, so that she would be able to get good medical treatment. She had fallen in the street once and broken her foot, and the expenses incurred were fairly heavy.

The policies were taken out at different times between May and September, were they not?—Yes. They were similar to newspaper insurances, I think, only a little better.

Have you ever taken out a policy for yourself?—Yes, I once took out a £1000 accident policy for myself.

Your mother's policies expired on the 20th of October, and there was no policy on the 21st nor on the 22nd until you went to the Cornhill Insurance Offices in London and got the policy extended to midnight the next day?—Yes. I told them we were travelling the next day and asked if the policy of 20th October could be extended to the 23rd. They asked if I wanted it until noon and I said it would not be much good,

Sidney Harry Fox.

as we should not have finished our journey by then. They said, " Shall we make it until midnight ? " I agreed, and they said that, as it was such a short renewal, they would not trouble about any premium.

Did you also call at Pickfords and take a coupon ticket ?— Yes, it cost me 2s.

What was the insurance for yourself and your mother on 23rd October ?—£3000 in the event of death, £18 a week if she had been disabled, probably £9 a week if only partially disabled.

Did you ever see anything hanging in front of the fire in your mother's room ?—Yes. She was rather careless in the way she placed her clothes. I have seen a pair of combinations hanging over the chair as if to air in front of the fire, not only in Margate, but in other places.

If your mother had the opportunity would she wash out some of her clothes in the bedroom ?—I think so, yes.

After you left your mother sitting in the armchair, with the eider-down round her shoulders and the newspaper, until the moment when you went into the room and found it full of smoke, did you ever go into your mother's room ?—I never went inside the room.

Did you ever grip your mother's throat upon the bed ?— Never, sir.

Did you set fire to that room ?—I certainly did not.

With regard to these sham fights you had with your mother, they were just playfulness ; you were doing your best to cheer her up ?—Yes, we often played together. It used to amuse her. I would sometimes hold her hands—she was rather strong in the arms—and I would let her purposely release herself.

Had this taken place all the time you had been with her ? —Always.

Cross-examined by the ATTORNEY-GENERAL—How much money had you on the evening of 23rd October ?—I cannot say exactly, but approximately £1.

Had your mother any money ?—So far as I know, she had no money.

Did you get any money in London ?—I borrowed £1 from a friend, Mr. Gordon Campbell, the previous afternoon

182

Evidence for Defence.

Sidney H. Fox

before half-past four. I am prepared to give his address if necessary.

Was that all you borrowed? Was that all the money you had?—I borrowed no other money in London, but I had some loose change—probably about £1. I came back to Margate by train, and on the Wednesday afternoon I cashed my mother's and my own pension at Dover.

If your mother had not died on the night of the 23rd, what were you going to do on the 24th?—On the following day it was our intention to go to London. It was my intention to stay in London with a friend, and my mother was going to stay with some cousins named Rayner in Duncan Road, Highgate. I was going to stay with Mr. Luckson, a friend of mine.

Had any arrangements been made about those visits?—No, but we always had open invitations.

You and your mother had a joint income of 18s. a week? —Yes.

Had you any other source of income whatever?—No. I had pawned a good many things.

Was there anything left?—Our furniture in store in town and in store elsewhere. It could have been sold.

You mean to tell us you were visiting hotels and had money or money's worth all the time?—I do.

Where was your furniture stored?—With Messrs. Bowmans, London, N.W.1.

Under whose name?—In my name.

How long had it been there?—For about four or five years.

Would the storage charges not exceed the value?—No. I think the bill is about £6.

Where else had you furniture stored?—At Humphrey Brothers, Southsea.

Do you say that at the time you were pawning a safety razor for 1s. 3d. you had this furniture in London?—That is quite true.

Has that furniture not been sold?—Some articles have— about six.

Did a woman named Mrs. Parsby buy that furniture?— She bought several articles.

Sidney Harry Fox.

Did she agree to buy that furniture for £4 3s.?—She agreed to buy some for £4 odd.

Were there storage charges then of £7?—I cannot say. There are storage charges due now.

And did Messrs. Bowmans decline to allow the furniture to be removed?—That I cannot say. I have not seen Mrs. Parsby since.

When did Mrs. Parsby pay you for it?—In August, 1929. There are other things there which would cover the storage charges for £7 and far above.

If you really thought that, why were you passing bad cheques?—Mother's furniture was in London.

Did it seem a light thing to you to pass bad cheques?—No, sir.

Were you never pressed for your hotel bills?—No.

Do you say that at this hotel at Margate you did not intend to slip away without paying the bill?—It was not my intention to leave without any explanation. I was going to tell Mr. Harding I had not the money to pay, but that at a later date I would pay at the first available opportunity.

Did it occur to you that that plan might lead you into considerable trouble?—I do not think it would have done. I think Mr. Harding would have been prepared to wait.

How were you going to explain your failure to cash your mother's cheque?—Not sufficient funds to meet it.

How would you have dealt with the furniture and house at Lyndhurst?—I think it would have helped to give credit.

Did you anticipate that Mr. Harding might ask some awkward questions?—I did not anticipate that.

Do you remember the little matter of the cheque for £2 which you cashed at Woolls, the chemists?—Yes, that rather worried me.

You knew perfectly well what that sort of conduct was bound to lead to?—I did.

How were you going to deal with the matter of the cheque at Woolls?—My intention was to borrow the money from Mr. Luckson and send it to them. I knew the cheque was bound to come back.

Evidence for Defence.

Sidney H. Fox

Do you admit that the signature of Rosaline Fox on the cheque was written by you?—Yes.

In fact, it had been signed by you and addressed to a bank at which there was no account at all?—That is right.

Did you anticipate trouble about that cheque?—No, not if the money was repaid. It was in fact repaid.

It was paid from money you borrowed from your solicitor?—Yes.

Did you borrow the money from your solicitor by telling him a pack of lies?—I may have told him one or two untruths.

Did you tell him lies?—Yes.

About your telephone message to Mrs. Platt on 22nd October, do you admit that you did not intend to stay in London that night?—Yes, but I did that in order to obtain a loan.

Do you deny that the telephone message to Mrs. Platt that you were to be told, if you rang up, that your mother was ill and you were to return at once, was sent by you or for you, or that it was all part of your scheme?—Yes. I think the message was for some one else with a similar name.

This is no time for lies. You are on your oath?—I realise it.

And that when on oath you must stick to the truth?—I am telling the truth now.

Do you always stick to the truth when on oath?—I do.

The inquest was a solemn occasion?—It was a solemn occasion. No one realised it more than I did.

There you gave evidence on oath?—Yes.

Let me read you the first sentence—" My name is Sidney Harry Fox. Until now I have lived at 19 Cathedral Close, Norwich, and I am now moving to End View, Lyndhurst, Hants." Is there one word of truth in that except that your name is Sidney Harry Fox?—It is my name. It should be 19 Cathedral Street. The Lyndhurst address is certainly untrue.

Were you doing any work at the time?—No, I could not.

Your tastes, I gather, were, comparatively speaking,

Sidney Harry Fox.

expensive. You liked living in this sort of hotel, and you liked coming down to dinner?—No. I had had a lot of meals out, but not during the last week.

Everything valuable was pawned; you had 18s. a week coming in, and your expenses daily were vastly more than your weekly income?—During the last two months, yes.

That was the situation which confronted you on the night of the 23rd?—I never thought of that.

Do you mean to say on your oath that you never thought of it?—I do not say I never thought of it. I had, of course, because I had not the money to pay.

You had no other income?—My mother had money besides from friends. She had had gifts and loans from a friend, Mrs. Morse.

Who is Mrs. Morse?—She is a very well-to-do Australian lady. She was over here for three years, and lived with us whilst at Southsea practically the whole time. She returned to Australia at the end of last year.

Did she return to Australia shortly after or shortly before your mother's death?—I do not know the day she sailed.

You know a good deal about Mrs. Morse?—I do. She has lived with us.

She was a married woman living apart from her husband, Captain Morse?—Yes. He had business abroad.

And Captain Morse has instituted divorce proceedings against his wife?—Yes.

And you have been cited as co-respondent?—Yes, I have had the papers.

Is she now in Australia?—Either Hong-Kong or Australia.

Had she made a will?—Yes.

Had you seen it?—Yes.

What had she done with her money in that will?—She had left certain things to me, certain moneys.

Had there been any payment from Mrs. Morse to your mother from August, 1929, up to the date of your mother's death?—That I cannot say.

So far as you know, she received none?—So far as I know.

At the date when you made out your mother's will leaving you everything, what had she to leave you?—She had the

Evidence for Defence.

furniture in store, as I have told you, two diamond rings, three or four gold rings, and various pieces of jewellery.

Prior to the date of the will had you ever insured your mother against accident?—No, but I think she took them out herself before that. She told me she used to take out travel accident policies when she was going on a journey. It was entirely at her direction that I took the policies out, and it was she who wanted to know the meaning of " violent, visible, external means " on the policies. It was for that reason that I asked the agent the exact nature of the accidents which the policy covered.

Have you ever insured any one else?—Yes, in my position as agent.

Anybody in whom you had any interest?—Yes, Mrs. Morse, at her request.

Did you go into room No. 66 after the fire?—Yes, on two occasions. The first occasion I endeavoured to get in was when Miss Bickmore was sweeping up, to ask if she had found a necklace.

Why did you tell lies?—I told lies to impress them. That was my sole reason.

Why did you tell Miss Hopper and Mrs. Wager that the chemist had had to break the doctor's prescription down?—I do not remember saying that.

Do you mean us to understand that you deny saying that?—I do not deny it, but I do not remember saying it.

Did you say the chemist had to do it for fear of a fatal dose?—I do not deny that, but I do not remember saying it. If I did say it there was no ground for it.

Had you the question of an overdose in your mind?—No.

Did you see on the prescription the words " Chloroform water "?—I cannot say, as I did not read the prescription. I could not have done so had I tried. I did not know there was chloroform water in it.

How many doses of medicine were given to your mother?—I gave her one, but later in the day I found it had gone.

Gone? What do you mean?—The bottle was knocked over and the medicine spilt.

Was the bottle broken?—I do not remember.

187

Sidney Harry Fox.

Sidney H. Fox

Who knocked it over?—My mother.

Now that I have reminded you of this, are you still unable to remember whether you did or did not say to Miss Hopper or Mrs. Wager something about an overdose?—I cannot.

Had you an overdose in your mind?—No.

Had you ever, in connection with your mother, anything of that sort in your mind?—No.

Had you ever heard of a case in which a murderer had killed women by drowning them in a bath?—No, I cannot say I have.

Had you poisoning at a restaurant in your mind?—Yes. They were possible things which might happen to any one.

Did you say to the insurance clerk when you went for that first policy, " Would it include drowning in a bath "? —Yes.

Did you mention about poisoning from food in a restaurant?—Yes, I had a number of things in my mind.

Some fortnight before your mother's death, did the death of Walburgar Lady Paget take place?—Yes.

She was an old lady who died as the result of a fire?— I have never met Lady Paget. I do not know.

Is that what the papers said?—Yes, she was reading a newspaper in front of the fire when her dress caught fire. My mother read it out to me.

Did that make some impression on your mind?—No. I did not know Lady Paget. My mother knew her; they had met at the Red Cross.

After your mother's death did you not comment on the coincidence of their deaths to Dr. Nichol?—Yes. It came into my mind after I had collected my thoughts together.

Let me recall to you what you said about the medicine bottle being upset and your going to the chemist to get another. Did you think a spare bottle containing chloroform water would be useful in case of emergency?—I never thought of it. I did not know it contained chloroform water.

I want to ask you about that scorched cane chair from room No. 66 which you say was near the fireplace and which was used by your mother as a table on the night of 23rd October. Several witnesses have declared at the Police Court

Evidence for Defence.

Sidney H. Fox

that they never saw the chair, and it was eventually found in the front of the window near the wardrobe. If these witnesses are right the chair was not near the seat of the fire and yet that chair was burned. Did you move the chair? —I certainly did not. It would be impossible for any one to say definitely where the chair was with all the commotion that night.

Did you ever go into room No. 66 after the fire?—Yes, I did on two or three occasions. The first was when I had endeavoured to get in after the discovery of the fire, and the next day I went in when they were sweeping up the burned patch and asked if they had found a bead necklace which my mother had been wearing.

Did you realise when you opened the communicating door that the atmosphere in the room was such as would probably suffocate anybody inside?—If I had stayed in three or four moments I should have been suffocated.

So that you must have been greatly apprehensive for your mother?—I was.

Fox, you closed the door?—It is quite possible I did.

Can you explain to me why it was that you closed the door instead of flinging it wide open?—My explanation for that now is that the smoke should not spread into the hotel.

Rather that your mother should suffocate in that room than that smoke should get about in the hotel?—Most certainly not, sir.

Why, at a moment when you believed that your mother was in that room, did you trouble one twopenny-bit about the smoke getting into the hotel?—I have not admitted that I did shut the door. I very much doubt that I did.

Does it not strike you now as an inconceivable thing to have done?—Not in the panic I was in; I don't think it was.

I suggest the communicating door was closed. You don't dispute that?—I don't know.

Before rushing down you closed the door of your room?— I don't remember closing the door.

And then you passed the door of room No. 66?—I must have done so to get down.

Sidney Harry Fox.

Did you open that door?—Not then. What would have been the use?

Will you swear you did not?—Yes.

So that you left your mother, as you say, with the communicating door closed and with the door of room No. 67 closed; you passed the door of No. 66, but you did not open that, and you knew your mother was inside that room?—Yes, I did not stop to open the door. I rushed downstairs to get help which I think is quite a reasonable explanation.

Don't you think that before rushing down for help you might have flung the doors as wide open as you could?—No, I don't.

Why not?—Because I wanted to get help as quickly as possible.

Do you say you do not remember whether you closed your mother's door?—I hardly know what I did. It is all very well to try to pin me down to details, but I don't hardly remember what I did do. I was agitated at discovering the hotel on fire.

Discovering the hotel on fire? That was what made you agitated, was it?—Yes.

I should have thought that what would have made you agitated was your mother being in that room?—Certainly.

Which is it, now?—I do not remember. You cannot pin me down to detail. I cannot remember all that happened that night.

I suggest if you had wanted to preserve your mother's life you would have flung open the doors?—I tried to get in, and when I could not I dashed downstairs.

There was one thing between. You closed the door?—I do not remember.

Can you account for telling the witness Wager you did?—I cannot.

Your mother's dresses were found hanging behind the door?—Yes, I put them there.

Was your mother, then, sitting in her underclothes?—Yes.

But, Fox, you told the coroner at the inquest that you left your mother fully dressed?—That is partly the truth. I had taken her dress off for her, and I did not say so

190

Evidence for Defence.

Sidney H. Fox

because I considered it was an intimate thing to do. I did not mention it with all the people round about, although I am not ashamed of doing it.

And you departed from the truth because you did not want the world to know you helped your mother off with her outer clothes?—That is absolutely true.

I want to ask you a question about your mother's false teeth which were found in a basin and not in the glass. Why is it that any one who took the teeth over to the glass should not trouble to put them into the glass, unless they were in a desperate hurry?—The only answer to that is because she did not do so.

Do you know that a bottle of petrol was discovered in room No. 66?—I have heard it.

Is there any reason, so far as you know, why the bottle of petrol should have got into room No. 66?—No. I may have taken it there or my mother might have taken it. It was used for cleaning clothes on the Sunday, and might have been used since.

You see, Fox, if it had been difficult to start a fire it might have been handy to have a bottle of petrol near at hand?—I suppose it would, but I do not know anything about it, sir.

Why did you go out to purchase the half-bottle of port that night?—I bought it outside because I thought it would be cheaper.

You have told us you intended to leave without paying. Why not have had it put on the bill, in which case you would have had it free of charge? Why go and pay for it at an outside hotel?—Because I had sufficient money to pay for it.

Do you remember your mother having a French newspaper?—No. She had one or two circulars about motor coaches which had been given to her in France. She had them in her bag.

Does it strike you as an extraordinary coincidence that a month later there should be found, among the charred paper, some French paper?—If it was a French newspaper I cannot account for it being there.

Sidney Harry Fox.

Sidney H. Fox

You have heard that the pillow was found on a pedestal?
—Yes.

Did your mother sleep on the pillow?—As far as I know,
she always slept on the pillow.

And it was an odd coincidence that the pillow should be
found on the pedestal?—Yes.

Did you tell the coroner that you had had a "boxing
match" because you were apprehensive lest some bruise
should be discovered on your mother?—Certainly not. It
was friendly play. I held her hands and then let go.

Were you heartbroken at your mother's death?—Indeed,
I was.

Quite stricken down when you knew?—I don't think it is
necessary to ask.

Did Dr. Nichol show you all the kindness and consideration one individual could show to another?—Yes.

He took you up to the room where your mother was lying
dead?—Yes.

That was the most solemn moment of your life?—It was.

And then did you tell Dr. Nichol your mother had £24
in her bag?—Some time after I did, which was, of course,
untrue.

Were you still heartbroken when you told that lie?—Quite.

Why did you tell that lie?—I did not want it to be thought
she was staying there without any money.

That was the thing you intended to say the next morning?
—Certainly.

Were you scheming and plotting to tell this lie because you
thought you would have some claim upon the hotel?—Not
at all. It never entered my mind.

Did you think you would make another £25 while you
could?—Most certainly not.

Why did you always say Lyndhurst in your story?—Well,
we went there several times for the day when we were at
Southsea.

You made a statement about your mother having a fainting attack. If you had mentioned about your mother having
a faint attack this story about the sham fight would have
looked very stupid?—I never gave it a thought.

192

Evidence for Defence.

Sidney H. Fox

So you left out that bit about her having a faint?—I was not asked.

Mr. Justice Rowlatt—Perhaps it is fair to point out that Mr. Harding said Fox told him his mother was in a faint.

Cross-examination continued—With regard to the insurance policies, had you ever taken out policies on your mother's life prior to her making the will?—No.

Why, if you only wanted to insure your mother against accidents, did you take out one policy for death only?— I was not aware until the policy was actually delivered that it was only an insurance in the event of death.

Did it ever occur to you that it was a piece of amazing good fortune that you had the policies?—Never.

What was your real reason for taking out these policies? —I was apprehensive lest something might happen on a railway journey or by a motor coach.

Is the truth about these policies that you were desperately hard up for money?—I do not agree.

That you knew the life you were leading could only come to one end, and that quickly?—No. It would have ended the same day, because we were going to London.

That Mrs. Morse had gone to Australia, and you wanted to go to Australia?—I did not want to go to Australia, and I should never have gone in my mother's lifetime.

If your mother had died you were going there?—That was my intention.

Would you have gone to Australia if you could have raised the fare?—I should probably have been there by now.

Did you desperately want to get the money to pay your fare to Australia?—Certainly not.

Do you remember telling a prison official that you were a medical student?—No.

If you did so, that was another lie?—Yes.

[At this stage a man was brought into Court.]

Do you remember that man?—Yes.

Do you remember him saying to you, " Fox, you have described yourself as a student. What kind of student are you?"—No.

Sidney Harry Fox.

Sidney H. Fox

Has your memory gone?—I think at that time, taking into consideration everything that had happened and the horrible charge made against me of murdering my own mother, it was not to be wondered I could not remember everything.

Did you reply, " Medical student " ?—I do not remember.

Is it another lie?—If I said so.

Did you go into your mother's room on the night of 23rd October after she had gone to bed?—I did—to try to get her out.

Did you go in before there was a fire at all?—Certainly not.

Did you go towards the bed before there was any fire?—No.

And stretch out your hand against your own mother?—Most certainly not—horrible.

Did you then start a fire?—Certainly not.

Did you move that cane chair back to the window?—Most certainly not.

Did you go out of that room into your own room, shut the door, and then give the alarm?—No, no—decidedly not.

Did you destroy your mother on the night of 23rd October in order that you might reap £3000 from those insurance policies?—Most certainly not. It is a horrible suggestion—horrible.

Re-examined by Mr. CASSELS—Did you know that if you were to strangle a woman in her bed you could do it without leaving a mark?—No.

Or that it was possible to produce only such a bruise as could only be found and seen one day, and would disappear the next?—No.

Have you ever heard of a case of trying to drown a woman in her bath?—No.

Have you ever tried to drown your mother in her bath, or to give her any poison?—Never.

You have been asked very pointedly by my learned friend whether you strangled your mother for £3000. Were there occasions during the three to four months when your mother had been actually insured, in so far as a death claim is concerned, for £4000?—There were.

194

Evidence for Defence.

Sidney H. Fox

It has been suggested that you shut your mother in that room and left her to suffocate. Was there such a thought in your mind when you rushed downstairs for assistance?—Never. If I closed the door it was in the panic of rushing down to get help.

PRIDIE SINCLAIR, examined by Mr. CASSELS—I reside at 3 Alexandria Road, Brentwood. I have known the accused and his mother for four or five years. They stayed at my house twice, the first occasion, as far as I remember, being from January, 1926, for four months as paying guests, and again from October to December of that year. On the second occasion the accused had a broken leg. I have not seen them since 1926. The deceased appeared to be in a dazed condition—a kind of stupor—when I saw her in 1926. I have seen the accused playing all sorts of games with the deceased; they were both very affectionate and playful. The deceased used to take her teeth out at dinner and complained about them hurting her.

Mrs. EDITH FRANKLIN, examined by Mr. CASSELS—I reside at Denton Road, Holloway, and I have known the accused and his mother for ten years. On occasions during the last few years the accused would bring his mother to my house and leave her for a few hours and return for her. The last occasion was in July, 1929. The accused was always affectionate and devoted to his mother, and used to play with her, but he was never rough. He would get hold of her by the shoulders and pat her cheek.

Professor SYDNEY ALFRED SMITH, examined by Mr. CASSELS—I am Regius Professor of Forensic Medicine in Edinburgh University. I was formerly Professor of Forensic Medicine in the University of Egypt and Principal Medico-Legal Expert to the Government of Egypt. I have had a long experience of cases involving manual strangulation, and I have examined a large number of bodies exhumed in which the allegation was made that they had been manually strangled.

On Saturday, 8th March, I visited Sir Bernard Spilsbury's

Sidney Harry Fox.

Professor Smith

laboratory at University College, Gower Street, and saw all
that he had available connected with the deceased. I saw
parts of the neck, the larynx and gullet, and microscopical
sections of the tongue, the heart wall, the coronary artery,
kidneys, liver, thyroid gland and epiglottis, and I made
examinations of the parts shown to me. I have seen the
transcript of the evidence given at the previous inquiry,
and I have also heard the medical evidence given in this
Court. In a case of death from asphyxia I should expect
to find a bluish or purple colour of the lips and ears, and a
change of colour of the nails. If a person was strangled
quickly the signs would be less than if it was done slowly. I
should expect to find some froth, which may or may not be
bloodstained, about the nose or mouth; the tongue is usually
forced outwards, and the hands are usually clenched. These
are the ordinary signs of asphyxia. In manual strangulation, marks would be found of the fingers on the surface of
the skin of the neck—the indentation of nails and pressure
of the tips of the fingers. If the victim attempted to pull
away the hand of the murderer there would be the tendency
to scratch the neck. On opening the body I would expect
to find general signs of asphyxia, such as enlargement of the
vessels leading to the heart, congestion of the lungs, and
other organs of the body. The high blood pressure might
cause small spots of hæmorrhage on the surface of different
organs, such as the lungs, heart, and occasionally other
organs. The trachea, or windpipe, and the smaller air tubes
frequently contain froth which may or may not be bloodstained, and in addition one expects to find signs of manual
strangulation underneath the skin and in the tissues. You
may have bruises in the muscles surrounding the neck and
in the larynx. In addition, especially in elderly people, it is
common to get fracture of the cartilages of the larynx, and
particularly of the hyoid bone. As age advances the hyoid
bone becomes brittle and is easily broken, and this is one
of the most characteristic marks of manual strangulation. In
fact a fractured hyoid bone is most important in diagnosing
the cause of death in exhumed bodies.

[At this stage the witness produced two hyoid bones, one

Evidence for Defence.

Professor Smith

from a young person in which ossification had not properly set in, and one from an old person which was fully ossified.]

Was the hyoid bone ossified in this case?—Yes.

Was it brittle?—Yes, it was so brittle that Sir Bernard Spilsbury broke it in two places while taking it out or in examining it.

Was the thyroid cartilage ossified?—Yes.

Were any of the cartilages of the larynx damaged?—No.

Could any of those cartilages have resisted violence?—If they had been gripped by the hand in manual strangulation I would have expected them to have been smashed.

Did you find any sign of injury of any part of the tissues shown to you?—No trace whatever.

Were there any bruises at the back of the larynx?—No.

Could the larynx have been immediately preserved in such a condition that other people could have observed it in the same way as Sir Bernard Spilsbury observed it when it was immediately taken out of the body?—Yes, it could have been preserved in formalin.

If blood is diffused or spread into the tissues, so as to form a bruise, is it likely to disappear rapidly?—It cannot disappear. There was no bruise on the back of the larynx when I saw it, and I do not consider that there ever was a bruise there.

Sir Bernard Spilsbury says that he saw a bruise the size of half-a-crown behind the larynx when he exhumed the body. What do you have to say about that?—I think it quite possible that it was a patch of discoloration from post-mortem staining or putrefaction.

Is it easy to distinguish between a bruise and a post-mortem stain?—No, it is difficult to tell by the naked eye, and, after putrefaction has occurred, it is often impossible.

Would microscopic examination be advisable?—Certainly, no opinion is justifiable in such circumstances as these without the demonstration of effused blood, either by cutting out the patch or by microscopic examination.

Did you find any bruises on the thyroid gland?—There was no trace of bruising that I could see.

Sir Bernard Spilsbury says that there were bruises on the

197

Sidney Harry Fox.

Professor Smith

thyroid gland?—Sir Bernard Spilsbury is, of course, entitled to his opinion, but I saw nothing but a few stray red blood corpuscles such as might be found in a section of any ordinary thyroid.

You consider that these were of no importance?—I am convinced that they have no indication whatever of violence.

Did you find bruises on the epiglottis?—There was a spot of hæmorrhage the size of the point of a pin, such as might be found on five out of six cases in which the death was natural.

Concerning the bruise on the tongue which you saw, what was the size of that bruise?—It was about the size of a split pea.

And do you think that could have been caused by getting the tongue between the teeth?—Yes.

Could you say when it was caused?—It is difficult to say when it was caused, but it was certainly recent.

Is it possible that such an injury could have been caused by throttling and forcing the tissues up against the teeth?—Yes, but I do not think that could be done without signs on the tissues round about and the breaking of the hyoid bone.

Supposing this bruise had been caused by the grip of a murderer ——?—I should expect to find injuries in the throat. In cases of murder you usually get the whole of the hand grasping the throat. There is usually no delicacy of touch in a murderer; he is always violent. He would move rapidly. He would want to get his victim killed at the earliest possible moment.

Would you expect to find external traces of violence?—Yes, I would expect to find marks of the nails or finger tips on the skin of the neck and bruising on the tissues underneath.

Nothing of this sort was found?—No, there were no traces of violence on the surface of the body, on the tissues under the skin, or in the cartilages. Nor were there any of the ordinary signs of asphyxia either on the surface or in the internal organs.

Would the carrying of Mrs. Fox's body from the room

198

Evidence for Defence.

Professor Smith

and the subsequent artificial respiration produce some injury to the tongue?—It might.

Having seen and heard everything in this case, and with your experience of throttling cases, would you be prepared to give an opinion that throttling was the cause of death in this case?—I would not.

Would you be prepared to take such a responsibility?—I would not.

What have you to say with regard to the condition of the other organs of the body?—I think in this case you have all the conditions that would justify you in assuming that the body, without other definite signs, had died a natural death. The heart was in an advanced state of degeneration, the coronary arteries were dislocated, and the kidneys were cirrhosed. If there was any additional strain upon the already weakened heart, such as sudden violence, attempt at exertion, or fright, it would tend to precipitate death.

Waking up and finding the room full of smoke—might that do it?—Yes. I do not think that sufficient significance has been attached to the position of Mrs. Fox's body on the bed. The bedclothes were turned back, the legs were hanging over the edge of the bed, and the head was towards the back of the bed. It rather suggested that death had taken place just as she was getting out of bed.

If there had been throttling would it not suggest that some struggle had taken place?—Yes; but if a person was strangled in the position in which Mrs. Fox was lying on the bed the murderer would have had to lean well over the bed or cross his hands, which would have meant losing some power of gripping with the right hand.

Does the absence of soot from the air passages necessarily mean that the person was dead before the fire started?—No. She may have breathed for a certain length of time through the nose without getting those particles into the lungs.* There is another point, and that is that when artificial respiration was performed this woman was turned on her

---

* The mucous membrane of the nose was not examined by the Crown experts.

Sidney Harry Fox.

Professor Smith

face, and it is quite possible that a certain amount of carbon particles would be lost in the mucus which would run from the nose.

Have you ever known of a case of manual strangulation with fewer signs, or as few?—Never.

Would you take the responsibility of saying she had died from it?—I could not.

The Court adjourned.

Evidence for Defence.

Eighth Day—Thursday, 20th March, 1930.

Professor SYDNEY ALFRED SMITH, cross-examined by the ATTORNEY-GENERAL—You stated in your evidence-in-chief that you had a very long experience in cases involving manual strangulation?—Yes.

Were they cases of strangulation by a young man of an old woman as the old woman lay in bed?—I have had many cases of strangulation of elderly men and elderly women.

Will you try to answer my question?—I will think of the special conditions for one moment. Yes, I have had.

Do you mean to tell us you had not considered that question before you came to give evidence in this case?—I have considered the question.

Then I take it you have brought your notes of a person being strangled in bed?—No, I have not.

Was there one case, or more than one case?—I have had many cases of a somewhat similar nature. May I explain?

Please answer my question. It may be difficult for a gentleman who gives lectures to answer questions, but I want you to answer mine?—I had a case which occurred some years ago in the East. An elderly woman was strangled by her husband, a young man, as she lay in bed. The body was put into a sack, and the murderer tried to dispose of it afterwards.

Assuming the fact of a young man about to end his mother's life and trying to make it appear that the woman had lost her life in connection with a fire, it is perfectly manifest that he would have to guard against two things— leaving obvious marks upon the neck and any cry from the victim?—Yes.

That is very different from a case in which the murderer is going to run away or dispose of the body?—Yes.

Do you agree that a pillow would be a handy instrument to prevent a cry?—Yes.

Do you also agree that in a case of suffocation by a pillow there might be no external marks except those of asphyxia-

Sidney Harry Fox.

tion, although injury to the lips is fairly common?—Yes.

Biting the tongue is also fairly common?—Yes.

[The Attorney-General then read from " Taylor's Medical Jurisprudence," of which Professor Smith said he was one of the editors, passages dealing with cases of suffocation. (Eighth edition, volume I, page 656.) He quoted the following passage :—" None of these signs is at all characteristic, and the absence of all of them is no proof that death did not occur from suffocation."]

Do you agree with that?—I agree with it in general, but I will say this, that as a rule with these cases you get some signs of asphyxia.

You said a moment ago you must get these signs. Do you adhere to that?—Yes.

Then do you agree with the statement I have quoted?— I agree with it.

[The Attorney-General then read an extract dealing with internal signs from page 658.]

I refer you to the passage where it says, " Again it must be repeated that none of these features is constant or characteristic, and in a very large proportion of cases there is absolutely nothing to suggest the cause of death "?—I quite agree with that. Even if you have all these things there you would not be entitled to say that death was due to suffocation.

Do you think that is being quite candid with me? Is it not perfectly plain that the editors of this book are pointing this out, that in cases of this sort—death by suffocation—you may get no external appearances at all?—I agree with the passage, always taking into consideration that Taylor was dealing with the possibilities of instantaneous death. If death occurs instantaneously you get none of these things.

If you get instantaneous death it is not asphyxia. Do you say Taylor is not dealing with asphyxial death at all? —Taylor is dealing with smothering.

And that is death by asphyxia?—Yes. But if you get instantaneous death, however caused, you cannot get signs of asphyxia.

Is Taylor dealing with death by asphyxia?—Yes.

Evidence for Defence.

she might have taken down a certain amount of carbon monoxide, but it certainly did not cause her death.

Re-examined by Mr. CASSELS—If the form of manual strangulation was such that it could produce a bruise on the back of the larynx, in your opinion must it have produced other injuries by the pressure of the fingers?—Yes.

Supposing you had no external appearance of asphyxia and no internal appearance of asphyxia, what would you say then?—I would say that I did not know what the cause of death was.

Would it be possible to prove the presence of a bruise by merely looking at it?—It would be a physical impossibility.

Do you remember Sir Bernard Spilsbury saying that the heart was moderately enlarged?—Yes.

That there was failure of the heart muscle?—Yes.

And disease of the coronary artery of the heart?—Yes.

Those are conditions which predispose to sudden death?—Disease of the coronary artery is one of the commonest causes of sudden death.

You were shown certain slides by Sir Bernard Spilsbury made from the epiglottis. Did you see any bruises in those sections or anything suggesting strangulation?—What I looked at was evidence of a small hæmorrhage, which is common without manual strangulation.

Was it possible to deduce throttling from what you saw on the slide?—Absolutely impossible.

And if a pillow was used would you expect to find anything?—You commonly get a stain on the pillow, usually saliva or bloodstain.

At any rate you would expect to find in a case of manual strangulation some signs of violence, either external, internal, or both?—Yes. In my experience I have never known a case of manual strangulation with so few signs.

You referred yesterday to " sudden violence." What did you mean by that?—I meant violent effort on the woman's part, thus putting up the blood pressure.

By Mr. JUSTICE ROWLATT—Supposing the woman had been found lying dead in the position she was, with the body, externally and internally, in the condition it was, and there

205

Sidney Harry Fox.

Professor Smith

had been no question of a fire, could you have given an opinion as to the cause of death?—In such a case I should have been of opinion that she died from heart failure.

Heart failure just by pure accident?—Yes, my lord.

Dr. ROBERT MATTHEW BRONTE, examined by Mr. CASSELS —I was formerly Crown Pathologist for all Ireland. I have had twenty-three years' experience of post-mortem examinations, and I have conducted many thousands of such examinations. I visited Sir Bernard Spilsbury's laboratory with Professor Smith, and I agree with the evidence given by Professor Smith. From what I saw, and from the evidence of Sir Bernard Spilsbury as to the mark at the back of the larynx, I am prepared to say that it was not a bruise, and must have been a post-mortem change. If it had been a bruise it would have been there so long as the tissue or organ existed and would have been capable of demonstration. It would be impossible to make such a bruise without some external mark. I don't see how bruising of the inner tissues could occur without bruising of the tissues themselves. I agree with Dr. Weir and Professor Smith that no such bruise is to be seen in the thyroid. With regard to the epiglottis, Sir Bernard Spilsbury gave me a slide and I saw some blood through tissues, but it was impossible to say whether or not it was due to natural causes. No evidence has been produced in my hearing that Mrs. Fox died from asphyxia. Sir Bernard Spilsbury has omitted the usual signs one always gets in asphyxia. On the material available to me, my opinion is that Mrs. Fox died of heart failure as the result of disease of the vessels of the heart and disease of the muscles of the heart, accelerated by shock.

Was she in such a condition that fright would bring about sudden death?—Yes. I saw a section of the tongue corresponding to the third molar from the left side. The bruise on the tongue, which was about the size of half a pea, might have been caused very soon after death, but much more probably some time before death.

And as regards the use of a pillow, must there have been froth round the mouth and nose?—Yes, and it is inconceivable that the pillow was not stained by it.

206

Evidence for Defence.

Dr. Bronte

Cross-examined by the ATTORNEY-GENERAL—When were you first asked if you could assist in this case?—Mr. Hindle first asked me at 2.30 on Thursday, 23rd January, if I would assist him in this case. I said I could not say until I got the report of the medical evidence. I saw the evidence and I consented to assist him on 18th March.

You had not at that time seen any of the slides or specimens?—No.

You did not know what you were going to find?—Oh yes, from Sir Bernard Spilsbury's evidence.

Sometimes, you know, specialists with the best will in the world may take a preconceived view of a case and make things fit into it?—I do not think that applies to specialists in the line I specialise in.

It applies to most specialists, but perhaps not in your case?—If I had found all the traces Dr. Spilsbury said he found I should have been in entire agreement with him.

Are you agreeing with everything Professor Smith has said?—Practically.

Did you observe Dr. Weir did not agree with everything Sir Bernard Spilsbury said?—Yes.

That shows that Dr. Weir is a man of independent mind? —The insinuation is that I am not, I suppose. If so, I disagree with you.

I made no insinuation about you at all, sir. Do you know Dr. Weir as a very distinguished practising pathologist?—Yes.

He accepted without hesitation that Sir Bernard had seen that bruise. Do you accept it?—No. I only say I did not see it.

Are you suggesting Sir Bernard did not see what he said he saw?—Far be it from me to make such a suggestion.

Do you suggest that Sir Bernard Spilsbury was wrong, and that it was a post-mortem change?—I say it was not there when I saw the larynx. I cannot say what Sir Bernard Spilsbury saw.

If Sir Bernard Spilsbury made this mistake it would be a very elementary mistake to make?—No.

It is a sort of mistake that every laboratory assistant is warned against?—No.

Sidney Harry Fox.

Dr. Bronte

By Mr. JUSTICE ROWLATT—Then it really comes to this, that you did not see the bruise, and that you are not prepared to accept it?—I am not.

Cross-examination continued—Do you really say that, without any microscopical slide, you can by looking at an object subjected to putrefactive changes tell whether a bruise was present?—I shall answer in the affirmative, and go further and say putrefactive changes magnify the bruise and make it easier to detect. Sir Bernard Spilsbury himself, four or five years ago, gave similar evidence in this very Court.

Do you mean at the Thorne case?—Yes.

Did you give evidence that that unfortunate girl had hanged herself by a cord?—No.

Did you by your evidence support that theory?—Yes.

Did you say that you could see the marks of the cord on her neck?—Yes.

Did the jury accept that theory?—No.

Are you conscious of the fact that the textbooks do not agree with your statement that in cases of suffocation there must be signs of froth?—I am not. I feel myself fully able to proclaim my own opinion upon my experience. It is so long since I read textbooks.

Do you give it as your opinion that the pillow was not used for suffocation in this case?—Yes, because there were no froth marks on the pillow.

What is it that stains the pillow?—The mucus from the mouth and nostrils.

If you found every other sign of asphyxia except the presence of froth would you still say there had been no asphyxia?—No, I do not say that. If I found no external and internal signs of asphyxia I cannot say death has been due to asphyxia. I found no evidence of asphyxia.

You may get death from strangulation without marks on the neck?—Yes, but it is uncommon. In manual strangulation death results from shock and not from asphyxia.

[At this stage the witness was questioned about the degree of pressure on the throat necessary to cut off the air, and the Attorney-General stated that Mrs. Fox's thyroid cartilage

208

Evidence for Defence.

was in Court, and, if necessary, Sir Bernard Spilsbury would give a demonstration of its pliability. The witness said that the cartilage had been preserved in glycerine, which would alter it, and he would not, therefore, want a demonstration.]

If you heard Sir Bernard Spilsbury had been able to do it on the day of the post-mortem, would that alter your view?—The body had been buried some days.

So, whatever I show you, I shall not influence you?—Not as to facts I can swear to. Remember, I am on my oath. I have not the slightest doubt in saying that no one could suffocate me without damaging my throat.

[The Attorney-General proceeded to read extracts from a book about thugs, and witness said he did not know what a " thug " was.]

Well, a type of Indian robber. You have heard of Indian thugs?—Yes.

And you know that they have a specially constructed finger band so adjusted as to enable them to strangle a person without any sign?—I agree. In the case of people in such a condition as Mrs. Fox one frequently finds hæmorrhage in the epiglottis. The bruise on the tongue could have been caused two or three hours before death, or a couple of minutes after, and while the teeth were in the mouth.

LEONARD STANLEY BAKER, examined by Mr. CASSELS—I am a dental mechanic in Lewes. I have examined Mrs. Fox's false teeth. The springs they were fitted with were to support them in the mouth, as the gums had no suction. With only one spring they would be supported on one side and come down on the other.

Cross-examined by the ATTORNEY-GENERAL—The spring on the teeth was a cheap one, costing about sixpence.

Evidence for the defence closed.

Sidney Harry Fox.

Closing Speech for the Defence.

Mr. CASSELS—Members of the jury, when this case was opened last week it was described as being unparalleled in the history of the country. The case for the prosecution has been presented to you with the strength that one would expect from the presence here of the Attorney-General of England, and bit by bit it has been built up from the evidence of an enormous number of witnesses, dealing with various branches of the case. You will agree, whatever view you may take, that no point has been omitted; no circumstance, if it is capable of interpretation, which would be calculated to provide you with an impression upon the side of the prosecution, has been left out of consideration in this Court. You will, in the course of a few hours, retire to consider your verdict. Midst this mass of evidence to which you have listened you will have to sift the important parts from the unimportant, and I ask you, for the defence, to apply yourselves carefully and with all the attention of which you are capable to what I conceive, and I think you will conceive, to be the one real main issue in this case, and that is : did Mrs. Fox die at the strangling hand of her son from asphyxia, or did she die a death from natural causes in which the hand of her son took no part? The onus rests entirely upon the prosecution.

Take the medical evidence, and let me ask you this : does that evidence leave you in any doubt upon that real main issue? If it does, the accused is entitled to be acquitted. What did Dr. Nichol and Dr. Austin say on the night of the tragedy? Sir Bernard Spilsbury's conclusion was that she died from asphyxia. In asphyxia you would expect the eyes to be bulging, the tongue protruding, froth, &c. Sir Bernard agreed some of those things might be found and reasonably expected. Dr. Austin and Dr. Nichol both say they saw no signs of death by asphyxia, and there was absence of marks on the outside of the throat. Is that a circumstance which you are going to entirely ignore? We have had a certain amount of explanation of what might happen, and, supposing you are satisfied with that, we are some dis-

Closing Speech for the Defence.

Mr. Cassels

tance from the point upon the larynx where Sir Bernard Spilsbury says he found the bruise. There is no bruising of the tissues between. In that connection I would remind you of the phrase of Professor Smith that " there is no delicacy of touch about a murderer."

The accused has throughout been presented to you as a desperate man whose financial straits were calling upon him almost at that hour to do something of a drastic nature in order to improve his position. You may well think it is a remarkable performance, if the case for the prosecution is true, that he, not being a doctor or a man skilled in the manipulation of the throat, should have carried out this crime in such a manner that it deceived two doctors, who, within half an hour of the death, were casting their eyes upon the body and would have been capable of observing what had happened—deceived everybody who came on the scene that night and the next day, in such circumstances that no one could suggest he was responsible. Not only that, but to do it in such a way that the coroner ordered no post-mortem examination, and there did not occur in the mind of a single person who had an opportunity of considering the circumstances at the moment the slightest suspicion. Is it not amazing that whilst this case comes before you as one of throttling, you find the external signs are missing and the damage you would expect upon the structure of the throat absent? Is it not inconceivable that the crime should have been carried out in such a way that absolutely no outward or visible sign was available for observers after death? We are left to decide this case on the merits of a mark, the size of half a crown, at the back of the larynx, and upon a pinpoint of blood upon the epiglottis, both of which are put forward to you with all the authority of a distinguished pathologist as being bruises, or the signs of bruising. There was, of course, another at one time—another pinpoint mark, which, under a microscope was said to be a sign of bruising upon the thyroid gland— that mark which Sir Bernard Spilsbury still retains his opinion about, but does not desire to have as much importance attached to it as to the other two, because Dr. Weir,

211

Sidney Harry Fox.

Mr. Cassels

Professor Smith, and Dr. Brontë did not agree with him. If Sir Bernard Spilsbury is wrong about one thing, and bearing in mind the gravity of this case, might he not be wrong about something else? It will be a sorry day for the administration of criminal justice in this land if we are to be thrust into such a position that, because Sir Bernard Spilsbury expresses an opinion, it is of such weight that it is impossible to question it, and it must be accepted by the jury. Do not think I am making any personal attack upon Sir Bernard Spilsbury; but whoever the person may be, if he expresses an opinion in a Court of law he is liable to criticism, and it is right that one should be in a position to criticise it, and even to call evidence which would be in disagreement with it.

With regard to the half-crown bruise, you may well think it is unfortunate that in a case like this, where it must have dawned upon those who were investigating it that it was bound to be a difficult case, steps were not taken immediately that mark was seen to preserve it from the effects of any further putrefaction, and to have had it available for inspection by others. No person other than Sir Bernard Spilsbury has seen that mark, and I submit that that evidence rests upon the observation of one man at one moment, and no one can say that an individual, whatever his position and skill, is never likely to be mistaken. I know it will be said—would you expect that a man of his eminence would be likely to mistake for the mark of a bruise that which was in fact a post-mortem change? No one can claim for anybody infallibility. Is there sufficient for you to come to a conclusion on this one mark? In my opinion that bruise has been getting a place far too high—much higher than it really deserves—in the case for the prosecution, because, in order to bring it into a place in this case, you must propound theories, you must make suggestions, you must reconstruct, and when you get in the realms of theory, suggestions, and reconstruction, in a case of this kind, you are treading upon ground which is very dangerous.

Every morning Mrs. Fox's teeth were in a glass on the wash-hand stand except one night when they were knocked

212

Closing Speech for the Defence.

Mr. Cassels

off the stand. The dental mechanic told us that with one spring off, Mrs. Fox would have great difficulty in keeping the teeth in the mouth. Medical opinion has gone into the state of the physical condition of Mrs. Fox when she died. Leave out suspicion and motive here. Dr. Weir has said there was sufficient disease to account for death, and Professor Smith and Dr. Brontë agreed with him. Sir Bernard Spilsbury said the disease was not sufficiently serious. She had heart and kidney disease and hardening of the arteries. Are you left free from doubt? In my submission, if suspicion were removed there is ample justification for saying that Mrs. Fox died suddenly from fright and sudden exertion. If you were to examine the certificates of death of people who had died in this country between sixty and seventy years of age how many would be certified to be due to some of the things found in this woman?

With regard to the fire, I ask you to leave out for the moment, the suggestion that it was not an accidental fire, and consider the effects likely to be produced upon a woman of Mrs. Fox's condition, who, having gone to bed, was wakened suddenly by the presence of smoke and burning, and perhaps flames in the room. It might have been the case that some of her clothes had been left in such a position as to have caught fire. Don't you think she would have been frightened and have made an effort to rise and get out of bed as soon as possible? Perhaps she was wakened by a violent fit of coughing, and, remembering the nature and condition of her heart and arteries and other organs, I invite you to say that if you remove suspicion from this case you have ample justification for saying: "Here is a case of a woman who has died suddenly by fright and exertion which her heart was incapable of sustaining." There are many considerations before you can accept what has been put before you by the prosecution that it was not an accidental fire. The man who is supposed to have deliberately brought it about was the first to give the alarm and bring the hotel people into the room before it had a chance to do its work. A book, matches, and a bottle of

213

Sidney Harry Fox.

petrol were untouched, and surely the stockinette dresses would have been of more value to any one making a fire put on the flames than left hanging behind the door. If it was an intentional fire, it was another remarkable performance on the part of the accused that the police officers, the firemen, and guests in the hotel were deceived.

With regard to the cane-seated chair, can you imagine a more stupid act by a person who started a fire than to use a cane-seated chair at the beginning of the fire, get it partially burning, and then take it away, putting it by the window? The chair was never produced until the accused requested that it should be. It is not altogether outside the realm of possibility that the woman may have washed some clothes in the room and hung them over the cane-seated chair to dry. As regards the bottle of petrol, the Attorney-General said that it might well be that no petrol at all was used from that bottle. In a case of this gravity you must not jump to a conclusion without evidence that there was another bottle containing petrol from which the man sprinkled some after murdering his mother.

Motive has loomed large in this case. The insurances are matters of no little importance in this case. They have been put to you as being the driving power in this crime. You will not lose sight of the manner in which it has been put to you—a will made on 21st April, and the first insurance taken out on 4th May. What is the object of emphasising those two dates if it is not that at some time he would put the life out of his mother, which would justify a claim by him for the money due under the policies? If the accused had wanted to murder his mother, he had many other occasions when policies were in force. On the first day at the Hotel Metropole Mrs. Fox was insured for £4000 at death, which was a larger amount than on the day she did die. On 23rd October there was a £2000 policy which cost nothing to extend to that day, and a £1000 policy which cost 2s., and for another 2s. could have been made for £2000. During the whole of the twenty-four hours of 23rd October Mrs. Fox, if she died accidentally, might have provided for those who were left behind a sum of £3000. Why did this

214

Closing Speech for the Defence.

Mr. Cassels

young man not take advantage of the first of those twenty-four hours? If he had been a man with murder in his heart, what was to prevent him doing it in the small hours of Wednesday morning when the hotel was asleep, when there could not possibly have been any disturbance, when the last hour of the policies was twenty-two or twenty-three hours away, leaving for those who came upon the scene afterwards no trace and no sign of what had happened in room No. 66? You are asked to say that this man, murderously inclined, determined and desperate, capable of the most diabolical crime it is possible to imagine, killed the mother who had borne him, in the last hour of the twenty-four available. Do not supply to the weakness on one side of this case what you may think is the strength on another.

May I draw a significance from the gas fire? What easier than to fill the slot of the gas meter, and, while his mother lay asleep, to go and turn on the gas and leave her to suffocate in that atmosphere? What easier than to explain that this suffering old woman in turning out the fire had turned it on again?

The accused has been in the witness-box and subjected to a long and strong cross-examination. If this had been a case in which the charge was obtaining food and lodging by false pretences, if it had been a case in which the matter which you were investigating was whether he had passed as some one he was not, whether he rarely spoke the truth, whether he was a man who deceived everybody with whom he came into contact, out of his own mouth what a case there was! But on the real issue which you are trying, was he demonstrated to your satisfaction out of the cross-examination by the Attorney-General as a man who had murdered his mother?

Members of the jury, upon you rests the greatest responsibility in this case. If you are going to be satisfied in the years to come with a verdict of guilty—satisfied that you have not done wrong or made a mistake, and satisfied upon this evidence—don't let any word of mine cause you to depart from the duty which you owe to the oath which you have taken. But, members of the jury, remember what you are

Sidney Harry Fox.

trying, remember the terrific responsibility which rests upon you—be satisfied. If you are not, then it is your duty, and law and justice demand, that your verdict upon this charge of murder shall be one of acquittal.

[The Attorney-General did not return to the Court after the luncheon adjournment, and when Mr. Cassels had concluded Sir Henry Curtis Bennett rose to make the final speech for the Crown. He explained that public duties had called Sir William Jowitt away.]

Closing Speech for the Crown.

Sir HENRY CURTIS BENNETT—Members of the jury, it is the duty of prosecuting counsel to calmly bring to the notice of the jury the facts of the case, and it is the clear duty of the jury to give their verdict according to the evidence. The onus is upon the prosecution to prove beyond reasonable doubt that the charge is a true one. Most cases of this kind rest upon circumstantial evidence, for there are rarely eye witnesses of murders, but upon circumstantial evidence a case might be proved with greater strength than where there were eye witnesses telling a story in which you might believe.

Before Mrs. Fox made her will on 21st April of last year, leaving practically everything to the accused, there is no evidence that Mrs. Fox was ever insured except for the sum of ten guineas. That will having been signed on 21st April, on 4th May, a fortnight afterwards, we find that for the first time the accused was insuring his mother. I do not want it to be thought for one moment that I am suggesting that at that moment the accused intended to murder his mother. I do not know. It may well be that you will come to the conclusion that when he first insured his mother, the will having been made in his favour, he thought there might be some accident and that she might suffer. Perhaps he thought she might be killed in some accidental way which was not criminal, and he took steps to see, if that did take place, that she would be worth some money. If the reason given for taking out these policies is that that was because his mother

216

Sir Henry Curtis Bennett, K.C.

Closing Speech for the Crown.

Sir Henry C. Bennett

would not travel without a policy, you will notice that on the day the longest journey was to be undertaken, namely, 23rd September, the day when they travelled to Ostend, no such policy was in existence.

From May to October the accused and his mother were travelling from one hotel to another, sometimes paying nothing, sometimes paying a proportion of the bill. Different articles belonging to them were pawned, and the position became so pressing that articles were pawned for so low a sum as 1s. 3d. That was the position when they came to the Hotel Metropole, at Margate. He made excuses from day to day. A mysterious packet of papers was handed in to Miss Hopper. On 20th October Mrs. Fox was taken ill. The accused said she had had a faint. A prescription was written out by the doctor in the presence of the accused and sent to the chemist. That prescription contained eight ounces of chloroform water. I suggest that you should bear carefully in your minds when you are considering whether or not, from 20th October, at any rate, when the accused said that the chemist had to break down the prescription for Mrs. Fox, the accused had the death in some way of his mother in his mind. The accused is a self-confessed liar about minor matters, and so you have to look at his evidence on a vital matter such as this with great suspicion. Because a man has told lies, however, I don't ask you to infer that he is a murderer, but, I ask you to look very carefully at what he says. I submit that at the most important time of this narrative—the night of 23rd October—he was lying, and lying for a very good reason. Possibly his journey to London was without much profit, because all he got was £1 borrowed. He extended the policy for one and a half days. At 4.30 he telephoned Mrs. Platt. She said, " Your mother is ill. Come back to Margate at once." She refused to lend him any money. Do you believe him? At 8.45 that night the accused and his mother go upstairs. Shortly afterwards he got a paper. At 9.30 the accused went out to a strange hotel for a half-bottle of port. He said he gave a quarter to his mother. What was the purpose of the purchase of the half-bottle of port on the night that Mrs. Fox died? Upon

Sidney Harry Fox.

Sir Henry C. Bennett

that day, too, there was a purchase of a third bottle of medicine, the prescription of which the accused said had to be broken down in case of an overdose. The accused left Mrs. Fox about 10 p.m. He said he left his mother sitting in front of the fire, and that when he left the cane chair was facing the fire and on it were some grapes. It was close to the fender.

From 10.40 to 11.40, the time during which the Crown allege the accused murdered his mother, we know nothing except what we can gather from what was found afterwards. If the case for the Crown is right, your verdict must depend very largely upon what you find about this fire. If it was not accidental, there is only one person who could have lighted it. There is one person who had a very strong motive, if the case for the Crown is right, in lighting it. Was that fire accidental? If the fire was an accidental one, due to clothing on the cane chair catching alight, the chair must have been very near the fire. If, as the Crown suggest, it was an incendiary fire, started by the accused, he would have had an opportunity during the course of the fire to move away that cane-seated chair, if it had been standing, as it might have been, by the side of the armchair.

I should also point out on the morning of 24th October the accused said that he was going to Australia, where a woman he was fond of, who had made a will leaving him money, whom he insured, and who was a very wealthy woman, had gone. On 23rd October he had not a farthing to take him to Australia, and this poor old lady, in the condition in which she was, had no money. He was owing money everywhere. You may think that the money which would come from the insurance was not the only motive there was in this case. It is not incumbent upon the Crown to prove a motive, and very often they cannot, but in this case you have the strongest motive possible, I suggest, and it is a double one. It is not the duty of the Crown to prove the exact way in which this lady died. It is not the duty of the Crown, for instance, to prove whether she died a moment before strangulation would have taken place or a moment after. All we have

218

Closing Speech for the Crown.

Sir Henry C. Bennett

to do is to prove that she was murdered by the accused. Nobody will ever know how this murder was committed, but have you any doubt at all that it was owing to the holding by the accused—because it could not have been anybody else—of that old woman's throat that she died? Whether she died actually as the result of asphyxia, as the result of manual strangulation, or whether she died as the result of partial strangulation, and then heart failure, according to Dr. Weir, or whether she died as the result of the shock of the interference to her throat, nobody will ever know. But have you any doubt at all that she died as the result of violence to her throat? Don't be frightened by the remark of my learned friend, " Will you be happy in years to come if you find this man guilty? " You have got nothing to be afraid of. You have got to make up your mind upon the evidence. That is the only responsibility you have—to give a verdict in accordance with the evidence. And I suggest that the only one you can give in accordance with the evidence is that the accused murdered his mother on the night of 23rd October.

The Court adjourned.

Sidney Harry Fox.

Ninth Day—Friday, 21st March, 1930.

Charge to the Jury.

Mr. Justice Rowlatt—Members of the jury, in this case no question arises of manslaughter or anything of that kind. It is murder or nothing. The crime the accused is said to have committed is a very horrible one, and if he is guilty of it, he is guilty of a very cruel and treacherous murder.

Do not allow any repugnance to influence you. The circumstances are such that it would be foolish to pretend that they are not of the greatest suspicion. But the prosecution must prove the case beyond reasonable doubt. That does not mean beyond the possibility of fantastic imagination, but you must feel sure that the case has really been brought home.

It is a case of circumstantial evidence, and it has been said that circumstantial evidence may be very complete and convincing. Circumstances may point to one conclusion and one only, but if one circumstance is not consistent with guilt, then it breaks the whole thing down. You may have all the circumstances consistent with guilt, but consistent with something else too, and that does not prove it. What you want is an array of circumstances which point only to one conclusion, and, to all reasonable minds, to that conclusion only. Where there are a very great number of circumstances it is an infirmity of many minds—I have to guard against this myself—to fix upon one particular theory and make a pet of it. I warn you to beware of allowing yourselves to be obsessed by any one circumstance. Consider everything all together. That is the only way to deal with a case like this.

There are two broad facts which, in fairness to the accused, must be borne in mind. If the accused strangled his mother and lit the fire before the other guests in the hotel had gone to bed, he took a very big risk, because anybody might have smelt the fire and intervened at too early a stage. It has been emphasised for the defence that it never entered anybody's mind at the time that there was anything suspi-

220

Charge to the Jury.

Mr. Justice Rowlatt

cious in the fire and death. That is true, so far as it goes, but it must be remembered that the accused was a young man of very good address and apparently very much attached to his mother. Mrs. Fox was found in a room in circumstances enough to suffocate anybody, and while it might have looked as if there had been most extraordinary carelessness in letting the fire catch alight, there was nothing at that time in anybody's mind to lead to a suggestion of foul play. The officials of Margate knew nothing at all about the circumstances, nor did they know anything about the remarkable story of the insurance. When this day-to-day insurance began to be put forward, and it was stated that this death was a tremendous windfall to this young man, then, of course, they began to say: " This thing is not quite so simple as it seems. We must look into this," and they began to do so. It is only fair to the people at Margate to say that it was very easy to be wise after the event. Sir Bernard Spilsbury went down to Norfolk not to look for signs of strangulation, but, in the first place, to see whether Mrs. Fox was smothered by smoke; and, secondly, was there any poison in the body. That is how the case grew up.

The accused and his mother were living that extraordinary life in the hotel. The accused himself said quite frankly that they maintained their credit simply by an elaborate system of bluff. No prejudice ought to attach to the accused, however, for murder from the circumstance that he was a dishonest man. He is not being tried for that, but what has a very direct bearing on the question of murder is that in connection with this dishonesty he was absolutely without means.

The defence, on the question of the insurance, have pointed out that there were times when Mrs. Fox had been insured for £4000 as against £3000 at the time of her actual death. It has been said that if she had died then Fox would have come into more money. It is one thing to plot this kind of thing and another thing to find an opportunity for it. The nerve might fail, you know. It may be that the insurance was taken out with some idea that it was a good thing

221

Sidney Harry Fox.

Mr. Justice Rowlatt

to do, and with the circumstance that he insured his own life for many of the summer months it went to show that he might have said : " Well, after all, if I have an accident I shall get a weekly payment which will be quite comfortable if I were not too badly injured."

It has been said in regard to one of these insurances that he asked whether it would cover death in a bath or death by being poisoned at a restaurant. He said his mother told him to ask those questions. Of course, her death could only interest him, and you may think it rather a curious question to ask, but I cannot help thinking that it is rather a small point. But there is one point about these insurances. It does seem to me that from one point of view they may be said to be in his favour, because, supposing the woman had never been insured at all, but he had gone up on the Monday and insured her for the first time for the Wednesday, and the Wednesday only, I think it would be a more formidable case against them than if he were only doing what he had done for the last twelve months. It takes a little off the significance which might have attached to the last policy.

They appeared to be a most affectionate mother and son. It is not suggested that there was any evidence that he showed any hatred towards his mother. It may be possible that, if he committed this murder—so curious is human nature—he was willing to treat his mother with great kindness until he found it necessary to destroy her. Human nature is a curious thing, and it may be that if he did it, he did not want to be unkind until he had to destroy her. The change of rooms was suggested by the manager. That is another point in the accused's favour. He never asked for a room with a gas fire, and he never asked for communicating rooms, either at the Hotel Metropole or anywhere else.

It appears that the accused said some very curious things about medicine. The medicine was not in the least dangerous. What was suggested was that he had some idea in his mind that his mother might be found dead and that it would be useful to make some preparation rather impugning the medicine. The suggestion was a little crude, because it

222

Charge to the Jury.

Mr. Justice Rowlatt

was easy to see that the medicine had no harm in it. It was odd, too, because it showed that his mind was running on the Sunday upon a fatality. But there that question dropped.

Coming to the Tuesday (the day before the death) you are getting to the very kernel of the case and a very serious part of it. The theory of the prosecution is that the accused said to himself, " There is nothing for it. I must go to London, insure the life, do the deed, and collect the money —nothing else for it." When the accused went to London he was obviously in very great straits. He had taken an enormous risk. He had done a thing which would bring the whole pack of cards down in a day or two by getting £1 16s. on a bogus cheque from the chemist. But in spite of that extraordinary shortness of money he took out two insurance policies in London. As Mrs. Fox's death happened just before midnight, the extension of one of these policies to midnight on 23rd October might strike you as very remarkable. The accused's explanation was that it was to cover travelling during the day, but as they had no money to pay fares, as travelling policies they were wasted. There is no doubting the position that if Mrs. Fox died between midnight on the Tuesday and midnight on the Wednesday the whole aspect of affairs would change for him from a state of despair and utter difficulty to a state of affluence. It has been urged that if he was going to do the murder why did he not commit it as soon as he got back after midnight on Tuesday? That would have meant, however, that the fire would have had to occur a long time before Mrs. Fox had gone to bed, and it would not then have been possible to rouse the hotel to tell everybody of the fire. If it were a plot, one would have thought it would have been far wiser to do it on the Wednesday, when she had recently gone to bed and might have left papers by the fire.

With regard to the insurance policies, why did Mrs. Fox and her son not travel on the Wednesday? The accused said it was because he had a bad leg, but there is no evidence that he had ever complained of that, and you have to face the fact that he did travel that day to Dover. It is difficult

Sidney Harry Fox.

to see, too, how they could have got the money to travel, even if they could have got out of the hotel. As travelling policies, the policies were wasted. It is fair to point out, however, that with one exception the accused has, in substance, always given the same account of how he left his mother on the fatal night. The one exception is that while he told Inspector Palmer and the Coroner he left her fully dressed, in the witness-box he said he helped her to undress. There was certainly a change of front for some reason, which appears to him to be important, as regards this woman being dressed or undressed when he left.

The theory of the defence is that this fire was accidental before the death. What I want you to guard against is this—that although it is the essence of the story, and as the story necessarily involves the question of the origin of this fire, that does not mean that you have got to look at the fire all by itself. You must consider all the circumstances of the case which bear upon it, and at once it springs to the attention that one of the most important circumstances about it is what he did do when he discovered the fire. It is a matter for your careful consideration. He obviously pulled to the door, although the room was full of smoke. If the doors were closed you may think it a very remarkable thing. It is fair to say that he would be in a great state of perturbation if there was an accidental fire; but, in whatever state of perturbation you might be, not to open the doors when your mother is suffocating inside by the smoke which would escape if the doors were opened seems very odd. You may think it odd that he did not make a more determined effort to reach his mother.

As regards the appearances of the room after the fire, and the tests which have been made, I would only point out that there is no evidence that petrol had been used. Of course, the person who lighted a fire would try to make it look accidental, and it is stated that that was what happened in this case, and that the accused was not very successful. Another matter is the position of the armchair, which was over the centre of the fire. Was there a bonfire laid there? The defence say that the fire was creeping along the bottom

Mr. Justice Rowlatt

Charge to the Jury.

Mr. Justice Rowlatt

of the chair and that that set fire to the horsehair, and that dropped and made a bonfire—that the chair lighted its own bonfire. That is quite a fair suggestion. But what you have got to find out is how there came to be any fire there at all. The evening paper which was found laid flat could not have been used for kindling, but that does not show that another paper was not used for fuel. The position of the scorched chair found in room No. 66 is a very grave matter. If it was burned in the fire and moved to the window, where witnesses have said it was later found, before the first of them came into the room, then some one must have been present at the fire.

It has been suggested that the pillow might have been taken from under Mrs. Fox's head and used to smother her. Of course, if it was certain that she did sleep until her death on the pillow that night, and that it was gone when they came into the room and found her corpse, it would be very important. You cannot get that certainty. It is possible that she might have moved the pillow and that was how the teeth got adrift. It is just conceivable that when Mr. Hopkins pulled her off the bed he may have pulled the pillow off on to the pedestal. It is possible, and that is all I can say.

The position of the body on the bed was very curious. If Mrs. Fox had been wakened in a fit of violent coughing by reason of the smoke, and that coughing had caused her to die of shock, it is possible that before she died she made an effort to get out of bed, and that might have contributed to her death. On the other hand, if a murderer came to murder her, so far as the bedclothes are concerned, he might or might not have turned them back, but she could have got into that position in the course of the strangling, when he was tending to push her head away, and her legs might have come forward. What you have got to consider is whether the murderer would leave the body like that when he had done his work. Murderers do funny things. But a cool and calculating murderer, one would surmise, would make a little disposition of the body if he had time and if he kept his head. That is all one can say about it.

P

Sidney Harry Fox.

Mr. Justice Rowlatt

It is frankly confessed that so far as evidence of what was on and in the body is concerned, this is a case of slight symptoms and obscure causes. First of all, there were no external indications of asphyxia. There has been some little heat about that part of the discussions in the case. There were no external marks on the throat. Sir Bernard Spilsbury said it was quite possible there would be none, but you and I might think it difficult to believe it. If you had a murderer who was going to destroy a body he would not care what harm he did to it; or if you had a murderer who was going to hide himself and run away, he would not be very tender with it. But if you had a man whose plan was that he would leave the body there, and leave it in such a position that it could not be said that he had murdered it, of course he would go to work in the tenderest possible way, and would not do any injury to the throat if he could possibly avoid it.

As regards the brittle bone in the throat known as the hyoid, it is a very curious coincidence that that bone was not broken in this case. That is a very strong point in favour of the accused. As to the mark at the back of the larynx, alleged by the prosecution to be a bruise, there is no doubt that Sir Bernard Spilsbury saw some object there. It is unfortunate that those tissues could not have been preserved for others to see. They had putrified when Sir Bernard got them to his laboratory. The defence have said —and are justified in saying it—that that point rests on the testimony of what one skilled man observed, and observed at one moment only.

The medical evidence as a whole provides four possibilities: whether, according to Sir Bernard Spilsbury, it was a case of manual strangulation and nothing else; or whether, according to Dr. Weir, it was a case of partial strangulation followed by death from heart failure; or whether, according to the defence doctors, she had been in the smoke and had coughed badly, and that such coughing in the state of her heart would have caused sudden death; or whether she died suddenly from ordinary causes. I think we can rule the fourth possibility out. The theory of the doctors for the

226

Charge to the Jury.

Mr. Justice Rowlatt

defence assumed the presence of smoke while Mrs. Fox was still alive. Was there any smoke there while she was alive? The theory of Professor Smith depends upon the existence of smoke in that room. You must ask yourselves if there was any smoke. That is where the question of the fire becomes of immense importance.

After Mrs. Fox's death the accused continued his career of romancing, and it was said, perfectly fairly, that he had to keep it up. What he said about his mother's health is very important. He told the Coroner in the most deliberate way that his mother had no illness. What were the facts? She had been a whole year in hospital. Why should he go and say she was a woman in perfect health, and that he had never known her to have a day's illness? The suggestion was that she should be treated as a healthy woman suffocated by a fire and no inquiry should be made into the state of her body. That false statement is a very serious matter, having regard to the people he was speaking to at that time. With regard to the accused's alleged statement to Dr. Nichol on the night of the fire, he said he had just come down from seeing his mother's body and was much affected. He said there was £24 in his mother's bag, and said the same to Inspector Palmer the next day. The Attorney-General pointed out that for a young fellow who had lost his mother whom he loved so much in these dreadful circumstances and had only a few minutes before stood by her dead body, to come down and start telling lies about the money she had in her bag was an astounding thing. But he might be abnormal. Don't push it too far. This is a brand-new plot and a brand-new falsehood which he is starting now, and which he must have resolved to start since the fire, perhaps before the fire. Why? They were in the utmost difficulties, it is true. There was a £10 bill to be paid, run up by fraud, but the situation was solved by the death. Surely there was no necessity for this new lie. It may be that he is so perverted that even when an honest and innocent attitude could be taken up he takes this dishonest one. You cannot get away from the fact that it was a remarkable new departure to take in the circumstances.

227

Sidney Harry Fox.

Mr. Justice Rowlatt

As regards the accused's conversation with Mr. Millbank, the insurance official at Norwich, after his mother's death, why did he tell lies to Mr. Millbank unless he wanted to impress, and, as he thought, make the thing go through easy?

You have been asked to consider how you will feel in ten years' time. If that means it is a much more comfortable thing not to do your duty, seeking comfort in that way, it is only a form of self-indulgence. If you want real comfort, the way is to face your duty and do it. There is an end of it. Consider your verdict.

The jury retired at 1.11 p.m. After an absence of an hour and ten minutes they sent for Mrs. Fox's artificial teeth, and these were taken into the room where they were discussing the verdict.

At 2.43 p.m. the jury returned into Court and delivered their verdict, finding the accused guilty.

Mr. Justice Rowlatt pronounced sentence of death.

The ACCUSED—My lord, I never murdered my mother.

The accused was removed from the dock and the judge ordered judgment of death to be carried into execution by the Sheriff of Kent. He also directed that the jury should not be called to serve again for ten years.

APPENDICES.

APPENDIX I.

Proceedings at the Quarter Sessions.

Friday, 10th January, 1930.

The accused, Sidney Harry Fox, appeared before the Recorder (Mr. G. Malcolm Hilbery, K.C.) on six charges relating to alleged frauds, namely—

" Between October 16th and 25th did incur a debt and liability of £12 14s. 8d. with the Hotel Metropole (Margate), Limited, thereby obtaining credit by false pretences.

" Between October 16th and 25th, then being an undischarged bankrupt, did unlawfully obtain credit to the extent of £12 14s. 8d. with the Hotel Metropole (Margate), Limited, without disclosing the fact that he was an undischarged bankrupt.

" On October 21st did obtain £2 by false pretences from V. J. Woolls, Limited, at Margate, with intent to cheat and defraud.

" Between October 3rd and 12th did incur a debt and liability to the extent of £15 5s. with the Frederick Hotels, Limited, at the Royal Pavilion Hotel, Folkestone, thereby obtaining credit by means of fraud other than false pretences.

" Between October 3rd and 12th, then being an undischarged bankrupt, did obtain credit for £15 5s. from the Frederick Hotels, Limited, without disclosing the fact that he was an undischarged bankrupt.

" On October 10th did obtain £1 by false pretences from the Frederick Hotels, Limited, with intent to cheat and defraud."

A grand jury was empanelled. The Recorder then briefly outlined the charges against Fox. He said that Fox was alleged to have obtained credit at the Royal Pavilion Hotel, Folkestone, and to have presented a cheque for £10 signed as being drawn by Rosaline Fox. He received £1 and asked that the balance should be kept for him. The cheque was returned. That cheque had been obtained from the clerk at a branch of Lloyds Bank in Tontine Street, Folkestone, on the statement that Fox's mother had an account. He asked the clerk at the bank to strike out from the form Tontine Street, and put in the name of the branch at which he was then stating his mother had an account.

With regard to the charge of obtaining credit at the Hotel Metropole, Margate, that was somewhat similar. Fox was also alleged to have presented a cheque for £2 to the manager of a firm of chemists in Margate. The manager declined to cash it, but during the luncheon interval Fox returned to the shop and got the cheque cashed by an assistant. The cheque purported to be drawn by Rosaline Fox on the Norwich branch of Lloyds Bank, but there was no such customer or account.

After a retirement of eight minutes, the grand jury returned a true bill against Fox, who was then brought into the dock.

Mr. FRANK POWELL—I wish to say that since Fox was committed for trial upon the present charges he has been charged upon a warrant with the murder of his mother. As that is a charge which is not within the jurisdiction of Quarter Sessions, and is still to be investigated, I ask you to order that the indictment should be transmitted to the next Kent Assizes, and that the recognisances of the witnesses should be enlarged. You will probably agree that in an application of this sort the less I say the better.

The application was granted.

APPENDIX II.

Proceedings before the Magistrates.

Thursday, 9th January, 1930.

The Magistrates' Clerk read the charge: "That on 23rd October, 1929, you, Sidney Harry Fox, did feloniously, wilfully, and with malice aforethought kill and murder Rosaline Fox at the Hotel Metropole, Paradise Street, in the Parish of St. John the Baptist, Margate, in the County of Kent."

Mr. GEORGE HINDLE—I am instructed to defend the accused, and through me he pleads not guilty.

CHIEF INSPECTOR PALMER, of the Margate Borough Police— At 11.15 this morning I read the charge over to the accused and cautioned him. He replied: "It is absolutely untrue. I deny every word of it. I have nothing further to say until I have consulted my solicitor, Mr. George Hindle, of London."

Friday, 17th January, 1930.

Mr. SEFTON COHEN, on behalf of the Director of Public Prosecutions, in opening the case, said: Some of you may be aware that shortly before midnight on Wednesday, 23rd October last, the accused, who had been staying with his mother, Rosaline Fox, at the Hotel Metropole in this borough, was seen running downstairs from the first floor of the hotel, shouting for help, as he said he believed there was a fire and that his mother was upstairs. He was apparently in a state of considerable alarm, and from his attire, which consisted of a shirt only, it would appear that he had just left his bed. Some of the visitors staying at the hotel ran upstairs to the first floor and were led by the accused into his own bedroom, No. 67, which was full of smoke, then out of his bedroom, back into the corridor, and from the corridor into the adjoining room, No. 66, as the accused said his mother was in that room. This room was also full of smoke. The smoke was undoubtedly dense in room No.

233

Sidney Harry Fox.

Sefton Cohen

66, and one of the visitors, Mr. Hopkins by name, tied a handkerchief over his mouth and very pluckily entered the room on his hands and knees. It was in darkness, for the only light there was in the room appeared to come from a red glow on the opposite side of the room. In the darkness he came upon the legs of a woman, hanging over the side of the bed. He dragged the woman, who was lying on her back, off the bed into the corridor, when it was seen she was apparently lifeless and in a semi-nude condition. The police were very soon on the scene, and the body which was that, of course, of Rosaline Fox, was taken downstairs, and, after some attempt had been made at resuscitation, it was seen by Dr. Austin, and he found that life was extinct. There are two details in regard to the condition of this body to which I should draw your attention. The first is that there were no signs of it having been touched by fire and no visible mark of any injury whatever on it. The second is that there were no teeth in the mouth. It appeared from subsequent examination of this room that the deceased woman had gone to bed. Her dress was hanging up behind the door, her shoes were under the bed, her stockings hanging over the rail, and it was found that there was a complete set of upper and lower dentures lying in the wash-hand basin in the room. It is important that I should tell you that there was no money, jewellery, or luggage of any description in this room. The dense smoke, which I mentioned just now, had apparently come from the carpet which was burning under a large upholstered armchair standing to the right of the gas fire, and the chair itself was burning underneath. The accused man, who appeared to exhibit very considerable emotion on hearing of the death of his mother, was given a hypodermic injection by Dr. Nichol, who had arrived about the same time as Dr. Austin, and accused was placed in another bedroom. After the fire on the carpet of this room had been extinguished and the burning armchair had been dragged out of the room, still burning, the police proceeded to examine this room, with some of the fire brigade, and to take particulars from anybody who was in a position to give information. Inspector Palmer saw the accused in his

Proceedings before the Magistrates.

Sefton Cohen

bedroom and asked him if he could give an account of what
had taken place, for the purposes of a coroner's inquest, and
he did so. He said that his name was Sidney Harry Fox,
that he was independent, that his permanent address was
Lyndhurst, Hants, and that they had recently been on holiday
in France. He said his mother was a healthy woman, and
on this night she retired about 9.45 and asked for an evening paper, which he gave to her, to read for a few minutes
before going to bed. He then went on to say : " I lit the
gas fire for her and asked if I should wait and turn out
the light. She said : ' No, that will be all right.' She was
not undressed. My room is next to hers—No. 67. It opens
into her room, which is never locked. I came downstairs
and retired about 10.45 and went to sleep. I was aroused
about 11.30 by what I thought was a window rattling. I
got up and noticed smoke fumes. I closed my window and
went to her room to see if it came from there. I found the
room full of smoke. I saw a light near where the stove
would be. I entered the room, but was beaten back by smoke
and called a porter. I ran downstairs for the porter, and
a number of men went to the room. I saw a man drag her
out unconscious. I cannot say if she was breathing. She
frequently read a paper in her bedroom. I cannot say if
she undressed in front of the fire. She was a good sleeper."

In view of the condition in which the body of this woman was
found in this room full of smoke, and the absence of any visible
indication of injury, no post-mortem examination was made
on the body at all at that time, as the cause of death appeared
to be quite obviously suffocation from fire or from shock. At
the inquest held the following day, 24th October, a verdict
in accordance with the medical evidence was returned. Consequently the body of Mrs. Fox was buried at Great Fransham,
in Norfolk, early the following week, and the various articles
which had been found in the room were thrown on a refuse
dump from which afterwards some of them were recovered.
On 9th November, as the result of certain information which
came to the knowledge of the police, the body of this woman
was exhumed in the presence of Sir Bernard Spilsbury and
certain police officers. As the result of the internal examina-

Sidney Harry Fox.

Sefton Cohen

tion of the body of this woman, Sir Bernard found recent injuries to the deeper tissues of the neck and tongue which were not visible on external examination at all. From the absence of any indication of soot in the inner circuit of the air passages, and from the absence of carbon monoxide in the blood, both of which conditions he would have expected in the case of a woman dying from the effects of fire, Sir Bernard is of the opinion that death was not the result of the effects of the fire, and, further, that this woman died very soon after the fire had started, if not before. The recent injuries to the tongue which he found could, in his opinion, only be caused by the larynx being forcibly pressed upwards in the act of throttling at a time when the deceased woman was wearing her dental plates, and the recent injuries to the neck and tongue taken in conjunction with the other conditions which he found could only, in his opinion, be accounted for as the result of manual strangulation. In the opinion of Sir Bernard death was due to asphyxia by strangling by the hand. The absence of any marks of bruises on the throat may in your minds give rise to some doubt, but you will hear from Sir Bernard that the absence of marks is only evidence that this woman offered no resistance, and that if a steady pressure of the fingers is maintained in the same area for a period of two minutes after death no indication of bruising would appear at all on the skin of the throat. If, therefore, you are satisfied when you hear the evidence of Sir Bernard Spilsbury that death was caused by manual strangulation, you will have to consider two points : whether this could have come about by accident, or whether she could have strangled herself. I think the Bench can dismiss from their minds any possibility of accident, as in the circumstances there was no means by which such an accident could have arisen. And in regard to the possibility of suicide, not only is there no evidence that she had suicidal tendencies, but, in the case of strangulation by the hands, all power of grip would be lost when the compression of the windpipe commenced. Therefore, death by throttling is very strong evidence of violence at the hands of some other person. There remains only a third method by which this woman of sixty-three could have come by her death—that is,

Proceedings before the Magistrates.

Sefton Cohen

by the hands of some assailant. The evidence I propose to put before you points inevitably to the accused as the man who murdered his mother.

On the completion of the examination made by Sir Bernard Spilsbury and on the analysis of the remains by Dr. Roche Lynch and other inquiries, the accused was on 9th January charged with the murder of Rosaline Fox and brought before this Court, and remanded until to-day. It is only fair that I should tell you that when charged he emphatically denied the accusation.

Mrs. Fox was the daughter of a farm labourer, and at the time of her death was sixty-three years of age. She married a railway signalman on the Great Eastern Railway and had four sons, of whom the accused is the youngest. Two sons only are alive—the accused and the eldest son, who is now a hospital attendant at the Queen Alexandra Hospital, Cosham. What became of Mrs. Fox's husband or how they came to part, I do not know, neither is it material to this case, but it would appear that for some years the mother and the accused son had lived together. It is evident that in the beginning of 1918 they were not in good circumstances. Mrs. Fox was then in receipt of a pension of 10s. per week in respect of one of her sons, who had been killed in France. She was admitted to St. Mary's Infirmary, Portsmouth, as a sick and destitute person, and she remained there until March, 1929, when she was taken out. In the early part of 1928 Mrs. Fox and the accused man visited a cousin at the Alexandra Hospital at Portsmouth, and that is of some importance because you will hear on several occasions in the course of this case that before and after the death of Mrs. Fox the accused was at pains to explain that he had no relations living except cousins and that his mother and himself had recently come back from France, where they had been visiting the graves of three of his brothers killed in the war. The defence may be able to throw some light on that statement. The evidence which will be called is to the effect that one son was killed in the war, a second son was killed at Woolwich Arsenal, and a third son is alive and will be called.

According to the accused in his statement the mother was

237

Sidney Harry Fox.

Sefton Cohen

a healthy woman, and during the time she stayed at the
Hotel Metropole she appeared to be in good health, with the
exception of 20th October, when she had a slight indisposi-
tion. You will hear that she walked in what is described as
a shuffling manner and appeared to be somewhat more
feeble than one would expect from a woman of her age.
The accused is a single man, thirty years of age, and during
the period under review he does not appear to have followed
any occupation. He was in receipt of a pension in respect
of an illness aggravated by military service in this country
during the war. Witnesses will be called who had an opportunity of seeing mother and the accused together, and they
will tell you he appeared to be an affectionate son, treating
his mother with every consideration, and that on her death
he appeared to be quite overcome with grief. However, you
will draw your inference from the facts which are before
you. The only inference, I submit can be drawn from them,
is that his show of affection was either assumed or due to
remorse.

On Wednesday, 16th October, the accused engaged rooms at
the Hotel Metropole for himself and his mother for one
night, and they were given rooms Nos. 68 and 70 on the first
floor. Later in the week—on Sunday, the 20th—these rooms
were changed at the suggestion of Mr. Harding, the manager
of the hotel, Mrs. Fox appearing to feel the cold and there
being no gas fire in the room she occupied. From that
Sunday she occupied room 66, which had a gas fire and also
a door leading to room 67, occupied by the accused. These
two rooms are situated at the extreme west end of the hotel,
and you will learn that in addition to the communicating
door there are, of course, doors leading out on to the corridor
which cannot be opened from the corridor without a key.
The accused and his mother brought no luggage with them
when they came, and the accused explained that by saying
that it had been sent on from France to their future residence,
End View, Lyndhurst, Hampshire. He explained that they
had been in France visiting the graves of three brothers.
In conversation with the manager of the hotel on 18th
October, the accused asked the manager whether he could
recommend to him a good solicitor for insurance.

Proceedings before the Magistrates.

Sefton Cohen

Although these rooms were engaged for one night only, the accused and his mother stayed on at this hotel, the accused giving as a reason, first, that he had friends in the neighbourhood, and later that his mother was not well enough to travel. And so it came about that they were staying at the hotel on the night of 23rd October. On Sunday, the 20th, the accused appeared to be disturbed about the health of his mother, and he spoke to the manager about it with the result that Dr. Austin was sent for to come and examine Mrs. Fox. He found that there appeared to be nothing very much the matter with her, and gave her a prescription for a tonic. This was taken to Messrs. Woolls by the accused, and an 8-ounce bottle containing sixteen doses was made up and sent up to the bedroom of Mrs. Fox. Later in the afternoon of the same Sunday the accused told the clerk at the office of the Hotel Metropole that his mother was very much better, and that the services of a doctor would not be required again. On 21st October the accused purchased a second bottle of this tonic, and he proceeded to make a very odd statement to one of the clerks at the hotel when he came back with this medicine. He said that the chemist had said on the matter of doctors' prescriptions that they were sometimes very dangerous, as they prescribed an excessive amount of drugs, and that in this case the chemist had broken down the prescription given by Dr. Austin. You will hear that no such statement was made by anybody at Messrs. Woolls, and that the tonic was sent as directed by the prescription. On 21st October the accused said his mother was not well enough to travel and that he himself was going to London to cash a cheque for her. The manager offered to pass the cheque through the hotel accounts, but Fox said it was necessary for him to go himself. He went up on the afternoon of the 21st.

Now, it is necessary for me at this stage to interrupt the sequence of events as they took place at the hotel by telling you that the suggestion of the prosecution is that at this time the accused man was in desperate need of money. You will hear that towards the end of the previous month he had in his possession about £40 in notes, but it is quite clear that this had all disappeared long before 21st October, because

Sidney Harry Fox.

Sefton Cohen

on the 21st, in order to pay his railway fare to London, it was necessary for him to cash at the chemists' shop of Messrs. Woolls a cheque drawn, or purporting to have been drawn, by his mother for £2 on a bank where she had no account, and that on his arrival on the 16th at the Hotel Metropole he had been unable to pay his accounts at the hotels where he had stayed for the previous fortnight.

Before I broke in to tell you of the financial condition of the accused, I was telling you that he said on the 21st that it was necessary for him to go to town, and this he did after purchasing a second bottle of tonic for his mother. He went to town on the 21st and did not return to the hotel until late in the evening of the following day. On the night of the 22nd he and his mother, in accordance with their usual practice, dined together in the public dining-room. It is a matter which perhaps I should mention that to nobody at the hotel did he mention that either he or his mother was leaving on Wednesday, the 23rd, and, further, that as far as the prosecution is aware, no complaint was made by Mrs. Fox to the effect that she was not feeling well enough to travel on that day. In fact, it was noticed that on this day she appeared to be very much brighter than normally. On the 23rd the accused asked the clerk in the office what his account at the hotel amounted to, and he was told that it amounted to about £12. He then said he was leaving on the following day, the 24th, and that he would then settle his account. And to this witness and to at least one other witness he stated that when they left the hotel they were going to End View, Lyndhurst. Evidence will be called to show that there was no house called End View in the neighbourhood, and that there was no trace of any luggage or furniture having been sent to that place.

I think I should tell you something about Mrs. Fox's movements on the 23rd. She breakfasted in her room in accordance with her usual practice, and she appears to have spent the morning in the drawing-room. In the afternoon the accused goes out and buys a third bottle of tonic, and why he did so is not very obvious, because he already had two bottles each containing sixteen doses; and in the evening

240

Proceedings before the Magistrates.

Sefton Cohen

they dine together in the dining-room. Mrs. Fox had a good meal and drank half a pint of beer, and she was last seen by the waitress leaving the dining-room with her son about 8.15. In the statement of the accused he said that he went up to her room at 9.45, when she asked for an *Evening Standard*, which he got and gave to her. When he left her the gas fire was on and she was not undressed, and pre-sumably—as he made no statement to the contrary—she was in a normal condition of health. In this statement which I have read to you he entirely omitted to mention the fact that at 9.30 on that evening he purchased at the Hoy Hotel half a bottle of port. Dr. Roche Lynch will say that as a result of his analysis he found traces of a moderate amount of alcohol taken within an hour of her death. After having bought this half-bottle of port, and taking the *Evening Standard* up to his mother's room, the accused went down to the saloon bar of the hotel and remained there until 10.25. He had a few drinks of beer. He then went down to the lower saloon bar, where he had one further drink. He was seen by the night porter going upstairs to the first floor about 10.40. About an hour later he is seen running downstairs giving his alarm of fire. Afterwards, you will recollect, it is Mr. Hopkins and the other visitors of the hotel who find the body of Mrs. Fox in the bedroom and bring it out of the room and extinguish the fire, and not the accused man. That, again, is a somewhat singular piece of conduct. The fire appears to have originated in the centre of a burned and scorched patch of carpet, as the carpet and underfelt were burned right through in the centre of this patch. Those who helped to extinguish the fire will say that the fire appeared to be exactly underneath the large upholstered chair. The chair was badly burned underneath and scorched all round the sides and back. Be-tween the scorched edge of the patch of carpet and the iron fender in front of the fire there was a strip of carpet about 6 inches wide that was quite untouched by fire or scorched. The bedding and the body of the deceased woman were quite untouched by fire, and it may possibly seem a little odd that Mrs. Fox, whose body was found clad only in a

Q

Sidney Harry Fox.

Sefton Cohen

vest, should have got into bed leaving the gas fire alight, and that, if she were alive when the fire started and the smoke commenced to fill the room, she never gave any alarm. Although the woman slept in the normal way with her head on the pillow, the pillow was found on a cabinet beside the bed, and on the bed, where there was a clear impression of a body, there was a large wet mark that was a mark of urine. There were no signs of a struggle. On the dressing-table there was a small bottle, nearly full, which contained petrol, and you will hear that the accused was using petrol to clean his suit on the previous Sunday, and that there does not appear to have been any attempt on his part to conceal the bottle. On the chimney-piece were two bottles of medicine which proved to be the tonic. There was no trace of the bottle of tonic bought on the 20th. On the carpet was found a small portion of a woollen garment, and the rest was burned. This was identified by the accused as part of his mother's undergarment. The armchair was taken out of the room and dragged into the corridor after the fire had been put out, and there was found on the unburned top-seat a lady's handbag with a hole burned in the outside, but with the inner pocket uninjured. Inside there were two black stockings, partly burned. The chair was not burned through, so in all probability you will come to the conclusion that those articles must have been picked up by somebody and placed on the chair outside in the corridor. There was no luggage or jewellery in the room at all. Mrs. Fox wore no jewellery, and all the belongings she had were what she clothed herself in. There was nothing else at all.

While I am on this subject, I should tell you that after the accused had given Inspector Palmer his account of what had happened on that night, he asked the Inspector whether his mother's handbag was saved, as it contained a lot of money—£24 in notes. Inspector Palmer, as was his duty, asked for particulars, and the accused said that he himself had cashed a cheque on the previous day, drawn by his mother for £25 on Lloyds Bank, Threadneedle Street, City, and that he had given his mother £24 in notes. Evidence from Lloyds Bank will show that no

Proceedings before the Magistrates.

Sefton Cohen

such cheque was cashed, and that his mother had no account there. You will also hear that the accused made a further statement in regard to what I may call his social position which was quite untrue. He said his mother had bought this house at Lyndhurst, that their luggage had been sent on from France, and the furniture had been sent on from Norwich; that his father was the proprietor of Fox's Flour Mills, East Dereham; that he himself was independent, and that he was educated at Framlingham College, and so on. You will possibly ask yourselves what object the accused could have had in making these statements, which were untrue, unless it was for the purpose of impressing the police inspector that he was a man of position about whom inquiries were quite unnecessary—inquiries which might quite possibly delay the burial of his mother's body. Another curious thing about this statement is that although he gave this wealth of detail about himself, he does not mention the fact that he had on the previous day insured his mother's life against accident. This is a material fact.

Now, I have dealt with the facts so far as they are known to the prosecution as to what took place at Margate during the time the accused and his mother were at the hotel, culminating in the fire which took place on the night of the 23rd. You recollect that on the 21st he left the hotel and said he was going to London to cash a cheque, but what you will hear is that he was, on the afternoon of the 22nd, in a state of considerable difficulty as to how to find money to pay his railway fare to Margate. You will probably come to the conclusion that he did not succeed, if ever he tried, to cash the cheque for his mother. What did he do on the 22nd? You will hear that he called at the head office of Messrs. Pickfords and there filled in a form with the Ocean Accident Guarantee Insurance Company for a personal accident insurance for tourist and traveller policy, and filled it up for his mother at the Hotel Metropole, Margate. I should have told you that this particular policy can be, and generally is, taken out for one day only. By payment of 2s., cover can be obtained against accident involving loss of life, in which case compensation of £1000

Sidney Harry Fox.

Sefton Cohen

is paid. For the loss of an arm the compensation is £500, and so on for minor injuries. Having filled in this proposal form and paid the 2s. premium the accused asked the clerk to make out the policy to cover the full day of 23rd October up till midnight. On the same afternoon, the 22nd, he called at the offices of the Cornhill Insurance Company where his mother had been insured against accident on and off by the accused since 10th August. The last was for £2000 in the case of death and lesser sums for accident not involving death. The policy taken out by him on 10th August had been renewed from time to time up to 20th October, and therefore it was not in force on 23rd October. The accused stated, when he called at the office of the Cornhill Insurance Company, that his mother would not travel by train unless she was insured, and asked whether a personal accident policy which he had could be extended up till midnight on the 23rd. He was told that it could be. He inquired what the premium was, and they said that the period of extension was so short that no premium would be charged at all. By arrangement he called back again a little later, and was handed an endorsement of this Cornhill policy up till midnight on the 23rd. I should also tell you that there was in existence at the time a third policy in respect of Mrs. Fox, and this was for the relatively small sum of £10 taken out in the Wesleyan and General Insurance Company as long ago as 1913. It expired in August, 1928, and was revived in May, 1929, by the accused. Each of these three insurance companies received within a very short time of the death of Mrs. Fox a claim made by the solicitor acting on behalf of Sidney Fox, who is sole executor and beneficiary under the will of his mother, made on 21st April, 1929. Before leaving altogether the subject of insurance, it is material for you to know that the accused has at times insured his mother against accidents since May, 1929, that is, since the date of the will. Witnesses will be called and they will give their evidence with regard to these things. From the 11th September to 19th October the accused had taken out with Messrs. Pickfords, Limited, at least twelve similar one-day policies in respect of his mother. This Cornhill policy, taken out on 10th August, 1929, was extended from time to time on

244

Proceedings before the Magistrates.

Sefton Cohen

at least six previous occasions, the last being in respect of 20th October. You will hear also that there were other policies taken out by him on behalf of Mrs. Fox, the last being on 4th May, 1929, with the Eagle Star Insurance Company. What is the explanation of this insurance against accident taken out by the accused in respect of his mother? It may be that you will be of the opinion that they are consistent with a perfectly innocent motive. If so, of course, you will give the accused the full benefit of that view. But you may think, in the light of the evidence given to you, that he first expected that it was probable that some accident would happen to this elderly woman, who was so uncertain on her feet, and as time went on and nothing happened, he decided to take the matter into his own hands when a convenient opportunity presented itself.

The day following his mother's death, the 24th, he attended the inquest and gave evidence. He left the Hotel Metropole on the 25th, having instructed the office clerk in the hotel to see the solicitor who was acting for him in respect of these insurance claims. The account, which amounted to over £12, was accordingly forwarded to his solicitor. On the 25th and again a week later the accused was seen to be in possession of substantial sums of money of £25 and £14 odd respectively, which sums, it will be proved, were advanced by the solicitor acting for him in respect of the insurances. Before he left the hotel he told the clerk that he was going to the Royal Hotel, Norwich. There he did go and there he expressed his very great sorrow at the death of his mother. Later, one of the staff saked him his plans, and he said that as he had no relatives in the world except cousins he would leave the country and go to Australia, where he had friends. It is not part of my duty to prove motive for the commission of the crime. The circumstances of the case must be examined by you, and such considerations as normally affect human beings applied to them.

EDWARD THOMAS COX, photographer, Margate—On the instructions of the police I took six photographs of the interior of room No. 66 at the Hotel Metropole and also of the corridor.

Sidney Harry Fox.

Edward T. Cox

Cross-examined by Mr. HINDLE—I was accompanied by the police on each occasion.

JACK GODWIN TOMLIN SMITH, Borough Engineer's Office, Margate—I went to the Hotel Metropole on two occasions at the request of the police and I took certain measurements of rooms 66 and 67.

VERA WINIFRED ALWYN HOPPER, book-keeper and receptionist at the Hotel Metropole, Margate—I first saw the accused at the hotel at about 6 p.m. on 16th October. I was then in the office. He asked for two single rooms for himself and his mother for one night. I asked him if he would like rooms with a sea view, and he said he would rather not as it was cold at the time. He wanted the rooms to be together. There was nobody with him when we had that conversation. Eventually rooms 68 and 70 were booked, 68 being for the mother. These rooms were on the first floor. The accused signed the visitors' book in my presence. I saw Mrs. Fox a few minutes later going upstairs to the room; she did not speak to me and I did not see her to speak to at any time. I did not know who Mrs. Fox was, but assumed that she was the mother of the accused. She did not come down to dinner that night, but went to bed. The accused came down to dinner. After dinner I had a conversation with the accused, and he told me he had been to France to see the graves of three of Mrs. Fox's sons who were killed in the war.

Did you know whether they had any luggage when they arrived at the hotel?—He said that their luggage had been sent on, but he did not say where the luggage had been sent from or to. I next saw him on the following morning when he asked if he could get the rooms for another day, giving as his reason that he had some friends he wanted to see. The previous night he had given me a small packet and asked me to put it in the safe. He did not tell me what it contained. On Friday, the 18th, the accused told me that his mother was unwell and had a headache. He asked if they could stay on, and I said that that could be done. He asked me about his bill every day, wanting to know how

246

Proceedings before the Magistrates.

Vera W. A. Hopper

much it was, and I told him. The accused got the packet from the office for a time and brought it back in a different envelope. I do not know whether that was on the Sunday or the Monday. On the Sunday the accused told me that Dr. Austin had been joking with his mother, to cheer her up. I did not see a prescription that afternoon. I do not remember the accused going out that afternoon before the doctor had been, but he told me that he had been to a chemist, who had told him that the doctor's prescription would have to be modified, or a word to that effect, " in case an overdose was fatal," or, it may be, " for fear of an overdose having bad effects." Later the accused asked me to ring the doctor up the following morning because he did not want him to call again as his mother was better and leaving that day. On Monday, the 21st, the accused told me that his mother was better. That night he told me he was going to town to change a cheque. He offered it to me and I replied that I would see the manager. He then said : " Don't trouble, I will change it." He went away that night and came back the following night. He got his bill on the Sunday at lunch time, which then amounted to £5 16s. 11d. On the following Wednesday evening he asked me about the account and I told him that it was £10 11s. He said he would be leaving the hotel on the next day to go home—Canterbury it was in the register, and I imagined it was there. He said it was a new home. I asked the accused whether his mother had a nice coat for travelling in. I said he could have the loan of my fur coat for his mother and she could post it back. He then said he had written home for his mother's own fur coat and that it would be there in the morning, but nothing arrived the following morning. I saw the accused on the morning after the fire. He appeared to be very unhappy about his mother's death.

Did he say anything about why it was that he had not looked in to see her last night or anything of that sort?— He said he did not want to disturb her, as they had been going to get up early the next morning to go away by train. On the 24th he asked me for the package, and opened it in the presence of myself and another. It only contained papers.

Sidney Harry Fox.

Vera W. A. Hopper

On the 25th he left the hotel. The account was then £12 14s. and it was still unpaid. When he went on the 25th he gave the address of a hotel at Norwich for letters to be forwarded. I afterwards received a letter from him written on the Norwich hotel paper.

Cross-examined—Was it the accused who asked for communicating rooms?—Yes.

I suppose you have had mother and son staying at the hotel before?—It is nothing unusual. There was nothing unusual in asking for communicating rooms. I saw the accused and his mother pass the office, but did not take much notice of them, as I was busy with my work. They seemed to be on perfectly affectionate terms. The first rooms they occupied did not have gas fires in them. So far as I know, it was Mr. Harding who suggested that she should move.

ROLAND REUBEN BAIRD—In October last I was a page at the Hotel Metropole. I remember the accused staying there with his mother. On Sunday, 20th October, I took a prescription to Messrs. Woolls, Cecil Square, and brought a bottle of medicine back to the hotel. I gave it to the chambermaid, Miss Louise Bickmore. I cannot remember at whose request I went for the medicine. I did not pay for the medicine. On Wednesday, 23rd October, I went to the chemists for another bottle of medicine, which I took into room No. 66 and placed on the mantelpiece. While I was at the hotel I saw the accused go out with his mother once or twice. They appeared to be on affectionate terms. I did not have much conversation either with Mrs. Fox or with the accused. He told me he had been to Australia, but not of late. He also told me he had just come from France, where they had visited the graves of his three brothers.

LOUISE ELIZABETH BICKMORE, chambermaid at the Hotel Metropole—I first saw the accused when I took him early morning tea on Thursday, 17th October. He was then occupying room No. 70, and his mother was in the adjoining room—No. 68. I took them early morning tea every morning

248

Proceedings before the Magistrates.

Louise E. Bickmore

while Mrs. Fox was alive. On 20th October they changed their rooms, and Mrs. Fox had room No. 66, where there was a gas fire, and the accused was in room No. 67, where there was no fire. On the first morning the accused came into the corridor and gave the order for his mother's breakfast. Mrs. Fox had her breakfast in bed and the accused came downstairs. Whilst she was occupying room 66, she got up at lunch time. On Monday, the 21st, she stayed in her room all day, and had dinner there. On the Tuesday she got up at 12.30 and went down to the drawing-room, where she remained all day. On the Wednesday morning the accused went up and fetched his mother down to lunch. I next saw the deceased at 7 o'clock in the evening when I went into the room and saw her sitting by the gas fire with a newspaper. Hot and cold water was laid on in the room, and the accused was wiping his hands. He was on the other side of the grate. A few minutes after seven the accused and his mother went down to dinner and passed me in the corridor. I put a hot-water bottle in the deceased's bed at a quarter past eight. The gas fire was then out. I swept out the rooms every day. I never found any matches or cigarette ends. I remember on the Wednesday morning, the 23rd, when I took up early tea, noticing that the communicating door between rooms 66 and 67 was locked. The door was bolted from room 66 side. I unbolted the door to take in the accused's tea. I do not remember it being locked on any other occasion. On Sunday, the 20th, I was off duty for a time, and before I went out I knew that Mrs. Fox was unwell. Dr. Austin called during the day.

Did you notice anything peculiar about her walk?—She walked with a shuffle. I sometimes helped the deceased to descend the stairs. She was very quiet and did not talk much. In the day time she wore two stockinette frocks, one over the other. She sometimes wore over them a coat and a fur. She wore no jewellery. When I went into the bedroom in the mornings the deceased was lying on the left-hand side of the bed, nearest to the door. She had a pillow under her head.

Did you ever see, when you went in in the mornings, the

Sidney Harry Fox.

Louise E. Bickmore

pillow lying on the pedestal cabinet by the side of the bed?—
Never.

Or at night?—No. When I took the sheet off on the 25th
of October there was a stain on it which had never been
there before. I first knew that the deceased had dentures
on the night of Monday, 21st October, when she asked me to
put them in a glass of water for her. They were both upper
and lower dentures. The next morning I gave them to the
deceased before she had her breakfast. When I took her a
cup of tea on the morning of Wednesday, the 23rd, I saw
the dentures lying on the floor by the side of the bed and
gave them to the deceased. The next occasion on which I
saw them was on Friday, the 25th, when they were on the
wash-hand basin. When I last saw the teeth they were joined
by a spring, and there was no broken tooth on either of the
plates. After the inquest I asked the accused what I was
to do with his mother's clothes and teeth. He told me to get
rid of them or to give them away, as they were of no
use. I gave the teeth to Teresa West, a maid at the hotel,
but I afterwards received them back from her in the presence
of Inspector Palmer. One tooth was then broken off and
the spring was broken. All of the deceased's clothes were
given to Teresa West, with the exception of her coat and
fur. The two dresses were of no use and were destroyed.
The deceased had only one pair of shoes.

Friday, 24th January, 1930.

Louise Elizabeth Bickmore (recalled and further examined)—I never had occasion to enter the room when the
deceased was undressing in the evening. Before she got up
in the morning I have seen articles of her clothing lying
about, generally on the armchair near the fire. The accused
never had any luggage of any sort in his room, nor did
he appear to have other clothes than those he wore. He did
not wear a nightgown or pyjamas of any sort. He appeared
to be a devoted and affectionate son. On Monday, 21st
October, the accused left the hotel about 5.30 p.m. At lunch

Proceedings before the Magistrates.

Louise E. Bickmore

time that day he asked me to look after his mother while he was away, and he gave me 7s. 6d., but did not say it was for anything in particular. On the same occasion I recollect that I saw the accused take a bunch of grapes to his mother. The last occasion on which I went into room No. 66 before the fire was about 8.15 p.m. on Wednesday, when I took up the hot-water bottle for the deceased's bed.

Cross-examined by Mr. HINDLE—How many times have you been interviewed by the police?—I do not think I can remember, but not very many times.

You remember the accused going to London on Monday, 21st October. Do you know if he telephoned from London to inquire about his mother?—He did. He telephoned again the next morning. He always appeared to show his mother every possible consideration. When the deceased moved to No. 66 she took the bottles of medicine and what other things there were from one room to the other. I did not know that it was Mr. Harding, the manager of the hotel, who suggested that the deceased should change rooms. I can only remember the keys of rooms Nos. 66 and 67 being outside on one occasion, and that was when I left them there myself on Monday, 21st October.

Did you notice the next morning that the communicating door was bolted on the deceased's side?—I cannot remember.

The accused was not there that night?—No.

You went into the deceased's room the next morning whilst he was away?—Yes. I did not notice whether the door was bolted. There was a chest of drawers standing in room No. 66 against the communicating door, which was moved to another position on the Monday the deceased went into the room.

Re-examined—I usually used my master-key for entering room No. 66.

That rather indicates, does it not, that the key could not have been on either side of the door?—Yes. I only saw the key once, and that was on the chest of drawers.

TERESA WEST, staff maid at the Hotel Metropole, Margate —I remember the deceased dying in October last. On the following Friday morning, the 25th, Miss Bickmore gave me

251

Sidney Harry Fox.

Teresa West

two old silk cashmere frocks, a pair of black shoes, a pair of silk stockings, and an upper and lower set of false teeth. The shoes and stockings I afterwards gave back to Miss Bickmore. I identify the articles now shown to be as the articles I refer to.

By the CHAIRMAN—I destroyed the two old frocks and I handed the two sets of teeth back to Miss Bickmore in the presence of Inspector Palmer. The teeth were not in the same condition as they were when I received them. One tooth was missing and the spring was broken. I dropped them. There was only one spring attached to the teeth.

Mrs. GWENDOLINE BUGG, 56 Milton Road, Margate—I am employed at the Hotel Metropole as a waitress. I know the accused as a visitor to the hotel during October. I waited on him and his mother at meals in the dining-room. The deceased never breakfasted in the dining-room, but I sometimes took coffee to the accused there. That was all that he had at breakfast time. When the accused was in the hotel, he would lunch with his mother in the dining-room. The deceased never lunched in the public dining-room without the accused. When the deceased was in good health they dined together in the dining-room. The deceased did not dine downstairs on 16th October, but on 17th, 18th, and 19th October she dined with her son in the dining-room. On Sunday, the 20th, she did not dine downstairs, and on the following day the accused was away. On the 22nd the accused returned from London at night and they dined together. The deceased ate good meals on Wednesday, the 23rd, and seemed quite as usual. Her eyes were kind of fixed, and she always walked with a wobble or shuffle. She always had to be led. Apart from that she seemed to be in her normal state of health on the Wednesday. The accused appeared to be quite affectionate to his mother during lunch and dinner on the Wednesday. At dinner time the deceased had half a pint of bitter. She had a good dinner that night. I last saw Mrs. Fox when she was leaving the dining-room with her son on the Wednesday evening. I saw the accused the next day at lunch time.

252

Proceedings before the Magistrates.

Did he tell you anything about himself on that occasion or any other occasion?—Yes. I told him I was very sorry to hear how his mother met her death, and asked him what he was going to do. He said: "I do not know, but I do not think I shall stay in England, as I have only some cousins at Norwich. I shall probably go to Australia." He said he had an uncle who had died a few months previously. He did not tell me anything about his home. I saw him again at lunch time on 25th October, when he gave me half a crown and said: "That is all I have at present, Gwen, as you know how things are. I shall be returning very likely next week."

Did he say anything about any money being lost?—He said his mother's handbag was burned in the fire with £24 in it.

Cross-examined by Mr. HINDLE—I cannot say when I first gave my statement to the police.

JOSEPH HENRY HARDING, manager of the Hotel Metropole, Margate—The accused and his mother stayed at the Hotel Metropole from 16th till 25th October. On Sunday morning, 20th October, the accused came to me and said that his mother was in a faint. That was about eleven o'clock. I gave him some sal volatile, and at my suggestion Dr. Austin was sent for. After the doctor had examined her the accused sent a prescription to the chemist by the page-boy. On that Sunday, owing to the fact that Mrs. Fox appeared to feel cold, I suggested they should change their rooms, and they got rooms 66 and 67 instead of 68 and 70. A little later on that Sunday the accused told me that his mother was better. On Wednesday night, the 23rd, I went to bed in the ordinary way, but after I had retired I was aroused by an alarm of fire. I went to the end of the corridor on the first floor. At the moment of my arrival the deceased was being pulled out of room 66 by one of the hotel visitors. I did not see the accused at that time. The deceased was clad only in a vest of some description, and when I saw the accused on the landing a couple of minutes later, he was also dressed only in a vest. I was present when the body of the deceased

Sidney Harry Fox.

Joseph H. Harding

was carried downstairs by the police. The accused was following closely behind and was very distressed. The body was afterwards examined by Dr. Austin. When I looked through the door of room 66 I noticed that the carpet was alight. The room was full of smoke, and the gas fire was not alight when I looked into the room. I requested that the armchair be brought out into the corridor and that was done while I was there. That also appeared to be alight underneath. The fire on the carpet and the underneath part of the chair was extinguished by visitors. They obtained jugs of water from room 67 and the maids' pantry adjacent. After the body had been examined by Dr. Austin, it was taken up to the top floor and placed in room 126. The door was locked and the key was handed to one of the police officers. About one o'clock in the morning I went up to room 126 with the accused because he desired to see the body of his mother. Dr. Nichol came up with us. When the accused had seen the body of his mother, the door of room 126 was locked, and I again handed the key to the police. The body of the deceased remained in room 126 until Thursday, the 24th, when it was removed by the undertakers in my presence. The room was entered on that day by the Coroner and some police officers. The accused appeared to be in a very distressed condition. After the fire he was taken to room 42, where he slept; he was attended by Dr. Nichol. I was in room 66 when the police arrived a few minutes after the alarm of fire was given. When I went into the room with Inspector Palmer and other officers I noticed a set of false teeth in the wash-hand basin. I did not move anything. There was a monthly magazine lying on the carpet some distance from the chair towards the window, not in any way burned. There was also some partially burned newspaper close to the chair. The carpet and underfelt were burned through, and the floor board just scorched. The fire did not touch the bed or clothing. There was a pillow on the top of the pedestal by the right of the door. The bedclothes were turned back on the left of the bed, and there was the impression of a body on the bed. There were clothes hanging on the door. The accused left the hotel on

254

Proceedings before the Magistrates.

Joseph H. Harding

Friday, the 25th October. He did not at any time tell me he had insured his mother against accidents.

Cross-examined by Mr. HINDLE—From what I saw of the accused I formed the opinion that he was a dutiful and affectionate son. It was about midnight, as far as I can remember, when I entered room 66 on 23rd October. Some five or six guests and the firemen had been there before I entered.

Mrs. ELIZABETH WAGER, 18 Dane Park Road, Margate— I am a widow and I am employed as a barmaid in the saloon lounge at the Hotel Metropole. During the time the accused was at the hotel, I knew him as a customer at my bar. He came into the bar about 6 p.m. on the 23rd, and said he had been to Dover that afternoon. I saw the accused again before he went in to dinner. He remained in the bar from about 6.30 until about 7.30. As far as I can remember, he then went in to dinner and I next saw him about a quarter to ten, when he came into the bar for an evening paper. He told me that he wanted the paper for his mother. He borrowed a copy of the *Evening Standard* and then went away from the counter in the direction of the staircase. About ten minutes later he returned to the bar and it was then about five minutes to ten. He remained in the bar until it was nearly closing time. He had one or two bitters and I saw him leave about 10.25. I did not see him again that night.

Was anything said by him about the state of his mother's health on that Wednesday?—He said she was much better. In the same conversation before dinner, at the saloon bar on the 23rd, he said they had been having a sham fight, as they generally did when she was all right.

GEORGE ARTHUR IRVINE, relieving officer for the parish of Portsmouth—Mrs. Rosaline Fox was admitted to St. Mary's Infirmary on 20th February, 1928, as a sick and destitute person, and remained until 27th March, 1929. No money was received for her maintenance, and the only income she had was a needs pension of 10s. a week for a son killed in the

255

Sidney Harry Fox.

George A. Irvine

war. On 6th December last the document now produced was written out by the accused in my presence.

Mr. SEFTON COHEN—This document authorises the disposal of certain articles of clothing. It is produced on a question of handwriting only.

Cross-examined by Mr. HINDLE—I am quite aware that this is put in for identification of handwriting, but have you a list of the effects?—I have got the effects in my possession and Inspector Palmer has the list.

FREDERICK THOMAS ROBERTS, night porter at the Hotel Metropole—On the night of 23rd October I saw the accused going upstairs to the first floor at 10.40 p.m., having apparently come from the lower bar. I next saw him at 12.10 a.m. coming downstairs, following his mother, who was being carried down. He looked very agitated. It was my duty to answer night bells and there was a push bell in every room. Between 10.40 p.m. and 11.40 p.m. I was on the ground floor.

Cross-examined by Mr. HINDLE—When you say you saw the accused agitated, do you mean he was overcome and distressed?—He was crying.

He was overcome?—Quite. He was agitated.

WILLIAM HENRY SMITH, hall porter at the Hotel Metropole—I knew the accused as a guest at the Hotel Metropole. On Tuesday, 22nd October, I received a telephone call from London from the accused, inquiring as to the condition of his mother. On 23rd October I arranged, at the request of the accused, for the collection of a bottle of medicine from Woolls, the chemist. As far as I can remember that would be about 6.30 in the evening. When the alarm of fire was given I went to the bedroom. There was a number of people in the corridor. I saw smoke on the landing, and there was smoke in room 66, but I did not see if there was any in room 67, because that door, as far as I remember, was not open. The chair was in the room when I got there. I did not see the accused at the time, but I had a conversation with him on the following day. He said that he had lost some

256

Proceedings before the Magistrates.

William H. Smith

brothers and was alone in the world. There is a gas fire in room 66; it is a penny-in-the-slot gas meter. The gas meter was emptied in my presence during the latter part of November, so far as I remember.

FREDERICK JOHN PALMER, manager at the Tivoli Road branch of Messrs. V. J. Woolls, Limited, chemists—About 2.30 on the afternoon of Sunday, 20th October, I received a prescription from a page-boy and dispensed it in an 8-ounce bottle containing sixteen doses. The prescription was made out in the name of Mrs. Fox, Hotel Metropole, and I gave the medicine to the page-boy. I retained the prescription in order that it might be entered in the prescription book. I did not see the accused on that day. This prescription was just a simple tonic.

JAMES ELGAR FARMER, manager of Messrs. Woolls's shop in Cecil Square—About 6.30 p.m. on Sunday, 20th October, the accused came into the shop and said he had had a prescription made up earlier in the afternoon which had not been paid for. He tendered a cheque in payment, but I refused to change. The cheque was made out on Hotel Metropole paper and signed "Rosaline Fox." The cheque only bore one penny stamp at that time. When I declined to accept the cheque the accused left the shop.

Did you make any statement to him to the effect that doctors' prescriptions are sometimes dangerous?—Nothing whatever.

Or that you had been compelled to break down the prescription given by Dr. Austin?—No, I never mentioned it. The prescription was not broken down in any way; it was a drachm and a half of nux vomica, half an ounce of sal volatile, and chloroform water up to an 8-ounce bottle. I gave the prescription to the accused on the Sunday, and he took it away with him. He came into the shop again about 10.30 a.m. on Monday and ordered another bottle of the same medicine. He also purchased a bottle of cascara tablets. He offered in payment the same cheque, and I again refused it. The prescription was to be made up and he was to return at mid-day for it. I went to lunch at twelve o'clock

Sidney Harry Fox.

and when I returned Miss Allen, an assistant, told me she had cashed a cheque for the accused. About 10.30 a.m. on 24th October the accused again called at the shop. He said that if the cheque did not go through the bank, I was to refer it to a solicitor in the Square, who would see the matter through. The cheque was ultimately returned marked " No account," and the money was repaid by a solicitor acting on behalf of the accused. An 8-ounce bottle of this medicine taken during the daytime would last about five days, and if taken at night-time as well, about two and a half days.

Cross-examined by Mr. HINDLE—There was no discussion between the accused and myself about the doctor whose name has been mentioned.

MARGARET CATHERINE ALLEN, assistant with Messrs. V. J. Woolls, Limited—Shortly after mid-day on 21st October the accused brought a cheque into the shop. He said he wanted it changed, and that I was to take out of it the cost of two bottles of medicine and a bottle of tablets. The accused said : " It is quite all right. I saw Mr. Farmer about it, and he told me to go to the bank. I have been to the bank, and they said it would be quite all right if I affixed another penny stamp and endorsed it, which I have done." I deducted 4s. for the medicine and tablets, and gave the accused the balance of £1 16s. I also gave him a bottle of medicine which was ready.

HAROLD FREDERICK BYWORTH MORGAN, manager of the Hoy Hotel, Margate — On Wednesday, 23rd October, at 9.30 p.m., I sold a half-bottle of port to the accused. The price was 3s. The bottle was wrapped in a " Johnny Walker " brown wrapper—a half-sheet. This particular port is bottled on the premises from bulk. I am the only person, locally, who uses the red tops on bottles of this kind. The bottle was supplied with a white leadfoil covering or capsule similar to that produced.

Cross-examined by Mr. HINDLE—Is not 3s. for half a bottle of ordinary port very cheap?—No, not in Margate. We have five kinds cheaper than that.

Proceedings before the Magistrates.

Friday, 31st January, 1930.

SAMUEL FRANCIS DOUGLAS HOPKINS—I am a commercial traveller. I was staying at the Hotel Metropole on 23rd October. After dinner I went to a place of entertainment and returned to the hotel about 11.20 p.m. I sat for some time in the lounge; there were no other people there. About twenty minutes to twelve I saw the accused running down the stairs from the first floor, crying: " Where is the ' boots '? I believe there is a fire. Where is the ' boots '? There is a fire." He said his mother was upstairs. He had only a day shirt on, and appeared to be very agitated and distressed. I called the " boots," then I shouted down to the people in the billiard saloon that there was a fire, and seeing that they were coming I immediately turned round and went after the accused who led me upstairs. When we got to the first floor, he turned to the right and went along the corridor, and then turned to the left. The other people were following me. The accused went to room No. 67. I think the door was shut, but I could not see properly because he was in front of me. I could not see whether he had a key, or whether the key was in the door. When he had opened the door he went into the room and I followed him. The room was full of smoke. There was no light in it. I went into the room a few feet and turned back because of the smoke, and the accused followed me out into the corridor. When the door of the room was opened, a lot of smoke gathered in the corridor. The accused did not say anything when he was in room 67 with me. When we came out into the corridor, he pointed to the door of room 66 and said, " My mother's in there." He went to the door of room 66 and opened it. I rather think the door was closed. I did not notice any key in the hand of the accused.

What did he do when he opened the door?—He was standing on the left side of the door. I entered the room a few feet, but turned back because of the smoke.

Was there a good deal of smoke in the room?—It was very thick indeed.

When you went into the room a few feet, did you notice

259

Sidney Harry Fox.

Samuel F. D. Hopkins

whether there was a light on in the room at all?—No light, but a glimmer on the left, which I thought was from the gas fire or the glare of the flames.

What did you do when you came out into the corridor again?—I made another attempt to enter the room by putting a handkerchief over my mouth. I went in a few feet, but withdrew again because of the smoke. I then went down as low as I could on my hands and knees and crawled into the room, having put the handkerchief away. I noticed there were 5 or 6 inches of clear air above the floor—a clear space right across the floor. I groped about with my right hand and came across the legs of the deceased hanging over the side of the bed. I could not see the legs before I touched them, and I could not see them afterwards because of the smoke, but they were not touching the floor. The body was not visible at all. I immediately stood up, put my hands under the deceased's arms, and dragged her off the bed. I did not notice whether the body was covered with bedclothes or not. The deceased was lying on her back, and I placed her in the same position—on her back—on the floor. Having got the body on the floor I then dragged it outside into the corridor. I did not touch any other portion of the body except under the armpits and the legs. The deceased was wearing only a small singlet. I did not notice any signs of life; I could not say whether the body was warm or not. I could not say whether the head was lying on the bed.

When you first entered the room, you say the accused was standing on the left of the door. I want to know if you can tell us something about him. Was he in the room again at any time?—He was not in the room again, and I did not see him again either in room 66 or out in the corridor. I heard him speaking, however. As I laid the deceased on the floor in the corridor I heard him say, " My mummy; my mummy." When I got the body of the woman outside in the corridor, I laid her on the floor and took my raincoat off and put it round her. Having placed the raincoat over the body, I endeavoured to get the lady along the corridor to the top of the stairs because of the smoke in the corridor.

Proceedings before the Magistrates.

Samuel F. D. Hopkins

Mr. Miller helped me for about a yard or two, and then I did it on my own again. I got her to the top of the stairs, and then I collapsed. I do not know anything of what happened afterwards.

By the CHAIRMAN—Did the accused help in any way to get his mother from the room or along the corridor?—No.

Cross-examined by Mr. HINDLE—The accused came downstairs about twenty minutes after I got into the hotel. I was talking to a commercial traveller at the time. I made a statement to the police shortly after the occurrence that night. It was taken down by Inspector Palmer. What he took down then I gave at the inquest the next day. I have seen Inspector Palmer about three times since I gave him that statement on the night of the 23rd. The case was not mentioned on those occasions, because he had my statement on the night it happened.

You saw the accused running down the stairs and he was very excited?—Yes.

He looked as though he had almost lost his head?—Yes.

Are you quite sure that he had a day shirt on or was it merely a vest?—The garment looked like a day shirt. Anyhow, it was a shirt, a plain shirt.

I put it to you that he had nothing but a vest on. Would you like to go so far as to say it was a shirt?—I was more interested in his face. He was so terrified, and I was not looking at anything but his face.

Did you have a little difficulty in understanding the man when he rushed down? Did you think he had taken leave of his senses?—I saw him running down, and I looked up and he said: " Where is the ' boots '? I believe there is a fire. Where is the ' boots '? There is a fire."

Do you remember, when you rushed to room 67, whether the accused shouted to you, " Not that room "?—I did not hear him. I followed him into room 67.

Did he shout out at any time that his mother was in the other room?—He pointed to room 66 when we were in the corridor.

You have said that room 66 was full of smoke. You could hardly see, could you?—I could not see at all. There was

Sidney Harry Fox.

Samuel F. D. Hopkins

nothing but a glimmer of light from the gas fire, or it may have been the smouldering fire.

So you turned back?—Yes.

Even when you got into this room and got to the bed you could not see, could you?—No.

Was the accused sobbing when he came up, and did he say : " My mummy; my mummy "?—Well, he said it in a very tearful sort of way.

The deceased was not a very light lady to handle, was she?—No, very heavy.

I take it you experienced the greatest difficulty in dragging her off the bed?—Yes, it was very hard for me.

I think she weighed something like 12 stones?—Yes.

HENRY DICKENS MILLER, a commercial traveller, employed by the Cellular Clothing Company, London—I was staying at the Hotel Metropole on the night of the fire. At about 11.40 in the evening I heard some one shouting " Fire," and calling for the " boots." I saw the accused coming downstairs shouting for the " boots " and calling out " Fire." At that time I was at the door of the billiard room. The accused was wearing a singlet and shorts. He did not say anything about his mother at that time. The " boots " did not seem to be hurrying too much, and Mr. Reed, two other gentlemen, and myself, then ran upstairs. There was very little smoke in the corridor, but some was trickling through the cracks of the doors of rooms 66 and 67. As I went into room 67, I did not notice the accused or Mr. Hopkins. The electric light was on in the room—I believe I switched it on myself. There was not a great amount of smoke in the room. Whilst in there I heard a voice from the corridor say, " My mummy is in there," meaning through the communicating door. I opened the communicating door, and turned the light on in room 66. As I opened the door, I was met by a dense volume of smoke; the light gave only a very faint glow because of the smoke. I entered room 66 a foot or so, but was beaten back by the smoke. I noticed Mr. Reed crawling on his hands and knees through the communicating door into room 66. Shortly afterwards I saw

262

Proceedings before the Magistrates.

Henry D. Miller

him pushing an armchair, which seemed to be smouldering underneath, towards the communicating door. About half left from the entrance there was a line of flame 6 inches to 7 inches high and about a yard in length. I noticed that before I saw Mr. Reed pushing the chair out of the room. I saw Mr. Hopkins dragging the deceased through the door of room 66. I assisted him to drag the body along the corridor for a short distance. Mr. Hopkins was holding the woman under the shoulders. When she was moved along by Mr. Hopkins she was on her stomach. I did not touch any part of the woman's body except her shoulders. I did not see her face until she was on the landing at the top of the stairs. Her mouth was then open, but I could not see any teeth. The face was very pallid. I did not notice whether the windows of room 66 were open or shut. The body of the woman was afterwards taken downstairs, and the next time I saw her she was in front of the hotel entrance door. She was lying on her face then, and they were trying artificial respiration. Coming downstairs there were two or three at the head and shoulders and one at the feet; she was held under the shoulders and arms. I do not know whether she was carried face upwards or downwards.

REGINALD LEONARD REED, a commercial traveller in the employment of Messrs. H. A. Brain & Son, 39 Skinner Street, Clerkenwell—I was in the billiard room of the Hotel Metropole at 11.40 on the night of 23rd October. After hearing a cry of "Fire," I ran down the stairs and then up to the corridor on the first floor. I had seen the accused at mid-day, but not that evening. I knew his voice well enough to recognise it when he called "Fire." When I reached the corridor, I went into room 66 from room 67, via the communicating door. The smoke in the corridor was fairly dense. The door of room 67 opening into the corridor was open. I did not notice if the door of room 66 was open or shut, but the communicating door between the two rooms was closed. The electric light was not on in room 67. I dropped on to my knees, crawled through, and saw immediately in front of me the burning chair. The flames

263

Sidney Harry Fox.

Reginald L. Reed

appeared to come from the side of the chair and underneath. I tried first of all to extinguish the flames with my foot, but I was not successful. I then picked up a little iron fender which was round the gas stove. I do not know whether the stove was alight or not. I dropped this iron fender again as it was so hot. I then dragged the chair back through the communicating door into room 67 and from there to the corridor. I noticed that there was a portion of the carpet alight; there were short flames coming from it, roughly, about 18 inches square.

When you first entered this room and saw the chair and fire underneath, was that anywhere near the bed?—The back was not quite parallel with the foot of the bed. I did not see the body being dragged out of the room. I saw it when it was at the main entrance. A policeman was trying artificial respiration. She was lying on her face. The following morning, at Inspector Palmer's request, I went with him to room 66 and placed the armchair in the position in which I found it the previous night.

Cross-examined by Mr. HINDLE—Room 66 was full of smoke when I entered it, but I was not overcome by the smoke. It was very difficult to see. I could just see a burning chair—it was difficult to see anything else.

Having seen the burning chair, you went back on the following day with Inspector Palmer and placed the chair into position again. Yet you say it was very difficult to see anything in the smoke?—I saw the chair quite plainly. I did not measure it, but I think the position was right within an inch or so. I had a vivid recollection of what took place on the previous night.

FREDERICK GEORGE FRENCH, sales engineer, in the employment of Metro-Vic Supplies, Ltd.—On the night of 23rd October I was in the lounge of the Hotel Metropole, and about 11.40 I heard a voice shouting " ' Boots! ' Fire! " I went upstairs to room 66, and there was smoke in the corridor. The corridor was lighted. When we were 2 or 3 yards from room 66 I saw the body of the deceased lying on the floor. She was lying face downwards with practically

Proceedings before the Magistrates.

Frederick G. French

no clothes on. I did not see the accused. Both the doors of rooms 66 and 67 were open. I looked through the door of room 66. The carpet was on fire; it was placed roughly 3 feet from the gas fire. The fire on the carpet was just in the nature of a smoulder with short flames. The electric light was on in this room. I did not notice whether the communicating door was open or shut. I did not go into room 67 that night. I attempted to stamp out the flames and turned off the gas fire. There was not so much smoke as fumes in the room; the fumes given off by the carpet were very pungent, making you cough badly. The windows of room 66 were tightly shut. The smoke was going into the corridor, and so, after ascertaining that the wind was not likely to produce flames, I opened the window nearest the gas fire and closed the door of room 66 behind me. That was to stop the smoke going into the corridor. I could only see very indistinctly owing to the smoke. The armchair which was taken into the corridor was smouldering on the side of the seat, more underneath it than on top.

Dr. ROBERT WILLIAM NICHOL, M.R.C.S., L.R.C.P.—On the night of 23rd October, as the result of a telephone message, I went to the Hotel Metropole at about 11.45 p.m. The body of a woman was lying in the entrance hall just inside the front door. She was lying on her back. When I arrived, Dr. Austin was examining the woman; she was dead. There was nothing especially significant to gather from her appearance. The lady's general appearance was quite usual; she did not differ in appearance from the usual dead person. She was composed and pale, and I was not struck by anything. I refrained from examining the patient, because I was not asked to do so by my colleague, and I just stood there; but as far as I could see there were no signs of burning. I think her lips were apart, but I did not notice any teeth in her mouth. I gained the impression that she had none; but, of course, I did not examine her. Later on I went up to room No. 66 with Inspector Palmer, Dr. Austin, the chief officer of the fire brigade, and one or two police officers. When we got into the room the gas fire had been

Sidney Harry Fox.

Dr. Robert W. Nichol

turned out and the window was open. The room was practically clear of smoke. The armchair was no longer there.

Was there anything about this area of burned carpet that
attracted your attention?—Yes, it seemed to be disconnected
from the most obvious source of the fire—the gas stove.

By that I assume that you mean that there was an unburned strip between the scorched area and the fender?—
Yes. The bed was not near the scorched area.

Did the bedclothes appear to have been pulled aside?—The
appearance of the bed was that the clothes had been pulled
well off towards the foot. The bed gave the impression that
a heavy body had lain on it for some while; in the middle
there was a long impression. There was a wet patch some
18 inches or more in diameter up at the middle of the bed,
and the bedclothes on the side nearest the door were dragged
towards the floor a little bit. It gave the impression that
a heavy body had lain on the bed and had been pulled off.

Did there appear to have been any struggle?—No. There
was no indication of a struggle on the bed apart from the
appearance of a body having been dragged off. Later I
went to see the accused, who was in a sitting room downstairs.

Did he appear to be agitated?—Not unduly when I first
saw him. After I had explained about his mother's death
to him, he become considerably more agitated — in fact,
extremely so. I was surprised to see a man so agitated.
As I say, he was not very agitated at first, but gradually
became more and more distressed as the news was broken to
him, and, finally, he became seriously distressed. I asked
him several questions, and told him that I was doing so
for the benefit of the Coroner. The accused said: " What
Coroner? " and I then explained that an inquiry was always
made in cases of violent death. At that he seemed to double
up. He then asked if he could see his mother again, and
he went upstairs with me to a room where her body had been
placed. He walked into the room in the most natural way
imaginable, remained there a few minutes, and then came
out again. We went downstairs together. He was to have
another room to sleep in, and I went with him to that room.
As he seemed very worried I gave him an injection of mor-

Proceedings before the Magistrates.

Dr. Robert W. Nichol

phine. Before I gave him the injection I tried to talk him into a calmer state of mind.

Did either of you mention insurance?—Yes, I did. I told the accused that the circumstances of the fire were not satisfactory and advised him to have a solicitor to watch his interests at the inquiry, especially if insurance was involved. I do not know why I said so, but I did. He did not ask me for the name of a solicitor; I suggested a name to him. With regard to my statement that the accused " doubled up," I wish to explain what I mean. The accused did not collapse because the Coroner was mentioned. I was trying to break the news of his mother's death gradually, and I did so by referring to an inquest. The accused collapsed when he realised by what I was saying that his mother was dead.

Dr. GERALD ROCHE LYNCH—On 7th December last I received from Sir Bernard Spilsbury two jars containing stomach and stomach contents. On the following day I received three other jars containing other organs from the same source. I examined the contents of the five jars and detected no trace of any poisonous or noxious substance in the organs. In the stomach and stomach contents I found a very small quantity of a substance which belongs to a group of bodies known as the alcohols. There are a number of alcohols known to medical science, and of these, the ethyl alcohol is present in beer, wines, and spirits. It is not possible to state definitely that the small quantity of alcohol in the stomach was ethyl alcohol. It is extremely probable that it was ethyl because the other alcohols are not found in food.

The evidence is that Mrs. Fox had half a pint of bitter beer for her dinner, some time between 7 p.m. and 8 p.m. If she died at approximately 11.30, I want to know whether you would expect to find any traces of it in the body?—I would not. In that period I would expect to find that the beer had become absorbed in the blood and tissues.

Assuming it to be proved that this woman died about 11.30 on the night of 23rd October, would your finding be consistent with the consumption by her of any portion of that bottle of port wine at about 10 p.m. ?—I should say that death would

Dr. Gerald R. Lynch

have been about one and a half hours after drinking the port, and I think it would have been consistent with her having taken about half or rather more than half a bottle of port wine. That is assuming that the alcohol I found was ethyl alcohol.

The Court adjourned.

Friday, 7th February, 1930.

Dr. ROBERT NICHOL (recalled), cross-examined by Mr. HINDLE—I did not examine Mrs. Fox. I did not see any signs of death from asphyxia or any marks of violence. I do not think the appearances were consistent with heart failure.

You probably have been told or know that the deceased lady had fainting fits. Would that indicate that she had a weak heart?—Not necessarily. It might. I noticed that Mrs. Fox was rather stout.

You also said in your evidence that you noticed a patch on the bed?—That was urine, of course. I did not think that patch was of any special significance. If the woman had been frightened, that might have caused it, but I do not think inhaling smoke would have had that effect.

I think you said that you left the examination chiefly to Dr. Austin, but I think you must have noticed something as a medical man. Did you see any froth or blood at the mouth?—Well, no, but she had been handled——

She had been handled considerably, had she?—Yes, as a result of being taken up and downstairs. The tongue had been brought forward to try and prevent the patient swallowing it.

By the CLERK—I do not know to what extent Dr. Nichol is able to give evidence on this point. This is what you were told, doctor, is it not?—I was told she was carried downstairs.

Cross-examination continued—You saw her downstairs, did you not?—Yes.

Apart from what you have said and what you were told, you noticed nothing else? You saw no signs of blood or froth at the mouth?—No. Might I add I did not examine the patient?

Proceedings before the Magistrates.

Dr. Cecil C. Austin

Dr. CECIL C. AUSTIN, M.R.C.S.(Eng.), L.R.C.P.(Lond.), Margate—On 20th October last, between 1.30 and 2 p.m., I went to the Hotel Metropole, as a result of a telephone message, and examined the deceased. She complained of pains in her body, and had a slight temperature. I put it down more or less to stomach trouble. I did not examine the heart and lungs, as I did not think it necessary. I wrote out a prescription—tincture of nux vomica, $1\frac{1}{2}$ drachms; sal volatile, 4 drachms; chloroform water, 8 ounces. There is nothing dangerous in the tonic or in the amount prescribed. As a matter of fact, had she drunk the whole bottle, it would not have hurt her to a great extent.

The statement has been made that the chemist had to break down the prescription. What do you say about that?—That was not necessary at all. I left the prescription in the room and told them to take it to a chemist. I arranged to call again on the following day, 21st October. That appointment was cancelled early on Monday morning. On Wednesday, 23rd October, about midnight, I was called to the Hotel Metropole by the police. I saw the deceased lying in the vestibule of the hotel near the entrance. She was lying on her back on the floor. I examined the woman and found that she was dead. I formed the opinion that she had been dead for twenty minutes or half an hour. The body, hands, and face were quite warm. While I was examining the woman Dr. Nichol arrived. As far as I could ascertain, there were no external marks of injury upon her; she was not burned. In the absence of any post-mortem I came to the conclusion, on account of the fire, that perhaps she had gone to sleep and woke up and found the room full of smoke; she then had a shock and fell across the bed. I concluded that she died of shock and suffocation. On the following day I gave evidence at the inquest.

Cross-examined by Mr. HINDLE—You did not see any signs of death from asphyxia when you saw the woman, and there were no marks of violence of any kind?—There were no signs of death from asyphxia. From what I saw, there were no marks of violence on the body, but I did not examine the whole of the body.

269

Sidney Harry Fox.

Dr. Cecil C. Austin

Were the appearances of the deceased lady consistent with death from heart failure?—Yes.

Did you see any sign of froth or blood staining at the mouth or nose?—No, none at all.

I take it that the tongue is well supplied with blood, so that, if there was any injury to it, it would bleed rather freely?—Rather profusely.

Supposing the tongue had been injured just before death, would you not expect to see some sign of blood staining?—You would.

However slight, it would be shown about the mouth?—It all depends upon the extent. It might be kept in the mouth.

If there was no blood staining, would that indicate there had been no recent injury to the tongue?—No. You cannot put it that way. The absence of staining shows one of two things: either that there was no injury at all, or that the injury was so slight that the amount of hæmorrhage was not sufficient to cause a strain.

You said at the inquest that, from what you saw, death was due to suffocation from inhaling fumes and smoke?—And from shock.

Re-examined by Mr. SEFTON-COHEN—Did you examine the tongue?—No.

You told my friend that, if the tongue had been injured before death, you would expect blood?—In the mouth, yes.

Would you expect to find blood in the mouth if the injury had consisted of bruising to the substance of the tongue without injury to the surface?—In what way do you say the bruising of the tongue was caused?

If the substance of the tongue had been bruised without injury to the surface, would you expect to find blood?—No.

GEORGE EDWARD BRAY, police constable in the Margate Police Force—At 11.50 p.m. on Wednesday, 23rd October, I was on cycle patrol duty, and in consequence of what came to my knowledge I went to the Hotel Metropole. I went up to the first floor where I saw the body of a woman lying on her back. There were about a dozen people round her, but no one was touching her. I went into room 66 from which

270

Proceedings before the Magistrates.

George E. Bray

smoke was dispersing. The fire on the carpet had been put out. One window was open and I opened the other. I did not see any teeth on that occasion. As the fire had been extinguished, I went out into the corridor again to render what assistance I could to the woman, who was lying in the same position as when I first saw her. I called for assistance, and with the help of four other men carried her downstairs and laid her on the floor, where I resorted to artificial respiration, after having turned her on her stomach. In carrying her downstairs, I held her under the armpits from behind the head and the other men held her round the middle and the legs. No one except myself touched her head or shoulders and no one at all touched her neck. She was carried down head first and face uppermost. I carried on artificial respiration for five minutes, and up to that time I did not see any signs of life. The woman's mouth was partly open when she was being carried downstairs, and there were no teeth in her mouth. I did not touch her tongue. While I was applying respiration Police Sergeant Fleet arrived, and, with his help and the help of a man named Hart, I moved the woman to the entrance door of the hotel, where Sergeant Fleet and I continued artificial respiration alternately.

In what way was she carried?—Face uppermost, myself at the shoulders, and Sergeant Fleet had the arms underneath. While the body was at the entrance door it was examined by the last witness. I did not touch the woman again after the doctor arrived.

HERBERT BRUCE FLEET, police sergeant in the Margate Police Force—Shortly before midnight on Wednesday, 23rd October, I went to the Hotel Metropole with Inspector Palmer and other officers. On arrival at the hotel I saw the body of a woman lying in the corridor almost at the foot of the stairs on the ground floor. She was lying on her right side and was being attended to by Police Constable Bray. She was not at that time turned over on to her face. The woman's mouth was open and the colour of her face was reddish blue. I telephoned for a doctor, and she was removed from the

271

Sidney Harry Fox.

Herbert B. Fleet

foot of the stairs to just inside the main entrance doors of the hotel. She was carried face uppermost, and at the entrance of the hotel she was placed on her back and then gently rolled over on to her face. After she had been rolled over, I felt in her mouth to see that there was no obstruction to the air passages. I then gave instructions for the doors to be opened for air, and at once commenced artificial respiration with Schäfer's method, which was continued for some time, until Dr. Austin arrived, followed by Dr. Nichol. On the instructions of Dr. Austin the body was turned over on her face. I saw the accused a moment before, but I did not know who he was, and he was not present when the doctor examined the body.

When you say you felt in her mouth to see if there was any obstruction of the air passage, did you notice whether there were any teeth in the mouth?—There were no teeth. The body was carried upstairs to room 126 on the top floor. It was placed on a bed, and the door locked, the key being given to Inspector Palmer. The throat was not touched by me or by any other person in carrying the body, or at any time when I was there.

Cross-examined by Mr. HINDLE—Was the spring of the false teeth damaged?—I did not notice.

Did you touch the teeth?—No.

ARTHUR WILLIAM KEMP, police constable in the Margate Borough Police—I went to the Hotel Metropole about midnight on 23rd October and saw the body of a woman lying face downwards just inside the entrance door. A police officer was trying artificial respiration. I felt the woman's wrist, but there was no pulse; her mouth was slightly open.

Did you touch her mouth in any way?—Yes. I put my fingers into her mouth, took hold of the tip of her tongue between my finger and thumb, and pulled it between the lips, and then let it go. There were no teeth in the mouth.

HERBERT WILLIAM GORE, partner in the firm of Messrs. Gore Brothers, undertakers—On the morning of 24th October the accused called on me at my place of business and

272

Proceedings before the Magistrates.

asked me to make the necessary arrangements for the burial
of his mother at Great Fransham, Norfolk. As a result
of arrangements with the accused, I removed the body of an
elderly woman from a locked-up room on the third floor of
the Hotel Metropole on 24th October and placed it in my
private mortuary. The body remained there until 29th
October, when it was placed in a motor hearse and driven to
Great Fransham Churchyard, where the burial took place
in my presence. I was present at the exhumation of the
body of this woman in the presence of Sir Bernard Spilsbury,
Chief Inspector Hambrook, and officers of the County Con-
stabulary of Norfolk. I opened the coffin and identified the
body as the body of the woman I buried on 29th October. The
funeral expenses amounted to £47 10s., and the accused told
me to send the account to his solicitor. In consequence of
what came to my knowledge I did not do so, and the account
has not been paid.

Sir BERNARD HENRY SPILSBURY, B.M., B.Ch.(Oxon.),
M.R.C.P.(Lond.), honorary pathologist to the Home Office—
On 9th November last, about mid-day, I attended with Chief
Inspector Hambrook of Scotland Yard at a churchyard at
Great Fransham, Norfolk. I there saw the Chief Constable
of Norfolk and other police officers. I found on my arrival
that the grave had been opened and the coffin uncovered,
and in my presence the coffin was raised from the grave and
taken to an adjoining room. The coffin was of polished oak,
with brass fittings, and it was dry and in a very good state
of preservation. On the lid there was a brass plate with the
name of " Rosaline Fox " upon it. The last witness, Henry
William Gore, was present when the coffin was raised. When
the coffin was taken to the room Mr. Gore identified it as
one made by him for the burial of Rosaline Fox. He raised
the coffin lid, and I detected no smell other than that of
sawdust, of which a large quantity surrounded the body. The
sawdust was clean and dry, and there was a layer of putty
between the coffin and the lid. The body was then removed
from the coffin. It was clothed in a short white vest, which
was also removed.

s   273

Sidney Harry Fox.

Sir Bernard H. Spilsbury

What did you find as the result of your external examination?—Externally the body was that of a short, stout woman; rather a heavy woman for her size. The hair was scanty and was grey and white; the nose was aquiline and had a faint scar on the bridge—evidently an old scar. Slight putrefactive changes were present externally. The wall of the abdomen was rather tight and was green in colour in its lower part. There were blisters on the back of the trunk, and there were putrefactive gas formations in the eyelids and under the skin of the breasts. The lower part of the face, the neck, the shoulders, and the upper part of the chest had a dark red colour. The rest of the face, the whites of the eyes, the arms and forearms, and the flanks had a brighter red colour.

Were there any post-mortem stains?—Yes, the so-called post-mortem stains were on the back of the trunk, and the thighs were also bright red in colour. The lips and the finger nails had a bluish red colour. There were no external marks of injury and no signs of burning.

What are the results of your internal examination?—In the head I found slight disease of the arteries of the brain. The brain itself and its coverings were healthy. The spinal column and spinal cord were healthy. The cavity round the heart was healthy. The heart was moderately enlarged, weighing 286 grammes. The cavities of the heart were dilated and almost empty. The heart muscle was soft, and there was a patch of disease called fibrosis in the wall of the heart. There was slight disease of the main artery—the aorta—on the wall at its lower end, and there was a patch of disease in the left artery of the heart itself, called the coronary artery, and the artery was slightly narrow at that point. The blood was thick and dark red in colour. The cavity round the lungs contained a little red fluid. The lungs were rather shrunken. They were deep red in colour and were congested at the back. There was some chronic bronchitis and emphysema was present in the lungs. The air passages were clean. They were bright red in colour on the inside, with tiny spots of darker red. There was no visible deposit of soot on the inner surfaces of the air

Proceedings before the Magistrates.

Sir Bernard H. Spilsbury

passages. There was a large recent bruise at the back of the larynx, or wind-box, between it and the gullet, where it softens. There was no injury of the cartilages or bones of the larynx. The thyroid glands in the neck had a deep red colour. The cavity of the abdomen, or peritoneal cavity, was healthy. The liver was small, and weighed 1.163 grammes. It was congested and had a slight putrefactive gas formed in it. The spleen was small and weighed 92 grammes. It was firm and congested. The kidneys were small, and weighed 197 grammes respectively. They were congested. The bladder was healthy, but empty. The coffin was quite dry inside. The tongue appeared to be normal, but on incision of it a recent bruise was found on its left edge midway between the tip and the back. The bruise was about a quarter of an inch in diameter and extended deeply into the tongue. It was not visible on the surface. There were no teeth or stumps in the mouth. The jaws were atrophied or shrunken and the gums were smooth. There were no false teeth in the mouth. The stomach contained about 4 ounces of partly digested food. That, I think, completes the account of the post-mortem examination.

Did you make any subsequent examination?—Yes. I made a microscopical examination of scrapings from the inner surfaces of the air passages. I found no deposited substance as a result. I made a spectroscopical examination of the blood, but no carbon monoxide could be detected in it. I also found some brown wasting of the heart muscle. The left artery of the heart was somewhat thickened and slightly narrowed by chronic disease. The left side of the thyroid gland was very congested and there was recent pressing on its surface. The membrane of the uppermost cartilage of the larynx, which is called the epiglottis, was congested and small hæmorrhages were found in it. There was much fatty degeneration of the liver microscopically, and there was some disease of the arteries in the kidneys, which resulted in wasting of parts of the kidney substances. This is a condition known as sclerotic disease.

Have you arrived at any conclusion as the result of these examinations and investigations?—I have. Most of the

Sidney Harry Fox.

Sir Bernard H. Spilsbury

pathological changes which I have described in the body, the shrinkage of the organs, the disease of the arteries in different parts, and the brown wasting of the muscle of the heart, are commonly found in elderly persons and are not in themselves serious. Fibrosis of the heart muscle associated with disease of the arteries may cause sudden death, but the disease of the artery found here was not sufficient, in my opinion, to explain the death. No disease was found in the body to account for the fatty degeneration of the liver. This condition may have been the result of alcoholic excess, but it was not due to excess within a few hours of death.

In the condition of a person dying from the effects of a smouldering fire in the room, what would you expect to find? —I should expect to find, firstly, a deposit of carbon or soot in the air passages, and in the blood of persons dying from exposure to such a fire I should expect to find the presence of carbon monoxide gas. The absence of these two conditions leads me to the conclusion that the deceased has not died from the effects of the fire in the bedroom.

Can we leave that now and go on to the injuries?—Yes. The injuries which I found in the deeper structures of the neck and the tongue were of recent formation. By recent I mean, of course, shortly before death. The bruising on the surface of the left side of the thyroid gland could be produced by firm pressure between the thumb and fingers applied to the larynx or wind-box. The congestion of the air passages with the hæmorrhage, such as I found in the epliglottis, would also result from such pressure. If the larynx was forcibly pressed upwards towards the floor of the mouth in the act of throttling, the tension produced in the tissue between the larynx and the œsophagus, or gullet, might be sufficient to cause bruising such as that found here. Such upward pressure upon the larynx would forcibly close the jaws and might cause the tongue to be bitten. In my opinion the tongue could not have been bruised between toothless gums, and the deceased must have been wearing plates when that injury was caused. The plates would readily be displaced in the mouth by the act of throttling.

Have you ever found that bruises occur in the neck in

276

Proceedings before the Magistrates.

Sir Bernard H. Spilsbury

the case of manual strangulation?—Yes. Bruises usually occur on the surface of the neck in cases of strangulation by hand. If the victim offered little resistance, and the fingers were pressed in the same position until death occurred, there might be no external marks on the neck afterwards. That has partly to do with the cessation of the heart beating. In the first place, the amount of pressure required to close the passage of the wind-box when pressure is exerted from side to side may not be sufficient to produce bruising on the skin, but if the skin is crushed by the force employed, blood will not escape to form bruises as long as the pressure is maintained in the same areas. I think that answers that part of it.

How, in your opinion, can the injuries found in the neck and tongue be accounted for?—Only, in my opinion, as the result of manual strangulation. The injuries to the structures of the neck and tongue could, in my opinion, only have been produced by strangulation by the hand. The cause of death, in my opinion, was asphyxia, due to manual strangulation.

What do you say in regard to whether these injuries could have been produced by suicide or attempted suicide?—Well, for all practical purposes, it is impossible for persons to strangle themselves with their own hands. That is a generally accepted conclusion. As soon as consciousness is lost in the act of strangulation the hand will tend to release its pressure, and it is unlikely to go far enough to cause death. The grip of the hand would relax.

What do you say to the possibility of the injuries having been caused accidentally?—It is difficult to say how manual strangulation could have occurred unless the person responsible for the accident gives an account of it. There are few recorded cases of manual strangulation by accident, but they are accounted for by such things as gripping the throat in play too tightly. In those cases full accounts have been given of what exactly occurred. The presence of the wet patch on the bed is consistent with my finding that death was due to manual strangulation or a violent death from other forms of asphyxia, or with sudden death from other forms of violence and severe nervous fright.

277

Sidney Harry Fox.

Sir Bernard H. Spilsbury

Cross-examined by Mr. HINDLE—The face was not swollen up except the eyelids, which were blown up with gas. The lower part of the face had deep red coloration and the upper part a brighter red coloration. The tongue was not protruding, and there was no appreciable putrefaction of the tongue at all. The nose and mouth were absolutely dry. There was a little blood in the right heart cavities, but the left cavities were quite empty. The blood was not clotted—in fact, I found no clotted blood at all in the body. Generally speaking, there was discoloration of the body. There was no appreciable softening of the deeper tissues of the skin; there could not have been very much or I should have made a note of it. I should say that for the period of death the body was free from softening. The muscles were normal; they had rather a dark red colour which one usually finds in that stage after death.

Did you notice any hæmorrhage of the tongue?—No. To the best of my recollection the mouth and tongue were dry. After a body has been handled as this was shortly after the time of death, it would not be surprising to find nothing in the mouth. It was laid on its face for artificial respiration, and if there had been any fluid in the mouth or nostrils it must have run out. The injury to the tongue was rather deep, and I did not find it until I made transverse cuts across the tongue.

If the injury to the tongue had been caused, as you suggest, by manual strangulation, would there not be some blood?—Only if the surface of the tongue was injured. A bruise in the substance could not possibly produce any bleeding on the surface if the surface was intact.

You have described the injuries to the deeper tissues of the neck. Did you actually find laceration of the tissues?—No. There was no evidence of any injury, for example, to the thyroid gland, and there was no tearing of the lining membrane of the larynx, only hæmorrhage in its substance. It is more difficult to speak of the hæmorrhage between the wind-box and the œsophagus. There might be some tearing there which would be hidden by the bruise, and I could not say whether there was or not.

Proceedings before the Magistrates.

Sir Bernard H. Spilsbury

Did you describe the size of the bruise to the tissue of the neck?—The bruise between the larynx and the œsophagus was, roughly speaking, about the size of half a crown. The bruise over the thyroid gland I cannot give the exact dimensions of, because the thyroid gland itself is deep red in colour, and one cannot see the edge of it. I can only say it covered the area of the microscopic specimen made. The bruises of the epiglottis were all small.

Were there any external marks of violence on the neck or mouth?—No.

Is it not extraordinary that there were no marks of violence on the neck if, as you say, sufficient force had been exerted to cause bruising to the tissues?—It is not. It is unusual in a case of manual strangulation, but that is another matter. By pressure on the skin bruising directly under the finger would be prevented so long as the pressure was maintained up till death.

I think you have clearly said that the absence of carbon monoxide in the blood and the absence of soot in the inner surfaces of the air passage indicates that death was not due to suffocation?—Yes.

Supposing there was complete combustion would any carbon monoxide be formed then—I mean, by complete burning?—If you have a very free access of air all round the burning area, then there would not be an appreciable amount of carbon monoxide forming.

You could get carbon dioxide?—Everything that burns produces carbon dioxide.

So that if there is complete burning, only carbon dioxide is formed, and not carbon monoxide?—Yes. In most fatal conditions that would be so.

I think you said in your evidence that carbon monoxide was formed?—I did not say actually it was formed. I only said there was an absence of carbon monoxide in the body. It does not follow that there was none produced in the room.

Let us take the recent fire. Must particles of soot always be present in smoke?—Charred materials of some kind—partly burned material. That, as a matter of fact, is what smoke is.

279

Sidney Harry Fox.

Sir Bernard H. Spilsbury

I think the exhumation took place about sixteen days after the woman died?—That is right.

When did you make your report?—On the 7th of December.

Can you explain the delay from the date of your report until a month after when this man was charged with murder?—No, sir.

Mr. SEFTON-COHEN—I am afraid this is not one of the questions you can put to this witness.

Mr. HINDLE—I do not know; I maintain that it is. My point is a simple one. The report was made as long ago as 7th December. Why is it nearly a month after before the charge of murder is preferred? Sir Bernard either knows or he does not know.

Mr. SEFTON-COHEN—This is a matter of comment which the witness cannot possibly answer. It is a matter for the prosecution to answer.

[The objection to this question was sustained.]

Re-examined by Mr. SEFTON-COHEN—Carbon monoxide is found in fires in cases where combustion is not complete and access of air is not good, especially in fires in confined spaces, such as rooms where the doors and windows are closed.

Would the presence of a gas fire in such a room assist or delay the production of carbon monoxide?—That would tend to increase the production by using up some of the oxygen in the room.

Does the presence of these bruises cause you to form an opinion that there was suffocation or strangulation in this case? You don't get bruises in suffocation, do you?—Certainly not about the neck. The only form of asphyxia in this distribution is that produced by strangulation by the hand.

By the CHAIRMAN—Are you of opinion that Mrs. Fox was dead before the atmosphere of the room became sooty?—Yes. If she had been alive in that air, I would have found some soot in the air passages.

JAMES JOHN GALER, police constable in the Margate Police Force—I went to the Hotel Metropole on the night of 23rd October, and just inside the front door I saw the body of a

280

Proceedings before the Magistrates.

James J. Galer

woman lying on her back. I remained with the body until it was placed on a stretcher and taken upstairs to room 126. I was one of the officers who carried the body upstairs. I did not touch the neck of the body, and I did not see anybody else do so. I am practically sure that no one touched the neck; I was standing by the body the whole time.

EDWIN NORRIS, police constable in the Margate Police Force—I helped to carry the body of Mrs. Fox from the entrance of the Hotel Metropole up to room 126, and from the stretcher to the bed in that room. I did not touch the neck or throat of the woman, and no one in my presence did so.

Cross-examined by Mr. HINDLE—There were three other policemen besides myself who carried the body upstairs. I did not see any other person touch the neck or throat. I do not think they could have done so without my seeing them.

FRANCIS JOHN REGAN, a member of the Margate Ambulance Corps, said he went to the Hotel Metropole and assisted in the removal of the body of the woman to room 126. He did not touch the neck, and did not see any one else do so.

HERBERT CHARLES SWISS, a ledger clerk at the branch of Lloyds Bank at 39 Threadneedle Street, London, said that there was no account at the bank in the name of either Rosaline Fox or Sidney Harry Fox. There had not been such an account for the past year.

WILLIAM PALMER, inspector in the Margate Borough Police—I went to the Hotel Metropole on the night of 23rd October in company with other officers. The body of a woman lying at the foot of the stairs was being attended to by Police Constable Bray and others when I arrived. I did not notice then whether there were any teeth in the mouth. When I arrived the accused was kneeling at the head of his mother's body; he was very distressed and was taken away on my instructions. There were a number of people outside room 66 when I went up to it, but no one was actually inside. There was a considerable amount of smoke in the corridor—

Sidney Harry Fox.

more than in the room in which the fire had originated. In the room two windows and two doors were open. The fire on the carpet was extinguished. On my return to the hall I saw that the woman had been turned over on to her stomach and artificial respiration was being given by Police Constable Bray. In room 66 I found a quantity of burned and scorched newspaper on the floor in front of the fender over an unburned patch of carpet. On a subsequent examination, when looking for any notes, I found some charred portions of a French newspaper. The seat of the armchair was stuffed with horsehair and there was a little wool in the arms and side padding. When the fender was placed in its usual position there was a distance of 6 inches of unburned carpet between the fender and the nearest scorch mark. The clothes on the bed had been turned back from the left side to the right.

Was there any mark on the bed to show that a body had lain there?—There was an impression on the left side. The bed showed no indication of a struggle. The pillow was on the bedside cabinet. There was no luggage in the room. I found some medicine bottles, one containing petrol, and the other two medicine. On the mantelpiece was a Dr. Barnardo's match-book, with two or three spent matches. In the washstand basin was a set of false teeth; they were not broken when I first saw them. As far as I remember, there was only one spring. There was no smell of petrol or gas when I entered the room. The gas fire was out. Round the grate and skirting was a considerable quantity of charred paper. I found the key of the room on the chest of drawers. Later I saw the accused in bed in room 42, and I took a statement from him.

Friday, 14th February, 1930.

Inspector PALMER, continuing his evidence, said—I questioned the accused and he said his name was Sidney Harry Fox, and he was of independent means. He said his permanent address was Lyndhurst, Hants, and that it was formerly 19 Cathedral Close, Norwich. He said: "We have recently been on holiday in France, where my mother has

Proceedings before the Magistrates.

been visiting the graves of my brothers killed in the war. She was quite well and a healthy woman, and I had never known her to have had a day's illness. She complained of a slight chill on Sunday at mid-day and Dr. Austin attended and prescribed a mixture for her. She generally retired about nine o'clock. She retired to-night about 9.45 to her room, No. 66, and asked for the *Evening Standard*, and I gave it to her to read for a few minutes before going to bed. I lit the gas fire for her and asked if I should wait and turn out the lights. She said, ' No,' and that she would be all right. She was not undressed. My room is next to hers— No. 67—and opens into her room. It was never locked. I came downstairs and retired about 10.45 and went to sleep. I was aroused about 11.30 by what I thought was a window rattling. I noticed a smell of fire. I closed my window and went to her room to see if it came from there. I found her room full of smoke; there was a light near where the stove would be. I entered the room, but was beaten back by smoke. I called for the porter. I ran downstairs for the porter, and a number of people went into the room. I saw a man drag her out unconscious; I can't say if she was breathing. She frequently read her paper in her bedroom. I can't say if she undressed in front of the fire. Neither of us smoke, and she was abstemious and a good sleeper.'' That statement was given in reply to questions I put to him. I took down in my notebook at the time the answers he made.

At this time I had no reason for suspecting the accused of any crime and therefore I did not caution him before asking him those questions.

During the time that he was giving you these answers to your questions was he calm, or did he break down?—When I first saw him he was calm, but while he was giving me those answers he broke down on two occasions and cried.

Were any questions put by you with regard to any property?—Yes. Having made the statement, he said to me : '' Have you found mother's handbag, as it contains a lot of money? There is £24 in notes, I know. I went to London yesterday to change a cheque for mother for £25 at her bank in London. We intended going to Lyndhurst

Sidney Harry Fox.

to-morrow.'' I inquired what bank it was, and he said, '' Lloyds, 39 Threadneedle Street.'' He also said : '' We have just returned from France after having visited the graves of my three brothers killed in the war.'' There was no mention made of any relatives besides brothers at this interview; there was nothing said about his mother's position. I then left the room and called for the handbag, which was brought to me by Police Constable Bray. One side of the handbag was burned, but the inner compartment was intact, with the exception of just one scorch mark about the size of a pea.

What time was it when you first commenced to ask the accused questions about the fire?—About 12.20 a.m. on the 24th. I should say I left him about 1 a.m. or shortly afterwards. I searched for the notes before I left that night, but I could not find any. I went back to the room with Bray and Mr. Harding, the manager of the hotel. I made a subsequent search with Mr. Harding, Sergeant Fleet, and Mr. Hammond, chief of the fire brigade. We searched the bed, but failed to find any traces of any torn notes or otherwise. There was a good quantity of burned paper and other material in the grate in front of the fire. It was all burned up except the small portions produced last week. These were lying on the unburned portion of the carpet. Before I left the hotel on the morning of the 24th I again saw the accused at about 12.45 p.m. The Coroner was there, also the chief officer of the fire brigade, Sergeant Fleet, and Mr. Harding. I said to him : '' There is no trace of any burned notes in your mother's handbag or in the room. Are you sure she had them?'' The accused replied, '' Yes, I gave them to her —£24 in notes—and she placed them in her handbag.'' I asked him, '' Are you sure of the amount?'' and he said, '' I went to London on Tuesday and changed a cheque for mother for £25 at her bank, with which to settle her hotel bill. I gave her £24 and kept £1 myself.'' I again inquired the bank, and the accused said, '' 39 Threadneedle Street.'' I then said, '' Have you any luggage?'' and he said, '' No. You see, it went straight through to Lyndhurst. We only came here for a day, but mother was not well enough to travel, so we stayed on from day to day.''

284

Proceedings before the Magistrates.

William Palmer

The accused having told you about the luggage being sent to Lyndhurst, did you ask him anything about the house there?—Yes. I said, " Lyndhurst is rather a large village. Is there no further address? Is there a name to the house? " He said, " Yes, End View. My mother recently bought it, and we have been abroad whilst it was being redecorated and the furniture removed from our house at Norwich." In the course of conversation he said his mother was independent and had a good income. He said his father died at East Dereham in 1913 and that he was then pro- prietor of Fox's Flour Mills, East Dereham. He said he was educated at Framlingham College, and that he was a boarder in East House and gave the name of a housemaster named Rose. He never mentioned to me or in my presence to anybody else at any time that he had insured his mother against accidents. On 3rd November, at 10.45 p.m., I saw the accused at Margate Police Station in connection with another matter. I then went through a number of documents handed to me by Sergeant Fleet with the accused. On 7th November I went to room No. 66, in company with Chief Inspector Hambrook and Detective Sergeant Ayto, of Scot- land Yard. In my presence the wrapper and lead capsule of a half-bottle of port were found by Chief Inspector Ham- brook in room No. 66. The bottle was found in room No. 67. On Saturday, 9th November, I received the teeth from the witness Bickmore, and on Monday, 11th, I went to London and handed them to Sir Bernard Spilsbury. I was present when certain tests were made by Mr. Hammond, the chief officer of the fire brigade, on 17th December. On 9th January I saw the accused at the police station, and in the presence of the Chief Constable and the two Scotland Yard officers I cautioned him, and said I was going to charge him with the murder of Rosaline Fox at the Hotel Metropole on 23rd October. In reply to the charge he said, " It is abso- lutely untrue, and I deny every word of it. I have nothing further to say until I have consulted my solicitor, Mr. George Hindle, of London."

Cross-examined by Mr. HINDLE—You will agree with me that quite a number of people had gone into room 66 before you got there on the night of 23rd October?—Yes.

Sidney Harry Fox.

William Palmer

You know that they had been in there putting out the fire, opening the windows, and moving the chair?—Yes.

Do you remember, in answer to my learned friend just now, you said you were present when Mr. Hammond made certain tests. May we now have the date of those tests? It is not on the depositions?—17th December. Tests were also made subsequent to that date.

By the CHAIRMAN—We have heard about the bag, one side of which is charred. We take it that there was no charred paper in it and that the inner compartment was not charred. Was it possible for any notes to have been extracted from it by a person from the time it was discovered until the time it came into your hands?—I should say not. The bag is not charred; there is a hole in it.

Was it lying about in the corridor, and was it possible for notes to have been extracted by any person?—I do not know, sir.

Before it reached your hands, what interval of time elapsed from the time of the fire?—I received it from the police constable at approximately one o'clock.

And during that period was it lying on the couch?—I believe it was in the possession of Bray for a considerable period. He could give evidence on that.

Mr. SEFTON-COHEN—The Bench will recollect that the £24 in notes referred to was, according to the statement of the accused, the proceeds of the cashing of a cheque drawn by his mother at 39 Threadneedle Street, where she had no account.

WILLIAM THOMAS BRUNGER, secretary of Framlingham College up till 31st December last, said he had searched the records of the college, but had found no record of a student at the college named Sidney Harry Fox. So far as he knew, there had been no East House at the college, and for the past thirty years there had been no master of the name of Rose.

GEORGE SAMUEL HOLMES, clerk in the employment of Messrs. H. C. Stammers & Company, New Flour Mills, East Dereham, said he had been employed at the mills for forty-

Proceedings before the Magistrates.

George S. Holmes

three years and knew the district well. He had never known of the existence of Fox's Flour Mills, and there had been no owner or director of the New Flour Mills by the name of William George Fox or William Edward Fox.

ARTHUR CHARLES BELLINGHAM, police sergeant, stationed at Lyndhurst, said he had made a number of inquiries in Lyndhurst and district, but had been unable to trace the whereabouts of a house known as "End View." There was no such house.

ARTHUR WILLIAM CROSS, a wheelwright, sexton of the Parish Church at Great Fransham, said—I knew the woman known as Mrs. Rosaline Fox. She was a native of Great Fransham. She married a man named William George Fox, who was a railway signalman at Great Fransham Station. Mrs. Fox had four sons, the accused being the youngest of them. The accused was at Great Fransham from early childhood until he was thirteen years of age. He was at Great Fransham School. I was present at the funeral of Mrs. Fox in Great Fransham Churchyard in October; I saw the accused there. On 9th November I was present when a coffin was removed from the grave in Great Fransham Churchyard, and I saw a body in the coffin after the lid had been removed. That was the body of Rosaline Fox.

HARRY HAMMOND, chief officer of the Margate Fire Brigade —Shortly before midnight on the 23rd October I turned out with my men, tender, and pump to the Hotel Metropole. On my arrival there I saw the body of a woman just inside the main entrance. I went straight to room 66, where I found the fire had been extinguished. There was a considerable amount of smoke in the corridor; there was very little in the room, the windows of which were open. I examined the room and saw the burned and scorched patch on the carpet. The seat of the fire was unquestionably under the armchair. I say that because the greatest damage was done there to the chair and to the carpet. The chair was burned principally underneath. Since the inquest—on the 17th December and again this month—I have made certain tests in the presence of Chief Inspector Hambrook, Inspector

287

Sidney Harry Fox.

Harry Hammond

Palmer, Sergeant Ayto, and other officers. I tried burning newspaper on a piece of carpet taken from room 66 with a piece of felt underneath it. I used about six sheets of paper, which were creased up and placed on top of a section of the carpet with felt and then a piece of sheet iron underneath, and then burned them. It was a woollen carpet and only the wool pile was burned. The tests were made indoors. Besides paper I also used horsehair, cotton wool, and newspaper—without petrol. The effect of that was that the carpet was burned only on the pile. I also tried burning paper on under-felt, which burned through very slightly in one place. I allowed the paper to burn away entirely to ash.

Did you try an experiment with a similar piece of carpet taken from room 66, on which you placed a merino vest soaked in petrol?—Yes. The effect was that the carpet was slightly burned through on the outer edges of the fire. The vest was all burned up, except a very small piece right in the centre, which protected the carpet. It took seventeen minutes for it to burn through. As a result of my experiments, with and without petrol, I found it impossible to burn the carpet. There was not a great deal of smoke during the test—the doors and windows were all closed. I tried to make a bridge between the gas fire and the carpet by a newspaper across the fender from the fire to the carpet. I lit the end at the gas fire; it gradually burned itself away across the fender from the fire and burned itself out. It scorched the pile of the carpet wherever it came in contact with it. There was a mark of scorching close up to the fender. I tried a similar test with a merino vest. In this case the pile of the carpet was burned rather more. The test with the newspaper had no effect on the fender. The vest burned the paint and blacklead on the face of the fender, and the paint was scorched and blistered. The blisters were obviously fresh.

What is the seat of the armchair covered with?—Jute; then there is webbing, metal springs, and horsehair. Horsehair is easy to light, but it needs some lighter and more combustible material to keep it burning. If all the windows and doors are closed, it makes the fire burn very slowly—more

288

Proceedings before the Magistrates.

Harry Hammond

of a smouldering fire. In the petrol test there was more smoke produced than in the other.

Cross-examined by Mr. HINDLE—I gave evidence at the inquest on Mrs. Fox.

Then nearly two months afterwards do I understand that you made your first test?—Yes.

I understand that you made a test as recently as this month?—Yes, on the 6th of February.

There were no tests between 17th December and 6th February?—No.

ROBERT ERIC HAWKINS, assessor in the service of the Ocean Accident and Guarantee Corporation, Ltd., London—Messrs. Pickfords, Ltd., general carriers, act as the corporation's agents for the sale of tourists' and travellers' personal accident policies. These policies are intended to cover persons killed or injured in travelling. One of these policies shown in this green proposal form is series 63, and that relates to one-day insurance travelling risks, for which the premium is 2s. a day. That covers twenty-four hours of a self-contained day, meaning from midnight to midnight, and under that series the compensation for loss of life is £1000. The maximum insurable under these personal accident policies mentioned in this proposal form is £2000. The proposal forms do not need to be signed by the insured; the policies do. I produce eleven proposal forms which have been filled in in the name of R. Fox, eight copies of policies and three original policies. With the exception of one, the policies have each been taken out for £1000, the remaining one being for £2000. I identify the letter dated 26th October, which was received by my company from Mr. W. F. Wilson, notifying a claim on behalf of the accused.

Cross-examined by Mr. HINDLE—Does your company issue thousands of those day policies, particularly in conjunction with travel tickets?—Yes.

They are usually sold by being canvassed for when persons buy travel tickets?—Yes.

Messrs. Pickfords are your agents and they canvass for you?—Yes. They get commission and are out to get all they can.

So there is nothing very unusual about it?—No.

T

Sidney Harry Fox.

Herbert C. Husson

HERBERT CHARLES HUSSON, employed by Messrs. Pickfords, Ltd., High Holborn—I remember that the proposal form dated 23rd October, submitted on 22nd October, which is in my handwriting, was filled in in my presence about 12.40 p.m. on 22nd October. The man who filled it in was the accused. He asked for series 63, which covers one-day personal accidents of all classes. He said he wanted the policy dated 23rd October. He did not mention any time. He paid a premium of 2s. The proposal form was forwarded to the Ocean Accident Insurance Co.

Cross-examined by Mr. HINDLE—Do you issue a lot of these tickets?—I won't say a lot—at our particular office only between a dozen and twenty a year.

But that is only one branch?—Yes, the head office.

ARTHUR ROBERT CAMM, deputy underwriter to the Cornhill Insurance Company, London—A man came to the company's office on 9th August with a traveller's tour and travel accident proposal form in his possession. When the man brought the form into the office it was already partly completed. It was signed, but the amount of the policy, the period, and the destination were missing. It was dated 9th August, 1929, and purported to be signed by Rosaline Fox. I would not like to identify the accused as that man. I inserted as the amount of the policy required, " £2000 p.r." I wrote Scotland under the heading " Destination," and for the period of the policy, two weeks. The premium was £1 5s. The name of the insured person was Rosaline Fox, and the address the Premier Hotel, Russell Square.

ERNEST BERTRAM CRUSE, clerk in the Renewal Department of the Cornhill Insurance Company, Ltd., London—I produce a policy of insurance in favour of Mrs. Rosaline Fox for compensation of £2000, dated 9th August, and covering the period from 10th to 24th August, 1929. There were two endorsements on the policy, one extending it to noon on 1st September, and the other to noon on 13th September. On 25th September a new policy was issued for Mrs. Fox. I produce a copy of the policy which is for Mrs. Fox, Grand Hotel, Dover, for the period from 24th September to 8th

Proceedings before the Magistrates.

Ernest B. Cruse

October for £2000 in case of death. On 22nd October the accused called at the office and asked that the policy should be extended until midnight on 23rd October.

Did he give any reason?—He mentioned that his mother was very nervous, and would not go into a railway train without being insured. There was nothing said by him as to why he wanted the policy to cover up to midnight. I found they were prepared to extend the policy without an additional premium. I arranged to prepare the necessary endorsement of the policy, and the accused called back for it in the afternoon. The endorsement slip stated, " Insurance expires midnight, 23rd October, and not as within stated."

Cross-examined by Mr. HINDLE—The policy in question elapsed on 20th October, but was extended from the time the accused came in until midnight on the 23rd.

THOMAS WILLIAM GRIFFIN, a clerk employed by the Wesleyan and General Assurance Society, Birmingham—On 10th November, 1913, a policy was taken out by my firm on the life of Mrs. Rosaline Fox, then living at Thornton Heath. The amount of the insurance was 10 guineas. The policy lapsed on 6th August, 1928. We received a letter from Mrs. Fox, purporting to be signed by Mrs. Fox, on 9th April, 1929. It was as follows : " With reference to my lapsed policy and your letter, please let me know how much I am in arrears. I will then forward you a remittance.—Rosaline Fox." The arrears were paid up and the policy was in force on the 23rd October. The last premium was sent on 14th October, 1929, with a letter purporting to be signed by Rosaline Fox. I received a letter dated 26th October from Mr. W. F. Wilson making formal claim on behalf of the accused.

Cross-examined by Mr. HINDLE—The policy was an old one. It was taken out by another son of the deceased woman, Reginald Fox.

HENRY GARLAND SHEPHERD, district superintendent to the Wesleyan and General Assurance Society—Towards the end of May last year I went to 19 Cathedral Close, Norwich. There

Sidney Harry Fox.

was no one at home, but I left a card, and next day the accused came to the office. I had a talk with the accused about a policy on the life of his mother. As a result, Mrs. Fox was examined by Dr. Leahy, and a new premium book was issued. Arrears amounting to 12s. 6d. were paid.

Cross-examined by Mr. HINDLE—I received instructions from the head office to see Mrs. Fox. I discussed the insurance with her, and she quite willingly submitted to a medical examination.

Friday, 21st February, 1930.

NORMAN HARRY THOMPSON, clerk in the Accident Department of the Cornhill Insurance Company, Ltd.—On the 15th or 16th of August the accused called at our office and paid the amount of premium on the policy produced—£1 15s. The policy was granted from the 10th of August till noon on the 24th of August. Shortly before the 24th the accused told me over the telephone that they wished the policy to be extended for a further eight days. On the 27th of August he called at the office and paid the additional premium of 12s. 6d., and I handed him the endorsement extending the policy till noon on 1st September. I then received a letter on 3rd September signed " S. H. Fox," enclosing the policy, and stating that Mrs. Fox desired the policy to be kept in force until the 13th instant, and that she was leaving for the south coast on Thursday, the 13th instant. On 6th September the accused again called at the office and paid a further 12s. 6d., and I handed him this further endorsement extending the policy until noon on 13th September. I received and replied to a telegram on the 13th of September, and I wrote confirming the reply which extended the policy until the 14th.

Cross-examined by Mr. HINDLE—All these policies you have been talking about this morning have lapsed, have they not? —Yes.

DAVID DEWAR BEATON, of the Renewal Department of the Cornhill Insurance Company—I received a letter on 23rd September in the handwriting of the accused asking for a

Proceedings before the Magistrates.

David D. Beaton

renewal for fourteen days of the policy issued in respect of his mother and enclosing a postal order for 12s. 6d. I acknowledged that on the following day, and stated that the policy had been renewed in accordance with instructions. The policy was in favour of Mrs. Fox, Grand Hotel, Dover, and the period of the extension was from 24th September to 8th October, 1929. It was made out to noon on both days. On 30th September I wrote reminding Mrs. Fox that the policy expired on the 8th prox. and inquiring whether any further extension was required. In reply, I received the following letter on the notepaper of the Grand Hotel, Dover, dated 1st October : " Mrs. Rosaline Fox presents her compliments and thanks to the manager of the Cornhill Insurance Company, and begs to state that she will not need an extension of the policy as she will be leaving here during the week-end for her own home." Accordingly the policy was regarded as having lapsed, and the papers were marked to that effect. On 8th October, in consequence of a telegram received from the Royal Pavilion Hotel, Folkestone, the policy was extended. On 9th October I had a telephone conversation with reference to the policy, and on the same day I wrote to Mrs. Fox confirming the conversation, and saying that the company were prepared to extend the policy until the 13th October for a further premium of 2s. 6d. On 15th October we received another letter, dated 14th October, on the County Hotel, Canterbury, notepaper. The letter was signed by Mrs. Fox and was as follows : " As the weather continues to be so fine I have decided to extend my stay on the south coast for another week, until the 20th instant. I enclose a postal order for 6s. 3d. for an extension of the policy to that date." On 15th October I wrote enclosing an endorsement for the extension of the policy until the 20th.

GEORGE WILLIAM MILLBANK, manager of the Norwich branch of the Cornhill Insurance Company—The accused came to my office on 29th October and said he was the son of a lady who was burned to death at a hotel in Margate recently. He said he wished to make inquiries in regard to an accident policy taken out on the life of his mother. He

Sidney Harry Fox.

George W. Millbank

told me that he was awakened during the night by smoke.
He went to his mother's room, which adjoined his own, and
found it full of smoke. He tried to enter, but was overcome
by fumes and ran out shouting for help. Another gentleman
came along, crawled on his hands and knees into Mrs. Fox's
room, and dragged her out. He said that before he went to
bed he left his mother sitting by the side of the gas fire
reading. A few days afterwards I arranged to meet him
in the lounge of the Royal Hotel, Norwich. I remember
asking him what his profession was, and he told me he was
an agricultural farmer with a farm in Hampshire. He
asked me how soon our company paid out our claims. I told
him immediately liability was admitted. I suggested to him
that, in his case, there might be some delay owing to the
formalities of probate. He asked me if I anticipated much
delay or trouble—I cannot remember which of the two words
he used. He told me he was the sole beneficiary of his
mother's will.

WALTER FREDERICK WILSON, a solicitor, of Margate—The
accused first consulted me professionally on 24th October.
I advanced £25 on the 25th of October by cheque. Subsequently I advanced £15 on the 28th or 29th October in
Treasury notes, sent by post. There was no other advance.

BRYAN JOYCE, clerk in the employ of the Sun Insurance
Office, Ltd.—I produce an insurance form which was filled
in on 26th August. It was for a travellers' and tourists'
accident policy for Mrs. Rosaline Fox, Strand Palace Hotel.
I would not like to say that the accused is the man who
filled in the form. The man called again on 28th August and
produced the proposal on which had been filled in in pencil
" 28/8/29. Rosaline Fox." The man paid 5s. premium,
and a policy was issued covering a period from 26th August
to 2nd September, the amount of the insurance being £1000
at death. On 3rd September a letter was received at the
company's office signed " S. H. Fox," and stating that Mrs.
Fox was desirous of keeping in force for a further two weeks
the policy which expired on 2nd September. The request
was not acceded to.

Proceedings before the Magistrates.

Archibald W. C. Seamore

ARCHIBALD WALTER CAMPBELL SEAMORE, a clerk in the head office of the Royal Insurance Company, Lombard Street, London—I identify the proposal form shown to me, which I remember was produced to me, already filled in, on or about 26th June last. It was a proposal form for an accident policy for loss of life for £2000 in respect of Rosaline Fox, 19 Cathedral Street, Norwich. The form bore the signature of Rosaline Fox on it when produced. I identify the accused as the man who produced the form to me. At that time there was a policy in existence which had been taken out by the accused in respect of himself—a monthly policy, extended from time to time, insuring him for the sum of £1000. I identify the copy of the policy produced as the copy of the policy issued for the period 26th June to 25th July in respect of Mrs. Fox. It was a £2000 policy and the premium was £2. This policy was subsequently cancelled by us before it expired.

STUART KENNEDY DUNFORD, of the Norwich branch of the Eagle Star and British Dominions Insurance Company— A proposal form was handed to me by the accused. I believed that the form had been taken away and filled in. The name of the assuree was Rosaline Fox. The policy covered £1000 death benefit and also a sum of £50 in respect of luggage. The policy was issued for the period 4th May to 4th June. After the proposal form was submitted, the accused came to the office several times. He asked what exactly was meant by an accident.

Did he suggest any accident to you?—I can recollect two distinctly. He asked whether, if his mother was drowned in a bath, would that be an accident within the meaning of the policy. He also asked if it would be an accident if she was poisoned by food in a restaurant. He may have made further suggestions, but those are the only two that I can recollect. I more or less evaded these questions. On 4th June a second proposal form was prepared in the name of Rosaline Fox. The copy of the policy produced bearing the office stamp, 13th June, was issued for the period 12th June to the 26th. It was similar to the first policy.

Sidney Harry Fox.

Arthur A. Baxter

ARTHUR ALBERT BAXTER, employed in the Accident Department of the Eagle Star and British Dominions Insurance Company, Ltd.—A policy was endorsed to cover a period to the 9th June, at the request of the accused. On 24th July the accused again called at the office and asked for a further policy on behalf of his mother for a period of one month from 27th July. The policy was issued, but was not called for, and therefore marked as not being taken out. Another policy was subsequently issued in respect of Mrs. Rosaline Fox—an accident policy for £1000 at death for the period from 8th August to 20th August. That was afterwards extended to 27th August. About the beginning of September the accused called at the office and asked for a further policy in respect of Mrs. Fox. The matter was considered and no further cover was granted.

GEORGE FREDERICK PALMER, assistant manager of the Law Courts branch of Lloyds Bank, 222 Strand, London, said that there was no account in the name of Rosaline Fox or Sidney Harry Fox at that branch last year. On 11th October last the bank received a cheque for £10, purporting to be drawn by Rosaline Fox which was returned marked " No account."

ALFRED CLARKE WILLIAMS, assistant official receiver for the Southampton and Portsmouth district, said that the accused was adjudicated bankrupt on 10th March, 1928, and was still undischarged. The liabilities had been returned at £267 1s. 1d., and assets nil.

ARTHUR JONES WATTS, principal clerk in the Ministry of Pensions Department—Mrs. Fox was in receipt of a pension of 10s. a week in respect of her son, Cecil James, who died of wounds during the war. The accused was in receipt of a life pension of 8s. a week. The pension was granted on the grounds of epilepsy aggravated by military service. The service was entirely confined to this country.

GERTRUDE PLATT, boarding-house keeper, King's Cross, London—The accused has stayed at my house more than once with his mother, and he was there on and off through August,

Proceedings before the Magistrates.

with the exception of a few days at the beginning of the month. They occupied two single rooms on the second floor; there was no communicating door between the two rooms. He brought no luggage with him. The accused said he was an insurance agent, and that he was employed in the City.

Cross-examined by Mr. HINDLE—The accused has stayed with me frequently with his mother. They were very affectionate towards each other, and always went out together.

GLADYS MEADMORE, reception clerk at the Grand Hotel, Dover—The accused and his mother stayed at the hotel on three occasions in September of last year. On the second occasion he paid his account for that and the previous visit, and he handed me between £30 and £35 in notes to look after for him. When the accused left on the third occasion there was an amount owing in respect of that visit of £3 5s., which was not paid. The accused and his mother did not have bedrooms with communicating doors.

Cross-examined—As far as I know, the accused and his mother were out together a good deal, and they were on good terms.

LILIAN HOUSE, chambermaid at the Grand Hotel, Dover— I remember the accused and his mother staying at the hotel in September last. After they left I found a bottle on the dressing-table in Mrs. Fox's room. There was a label on the bottle which read "Cleaning spirit; highly inflammable." I handed the bottle over to the police in the same condition as I found it.

Cross-examined by Mr. HINDLE—The bottle was found on 14th September, and it was handed to the police on 23rd January. From September to January it was kept in a cupboard at the hotel. I once took out about a tablespoonful to use for cleaning clothes. I have no doubt at all that the bottle produced is the one I found in the bedroom.

KATHLEEN EDITH CROSIER, receptionist at the Royal Pavilion Hotel, Folkestone—The accused and his mother stayed at the hotel from 3rd to 12th October last. On 10th October I received a cheque from the accused " Drawn to self by Rosaline Fox." He asked me to give him £1 and keep

Sidney Harry Fox.

the balance for him. The cheque was afterwards returned from the bank marked " No account." The accused and his mother left the hotel on 12th October without paying their account, which amounted to £15 5s.

FLORENCE BROWN, chambermaid at the Royal Pavilion Hotel, Folkestone—From 3rd to 12th October the accused and his mother occupied rooms Nos. 221 and 222. These rooms have no communicating door between them.

Cross-examined—Are there any rooms with communicating doors in the neighbourhood of rooms 221 and 222?—There are no rooms with communicating doors under my supervision, but there are plenty of them on the same floor. The accused showed every possible fondness for his mother.

LEOPOLD GEORGE BAILEY, clerk at the Tontine Street branch of Lloyds Bank, Folkestone—I handed a blank cheque to the accused early in October; he said it was for his mother. He presented to me a letter from some Australian bank. The letter was addressed to Mrs. F. H. Fox, Royal Hotel, Southampton Row, London, and he said Mrs. Fox was his mother. It was on the faith of that letter that I handed him a blank cheque. The address of " 171 Tontine Street, Folkestone," on the cheque, was crossed out by me and " Law Courts, 222 Strand, W.C.," inserted in its place as the accused said his mother's account was at that office.

FRANK MASON, proprietor of the County Hotel, Canterbury —The accused and an elderly lady stayed at the hotel from 12th to 15th October. They had no luggage except a small brown paper parcel. On 15th October I saw the accused and the lady leave the hotel, with this parcel, and I instructed my porter to follow them. The accused returned with the porter and I asked him if he was going to pay the account, which amounted to £4 16s. 5d. He said he had no money and was going to Dover, but would come back in the evening and pay the account. In the afternoon I received a telegraphic money order from him for £2; the balance has not been paid. There was no communicating door between the rooms they occupied.

Proceedings before the Magistrates.

Frank Mason

Cross-examined—Have you any communicating doors at Canterbury?—Yes, we have several rooms with communicating doors. They did not ask for a communicating door.

CORA CAPELLI, wife of Francesco Capelli, proprietor of the Savoy Restaurant, Dover—The accused and his mother stayed at our restaurant in August last for two nights. The bill on that occasion was paid. They afterwards stayed with us on 15th October, and the account amounted to 14s. 8d. I received 4s. 8d. from the accused, and he promised to come back and pay the balance later. He did not come back. All the rooms in the hotel are separate rooms; there are no communicating doors.

WILLIAM EDWARD FOX, monitor at Queen Alexandra's Hospital, Cosham—I am a brother of the accused. My mother married William George Fox, a porter on the Great Eastern Railway. She had four sons of whom I am the eldest. Cecil, the second son, was killed in France during the war, and Reginald, the third son, was killed at Woolwich Arsenal in November, 1915. The accused is the fourth and youngest son. I first learned of the death of my mother on 5th October from what I saw in a newspaper; I received no communication from my brother. My brother was educated at the parish school at Fransham. I know my brother's writing. [Shown the Woolls cheque.] That is not in the handwriting of my mother. The body of the cheque is in the handwriting of my brother, but I cannot say whose writing the signature is. It is not my mother's. [Shown proposal forms, letters, &c.] These are all in the handwriting of my brother. I know my mother's writing; it was very shaky. In 1928 it was just a scrawl, she could hardly write at all. These signatures are not hers—her signature spread all over the page. I have not seen her signature since 1928.

By the CHAIRMAN—The documents you have been shown are all within recent date—twelve months or so—and the signatures are firm. Are you prepared to swear they are not your mother's signatures?—Yes.

The accused was committed for trial.

12-III·40